Good Writing for Journalists

Narrative, Style, Structure

Angela Phillips

SAGE Publications

London ● Thousand Oaks ● New Delhi

First published 2007

SAGE Publications Ltd
1 Oliver's Yard
55 City Road
London EC1Y 1SP

SAGE Publications Inc.
2455 Teller Road
Thousand Oaks, California 91320

SAGE Publications India Pvt Ltd
B-42, Panchsheel Enclave
Post Box 4109
New Delhi 110 017

British Library Cataloguing in Publication data

A catalogue record for this book is available from the British Library

ISBN-10 1-4129-1916-9   ISBN 13 978-1-4129-1916-6
ISBN-10 1-4129-1917-7 (pbk)   ISBN 13 978-1-4129-1917-3 (pbk)

Library of Congress Control Number 2006927540

Typeset by C&M Digitals (P) Ltd, Chennai, India
Printed on paper from sustainable resources
Printed in Great Britain by TJ International, Padstow, Cornwall

CONTENTS

ACKNOWLEDGEMENTS

My biggest thanks go to the writers who have donated their work. Without them, there would be no book. Everyone I contacted gave without hesitation and without pre-condition. Thanks also to the editors who gave me their time to talk about writing: Ian Katz and Claire Armistead, of the *Guardian*, Ian Jack of *Granta*, Hilly Janes from *Times 2*, Mary Hadar from the *Washington Post*, Marcelle D'Argy Smith from her experience at *Cosmopolitan*, Dylan Jones from GQ and all the very many journalists who have visited Goldsmiths to talk to my students about their work. Thank you also to the friends, colleagues and students who have read and commented on the early drafts: Judy Holland, Tony Dowmunt, Ellie Levenson, Reva Klein, Laura Deeley and my daughter Rachel Sturrock.

INTRODUCTION

This is a book about the art of writing stories for newspapers and magazines. It is needed because, if the print media are to survive the internet age, they must evolve a distinctive role involving more than the basic skills of news gathering and reporting. Simple news stories can be done more easily and far more quickly via radio, television or the web. The future for print lies increasingly in the quality of writing or the depth of analysis. Newspapers are already moving in this direction. Where ten years ago the majority of features in a quality newspaper would be less than 1,000 words; today features of 2–3,000 words (or more) are not uncommon. Saturday and Sunday magazines proliferate, demanding well-written profiles and features. Balancing the increase in the length of features and profiles, there has been a massive growth in the number of short, personal and opinion pieces, some of them little more than 300 words, but all of them demanding fresh, original writing.

As Mary Hadar, a commissioning editor on the *Washington Post*, says: 'These days so much of what ends up on the front page is a feature. Even when you are covering a war, you want to experience it, the feel of it.' So, although this book concentrates on feature writing, it looks also at reportage and it includes pieces at full length because it is hard to get a sense of the shape and structure of extended features when all you get is a couple of paragraphs. In Part II of the book there are examples of writing that are powerful, memorable, colourful or funny, each with a commentary on structure, style and writing quality, encouraging readers to learn from the best practitioners. It is not meant to provide a blue-print for young journalists so much as a springboard. I hope it will inspire and encourage those who want to make their writing individual and memorable because it is this skill which will really mark out those who are most likely to 'make it' in a world over-crowded with information. To quote Hadar again:

> I was always watching other newspapers and magazines for a distinctive voice. Maybe a young writer doesn't recognise their own voice. You have to push them a bit. Push them on to the high wire without letting them fall.

But the book isn't only about writing. It is also about how stories are framed and constructed. It challenges the assumption that journalists merely report, impartially, what they see and hear (perhaps with a few literary techniques thrown in). It recognises that most newspapers and magazines recount events within the context of existing narratives of the world, which necessarily colour, not only what they report, but how they report it. This approach to the news has until recently remained firmly fenced into the section of the world labelled 'media theory'. Practitioners have attacked it for undermining the very values upon which the profession of journalism is founded. It is used here for two reasons. It will help students of journalism to understand how stories are constructed. That will make them better writers. It will also arm them with an understanding of how easy it is to accept a one-sided account as 'the truth'. By understanding how competing cultural narratives work, young journalists will perhaps be a little better equipped to resist pressures to conform, and may in turn help shape new and more inclusive narratives for the future.

Journalists have to be good narrators in order to hold attention in a world in which information streams unceasingly through our daily lives (written, visual, sound, or all three). Their job is to carry messages not just about things that we need to know in order to get on in the world, but also about who we are and how we are changing. The first kind of message, usually referred to as 'hard news', tends to be the subject of most books about the practice of jour- nalism. The second kind of message, about people – the things they do, the things they buy and the way they behave towards one another – are usually dismissed rather derisively as 'soft news'. People who read 'soft news' are thought to be either dumb or female (or both) and the inclusion of more soft news in 'serious newspapers' and television programmes is often described as 'dumbing' down (Franklyn, 1997) or feminising.

For those who believe that journalism has fallen off its moral perch, the central complaint is always that newspapers are too taken up with 'unwor- thy' tittle-tattle about celebrities and tragic stories about 'victims' (Bird and Dardenne, 1988; Franklyn, 1997; Sparks and Dahlgren, 1992; Sparks and Tulloch, 2000) and that serious news (of governments and wars, political organisations and the economy) is so oversimplified that people cannot make proper use of it. The view seems to be that real news events, like green vegetables, should be digested because they are good for us, and that any attempt to make them palatable is likely to rob them of their value. Even some of those who take 'unworthy news' seriously do so only because they are concerned that these stories are doing 'ideological work' which is aimed at keeping the down-trodden in their place.

This debate isn't new. Simon Jenkins, quoted in the *Guardian* (Engels, 1996) said: 'there is always a golden age of journalism and it was always when the person discussing the subject came into journalism'. Indeed, the concern about the right way to communicate important information goes right back to Plato, who thought that using representations to demonstrate ideas or psychological truths (*mimesis*) was dishonest and that more direct forms, in which the author *tells* the audience the story (*diegesis*), were purer and more truthful. The counter-view is that, since all information is always selected, there can be no pure and truthful form. In all cases, writers decide which questions to ask, and who they will speak to. They prioritise information that fits their own view of events. Those who find ways to 'show' rather than simply 'telling' their readers are merely trying to help them understand. As Wayne C. Booth (1961) suggests in *The Rhetoric of Fiction*, all stories are told, *mimesis* is just an illusion created by the story-teller.

If there is a difference between journalists today and journalists in that far-off golden age before we all 'dumbed down', it is not so much what we write about, but how we write it. There was a time when the well informed read more than one newspaper. Today the well informed read newspapers, periodicals, books, watch television, listen to the radio and, for instant news, they go online. With all that noise out there to compete with we have to work far harder than we have ever done before just to get a hearing. One way in which we do this is by creating an illusion of intimacy and involvement by using personal stories as metaphors and experiences as examples. Some writers, such as Colin Sparks (Sparks and Dahlgren, 1992: 41), see this as a problem:

> They [the popular press] offer the experiences of the individual as the direct and unmediated key to the understanding of social totality. The simple reality is that the nature of the social totality is neither constituted through immediate individual experience nor entirely comprehensible in its terms. ... Critical thought must ... necessarily involve the processes of abstraction even if the critical impulse itself is ultimately grounded in immediate experience.

Sparks' promotion of abstract thought over personalisation comes up against what Bird and Dardenne (1988: 78) described as the journalist's paradox: 'The more "objective" they are the more unreadable they become; while the better storytellers they are, the more the readers will respond and the more they fear they are betraying their ideals.'

There are certainly journalists who continue to be plagued by this dilemma, but there is also a new generation of journalists who feel less of a conflict (Bird and Dardenne, 1988: 78). They recognise that we no longer live in a deferential world. Our readers don't want to be talked down to from a lofty height. They want us to talk in terms they understand. They are more likely to find out about a subject if we have caught their interest rather than gabbling away high above their heads. This doesn't mean that journalism has simply become another form of entertainment. We have only to see how newspaper readership rises in times of crisis to recognise that there is a thirst for knowledge, and understanding, but readers also like to know what people are wearing and who they have fallen in love with.

Journalism is more than a means of bringing news about disasters and changes in government policy. It is also a critical weathervane for cultural change. Stories about celebrities may irritate but if we understand them as vehicles for cultural myths (Lule, 2001; Silverstone 1988), we can see that they play a part in both change and resistance. We play out our attitudes to race, gender, sexuality and so on through stories. The people our newspapers choose to feature may be celebrities but the stories they tell are age-old concerns about social norms and values. When a footballer's sexual exploits are splashed across the newspapers, they provide a vehicle for a discussion of social attitudes to fidelity. When the same sportsman is filmed doing a victory lap with his child on his shoulders, he is passing on a message about the changing role of fathers.

Kevin Kerrane and Ben Yagoda (1998: 13g), in their book *The Art of Fact*, define journalism as work that is 'animated by the central journalistic commitment to the truth', based on fact-gathering (not just working from memory or sensory observation) and timely. From this definition, they specifically exclude commentary and memoir. I agree that journalism must be based on evidence, but that evidence can also be drawn from our own memories and observations of our own emotions, as well as from the experiences, emotions and memories of others. It should be animated by the quest for truth, but tempered by an understanding of how difficult that quest can be. It should bring us news of how we feel as well as news of what is done in our name. This book is about writing about things that matter (and even those that don't matter much) so that they will be read.

PART I

THINKING ABOUT WRITING

1

LET'S HEAR IT FOR STORY-TELLERS

From narratives to stories

There is much debate about the exact definitions of narrative and story. Indeed, they are often used interchangeably. For the purposes of this book, then, story is a sequence of events in which some form of action takes place. In journalism, as opposed to fiction, that sequence of events has actually taken place or is likely to take place. A narrative, in the literary sense, would be the telling of that story in printed form. I use narrative in a broader way to describe a set of ideas (or discourses) constructed from the myths and legends that have shaped our cultures and communities, which then help us to construct the way we think about our world. I suggest that these 'meta-narratives' shape and also direct the way in which a story is presented. The narrative arc, or the narrative spine, refers to the foundation idea that runs through the story when it is presented.

Private stories

From infancy the job of any human being is to find out who they are through interaction with the people closest to them. They are told stories about who gave birth to them, who their families are, who to trust and who to fear. The information will be passed on via legends, folk tales and parables of heroes and bogey-men, martyrs and witches, fire and water.

> Learning how to ... construct stories, understand stories, classify stories, check out stories, see through stories, and use stories to find out how things work or what they come to, is what the school, and beyond the school the whole 'culture of education' is ... all about. (Geertz, 2000: 193–4)

When we notice changes to the expected patterns of our lives we re-count these as stories, drawing humour, drama and suspense from the unexpected disruptions. These stories allow people to connect emotionally and feel closer but they also pass on information about changes or warn of danger. As we grow up, and our knowledge accumulates, we learn to sum up people and situations quite quickly by keying into a range of signs and symbols that we then interpret according to our own preconceived ideas and the stories we have been told. These signs and symbols start to form an overarching narrative that helps us to interpret change, threat or danger.

We are all the unofficial biographers of ourselves for it is only by constructing a story, however loosely strung together, that we are able to form a sense of who we are and of what our futures might be. (Thompson, 1995: 210)

Collective narratives

Public stories have a similar function. They pass on important information, warn of danger and they also create a sense of connection. Through them we learn, for example, that crime will be punished and achievement will be celebrated. We mourn together when good people die and we celebrate when bad people are avenged. Journalists, novelists, dramatists all use the same basic material: they are describing what they have seen and heard and experienced. They all tell stories that arise from the culture in which they live, and in their turn contribute to a collective 'grand narrative' – a shared idea of cultural life.

To say that two people belong to the same culture is to say that they interpret the world in roughly the same ways and can express themselves, their thoughts and feelings about the world, in ways that will be understood by each other. Thus culture depends on its participants interpreting meaningfully what is happening around them, and 'making sense' of the world in broadly similar ways. (Hall, 1996: 2)

This shared idea is an expression of a particular ideology. In a liberal democracy, one of our shared ideas is that powerful people are fallible and subject to jointly agreed laws and standards. We tend to tell stories that fit in with this belief: stories of powerful people who have been found wanting and been reduced to our level. We also have a shared belief in the possibility of opportunity, so stories of people who have risen far above the place they were born into are also popular. These stories acquire the status of myth (Barthes, 1972: 119), contributing to our sense that power is not arbitrary and that individual success will be celebrated, as long as we don't abuse what privilege our society provides.

In societies in which the shared belief in social solidarity overrides the belief in individual freedom, we would expect to see lots of stories in which self-sacrifice is celebrated and selfishness is punished. For example, the central character of the Chinese soap opera *Yearning* was a poor and poorly educated woman. Her life is a series of trials but she was not redeemed at the last moment by the love of a wealthy man or a miraculous cure (as we would expect of an American soap opera); rather, her self-sacrifice was celebrated as a worthy end in itself (Rofel, 1999). In Chinese newspapers, stories about corrupt officials are popular but, whereas in a western democracy the emphasis is likely to be on the failings of the individual, in China the emphasis will be on the success of the system in rooting out corruption.

These collective narratives help us not only to decode and evaluate stories, but also to decide which stories are important. On the whole, the stories we tell are normative – they point out and punish those who deviate from the norm and celebrate people and events that confirm our sense of how things ought to be. This is not something we do consciously; it is embedded into our thinking to such an extent that it requires an effort of will to conceive matters differently. This tendency to uphold the *status quo* has often been commented upon by critical scholars because it is used to block out discussion about change and to pillory those who do not conform. Indeed, it may be argued that this tendency to check everything, uncritically, against our pre-existing knowledge (Hall, 1996: 646) means that we have a built-in tendency to be suspicious of people and ideas that are unfamiliar and that this suspicion can be used to create division instead of cohesion.

Narrative and the conventions of journalism

Journalists are like novelists in that they are story-tellers, but they are unlike them in equally important ways. We are bound by a different set of imperatives. We tell people about events which are actually happening in the world at that time. If every journalist were to disappear tomorrow, society would re-invent us the day after, and in doing so would almost certainly suggest that news needs to be:

- timely – be about something that has just happened, or is happening, or has only just been discovered, or which will have resonance at this particular moment,
- relevant – have meaning for their existing audience,
- important – tell us about things that matter to that particular audience,
- focused on change to the established order – new songs, new trends, new laws, new wars,
- evidence-based – stories cannot be invented but must be based on accounts of things that really happened and can be verified, and finally news needs to
- have impact – big is more newsworthy than small, close is more important than far away, bad news sells better than good news.

Only by operating within these conventions can journalists expect to be trusted by their audiences – and trust is important. Without it, those who own the newspapers, magazines and television stations have no product, that is nothing to sell that is different from advertising. It is the realisation of this bond with the audience that makes it possible for journalists to work within the commercial world and allows for the development of professional ethics – loose rules of conduct that set the boundaries of what is permissible. Where there are no rules governing journalism, or where journalists have lost trust, people start looking elsewhere for the information they need to govern their lives.

This collective agreement about the permissible boundaries doesn't stop newspapers being selective or biased in the way in which they present information. The imperatives of news conventions provide the driving force for story selection, but at an unconscious level journalists are also looking for stories that fit in with their own (or their employer's) idea (narrative) of how the world works, or examples of how it doesn't work but ought to work.

Things are newsworthy because they represent the changefulness, the unpredictability and the conflictful nature of the world. But such events cannot be allowed to remain in the limbo of the 'random' – they must be brought within the horizon of the 'meaningful'. In order to bring events 'within the realm of meanings' we refer unusual or unexpected events to the 'maps of meaning' which already form the basis of our cultural knowledge. Into which the world is already 'mapped'. (Hall, 1996: 646)

The job of making a story 'fit' is done by a process of selection and juxtaposition so that, as Paul Willis (1971) observed: 'Once an item of news has been selected for transmission to the public there is already bias, some selective principle, some value, quite apart from the way it is presented.'

Choosing stories

Some of that 'value' undoubtedly derives from the structures of power within which journalists operate. To begin with, most 'hard' news stories emanate from what are described as 'authoritative sources' – the government, the police, the courts and the business community. More often than not journalists present the views of whichever part of the establishment their newspaper tends to support. Where news decisions are not overtly political in character they will still be made on the basis of certain 'values'. If the newspaper they work for is socially conservative in its outlook, then stories will be selected to uphold a world view in which 'good' people are married before they have children, refrain from sexually promiscuous behaviour, are unlikely to be homosexual and are always prudent in their financial affairs. A more liberal newspaper might select stories that demonstrate the validity of relationships that are not sanctified by state or religion and highlight the needs of people who are socially excluded.

But these power structures cannot on their own account for the kinds of story that continually recur in the pages of newspapers and magazines. Very often an item is chosen for what I would call its 'narrative quality' and that quality may well take precedence over the importance of the information contained in it, the source from which it derives or even the political slant of the newspaper. Bird and Dardenne (1988) suggest that we could productively look at news in terms of myth or archetype. It is through myth, they suggest, that members of a culture learn values and definitions of right and wrong. By understanding news as a means of conveying the values of society rather than merely a means of conveying information, we can understand more easily what journalists actually mean when they say 'now that's a great story'.

Often those stories have a very simple story line that depends on a reversal of our expectations. Today I heard about a woman who had won the lottery but hadn't told her family. Her behaviour is unexpected but only because of our preconceptions: the story in our heads. Those preconceptions and our realisation that she is outside the norm arouse our curiosity. We want to know why she did that but we are already judging her within the narrative of our own morality. We may see it as a gesture of independence or as shamefully selfish. The way in which the story is written need not tell us explicitly what the journalist (or newspaper) thinks. Judgement will usually be subtly implied by the way in which the story is told (the narrative approach). For example, one newspaper will chose to interview a family therapist about the likely impact of such behaviour on future family relationships. Another might choose to get a comment from an organisation championing women's financial independence. Each narrative approach invites the readers to view the story in a different light (the preferred code [Hall, 1996: 58]) but the readers will finally shape the narrative for themselves, and make their own judgements in the light of the narratives in their own heads.

E X E R C I S E

Narrative framing

Using internet archives, look at articles printed on the same day in three different newspapers on the subject of: teenage pregnancy, gay marriage, education reform. Print them out and, using a marker pen, highlight all the quotes and pieces of information that are the same. Now look at sources of additional information and comment. List them for each piece. Look at the ordering of the information. Which sources are given pride of place? Who gets the last word? How does the choice of additional comment affect the 'narrative framing'? From this, can you deduce the kind of audience that the writer had in mind?

The stories in our heads

In a conventional narrative, a protagonist endures a series of disruptions that test his strength and character, followed in the end by resolution. Aristotle (1998) believed that a story must be resolved in order for it to work. Tzvetan Todorov (1977) argued that stories end when an 'equilibrium' has been established. Robert McKee (1999) writes that 'archetypal' stories always end in closure (though he describes different forms of story that end with only partial closure), and all the story types described by Christopher Booker (2004) have clear resolutions.

News stories are also about disruption and change and they often focus on people who have endured testing experiences, but they don't always have resolutions and, even for feature stories, the resolutions are provisional. They are being told while events are unfolding. Where they work towards resolution they may be overturned by a new set of events tomorrow. Nevertheless, I would suggest, it is possible to read news and feature stories within these conventions as episodes in an ongoing drama. In the real world we never know how events will unfold but we are continually trying to guess. In a sense, the whole purpose of news is to provide us with readings of the present that will allow us to make predictions of the future. In making our predictions we are using a ready-made set of possibilities (narrative structures). It is in this impulse towards controlling our world and making it seem predictable that we use stories. Journalists, who share the same human desire to make sense of things, are using the same stories when they try to explain what has happened, and what might happen as a result.

These narratives in our heads provide the impetus behind story structures and often the reason for choosing them. Sometimes events unfold neatly, mapped on to our expectations of story shape. Sometimes readers are lulled into the anticipation that a story will turn out a certain way, and then they are jerked awake when the writer (or life) pulls the archetypal rug out from under them, disturbing their expectations. Even if there is no obvious ending or resolution to a story, the expected, or desired, resolution is often implied in the way in which it is written.

Story archetypes

Journalists draw on the same set of basic characters, archetypes or myths, that are used by film-makers and novelists. They are the basic moral tales that guide human behaviour in all societies. They are told and retold in ways that conform to the needs and the norms of the particular society in which they are being written, and they are adapted as societal norms change. Some scholars and practitioners argue that there are a limited number of archetypal stories that recur throughout history and across cultures. Philip Parker (1999), a screenwriter, suggests eight. Christopher Booker suggests that there are seven. Their lists are very similar and deal with: justice (revenge), pursuit of love, tragedy, triumph of the spirit, coming of age, the quest. Lule (2001) suggests seven 'master myths': the victim, the scapegoat, the hero, the good mother, the trickster, the other world and the flood. (Though this seems to mix up archetypal characters and plots.)

I have boiled these lists down to five basic narratives. Using these narratives, I will demonstrate how they are used to shape stories by selection and exclusion. It is useful to be aware that the chosen template can overwhelm, or completely change the emphasis and interpretation of the information rather than simply framing it. It is equally important to see how much stronger a story becomes when there is a clear narrative idea framing it and giving it a coherence and drive. We will look for these narratives as we analyse the features in the second section of the book.

1 Overcoming evil

Many stories are told to reassure ourselves that good will prevail over evil. Good may be a matter of morality but morality and self-interest (individually or collectively) are often entwined. Evil in these tales may be represented metaphorically (serpents, storms, giants) or embodied by people who must be prevented by the hero(es) from invading the body of the nation and stealing its food, jobs, women, children … or sports trophies (think of the films *Invasion of the Body Snatchers, Men in Black, Superman*). At the end of the story the kingdom has been saved. However, the very nature of live news means that we don't always know how the story will end. We don't know whether evil will be overcome. We just write as though evil should be overcome and evil, in some newspapers, is just about anything that isn't clearly and identifiably 'us'.

While the nature of this myth is to reassure and rally people against the fear of the unknown, it can also be used very negatively to isolate and repel strangers or things we don't understand. Very often the 'evil' is actually a 'scapegoat' (Lule, 2001: 60). In Nazi Germany in the 1930s and in Rwanda in the late 1990s the state, working hand-in-hand with the media, cast a minority group (the Jews and the Tutsi) as evil monsters, ascribing to them everything that their societies most abhorred and setting them up to be massacred. George Packer, in his article on the Ivory Coast (see George Packer, pages 109–30) describes how a powerful elite uses 'malevolent stranger' stories to drive a wedge between communities and consolidate their own power.

The myth of the evil, invading stranger is a recurring theme in parts of the British press. In the mid-1980s one British newspaper summed up a demonstration by black people under the headline 'The Black Tide meets the Thin Blue Line', setting up an opposition between black people and the police and throwing in the additional allusion to the story of David and

Goliath. In this case, the police (the thin blue line) were established as the 'plucky heroes' – an interesting reversal as the police actually represent the power of the state. Through the 1990s and 2000s the newspapers have turned their attention to 'asylum seekers', who have been characterised as the evil invaders. A *Daily Express* front page (27 July 2005) is typical: 'Bombers Are All Sponging Asylum Seekers', thus managing to construct all asylum seekers, not as people seeking refuge from violence, but as representing violence.

However, globalisation is creating the need for a new way of expressing the concept of evil invader. An examination of news coverage in the aftermath of the 9/11 attack in America, and the July 2005 Tube and bus bombings in London, demonstrated a new version of the old theme. The old secure boundaries of 'us' and 'them', based on class and race, could no longer serve in a world in which the victims were of all nations, bound together in the face of a common threat. Newspapers struggled to find a new formulation, a way of being able to use the story form of the invading force and the heroic nation, while at the same time redrawing the boundaries. The choice of photographs, and stories of victims, seemed designed to represent a bigger, multicultural 'us', which would, by contrast, diminish and marginalise 'them'. The problem was just how to describe 'them'. Newspapers slid around, describing the bombers as Islamic while at the same time going out of their way to reassure readers that Muslims, as a group, were not to be feared. As a way of demonstrating this, most newspapers in the UK chose to feature the picture of a young Muslim woman – the first victim of the tube bombers to be buried. She was clearly one of 'us', not 'one of them'. But this, broader, more inclusive view, does not fit easily on to existing *mind* maps. The more common stereotype of Islamic people as 'violent irrational terrorists always on the lookout for murder and bombing outrages' (Said, 1994: 23) tended to recur – a recognisable stereotype to fit into an easily recognisable story. Of all the narrative forms, this tends to be the easiest to manipulate to a particular point of view because it relies for its effect on the creation of a shallow stereotype. We never really get to know the evil monster. If we did, we might find ourselves sympathising with it. And then it would turn into a quite different story, such as one of those described below.

E X E R C I S E

Examine the news coverage of a recent natural disaster over a period of a week. Who or what is the evil? How is it overcome? Who are the heroes? The villains? Note whether the roles change as the story unfolds.

2 Transformation

This category covers stories in which people are transformed by the experiences they undergo. Arthur Frank (1995) refers to transformation stories as 'Quests', and Booker calls them 'Journey and Return', in which the hero goes on a journey, faces many trials and returns, having been transformed by his experience. It is a narrative that holds out the possibility of redemption through personal effort. Twenty or thirty years ago it would not have been a very common theme for stories in serious newspapers, but it has long been the staple of mass-market popular newspapers and magazines where it is the basic story line of articles known generically as 'Triumph over Tragedies'. The protagonist may have experienced a personal difficulty, which takes him/her to the depths, but the reader knows that the resolution will always be up-beat. They will return having learned something important about themselves and (possibly) won the hand of a prince/princess as well.

A simple form of transformation is found in sports stories. Here the hero is offered a challenge. He or she works through the ups and downs of the season, the aim being to win the trophy and become the champion. Again it is the trials that the hero faces which create the drama: the tension of the match, the occasional failures on the way to victory. One of the reasons why newspapers don't like teams that win every match is that they flatten out this narrative and drive out the tension. Another form is the battle for the leadership of a party or country. First, the leader emerges through the tests that are set by his or her own followers. He or she then has to face the challenges from other leadership contenders. Finally, he or she faces the electorate and wins the country. Some struggles are rather more difficult than others. During the apartheid era in South Africa, Nelson Mandela became a hero to many people across the world. His quest was to overturn the apartheid regime and on the way he encountered many obstacles. He was accompanied, as in myth, by people who gave him help and strength, and in the end he won the keys to the kingdom.

But in the real world these stories are not straightforward because there can never be one single point of view. During the period of Mandela's struggle his position changed according to the point of view of the story-tellers. To white South Africa he represented evil to be overcome. Once he had assumed power, the myths started to be reshaped and he became a hero even to those who had initially feared him.

These are modern morality tales that remind readers that the inner values of strength, love and compassion are in the end more important than 'shallow' values of beauty and wealth. The transformation narrative is the bright side of what could be a tragedy (see below). Sometimes stories that look like tragedies to one person will be subtly reconfigured as transformation stories in the telling. One example of how news journalists used this form is in the story of George Best, the British footballer, who dazzled with his skill during the 1960s, and then spent much of the subsequent four decades in and out of trouble. These stories could have been told as episodes in a tragedy, but the basic fondness for him meant that the promise of transformation was the theme of almost all the coverage. Through every cycle of disaster the press were there wishing him well again, hoping that this time he would live up to the myth in which he had been cast. This was a comment from *The Times Online* (7 October 2005):

Yes, we think of him in terms of skill and the sheer beauty of the game, but courage … truly sums up Best and you can see that same characteristic in his approach to life. He just keeps on coming back. Long may it be so. (Francis Jones, London)

Transformation stories are also very often the template for personal columns. They may be funny, whimsical or sad, but the story arc is often about a journey through a transforming experience and the pay off is often the greater enlightenment of the writer. This form is often derided by those of the 'only hard journalism counts' school and yet it is enormously popular with readers because it provides the possibility of identification and the hope of transformation. Even the ubiquitous self-help features in women's magazines tend to fit into this over-arching narrative. They hold out the promise of transformation if you just take control of your life and …

E X E R C I S E

Find a feature that uses the transformation as a basic story form. How is it structured? Look for the way the narrative builds up from one hurdle to another. And then look at the way the writer 'signposts' the change in mood to tell us that we are going to have a happy ending. Now find a novel or film that also uses this framework. Compare the way in which they use this structure.

3 Tragedy

Aristotle (*Poetics*, 1998) saw tragic heroes as the architects of their own downfall. The hero is tempted in some way, by vanity, greed or pride, and becomes increasingly desperate or trapped by his or her own actions. The essential ingredient of a tragedy is the fatal flaw in the character of the hero. Note I am saying hero, not villain. The story structure requires that the central character is someone whom we respect. The story of his fall from grace depends on us identifying with him or her as a good person, someone we respect. Tragedies don't happen to people who have already been constructed as morally suspect. Bad people deserve the fate that awaits them. A classic 'villain' is nearly always a cardboard cut-out character, depicted without depth or subtlety. We don't need to know this person because he or she is merely a foil in a story about someone else. When we see good people fall, we are drawn in to their stories, we have an emotional connection and the story has the effect of a moral tale. This myth has enormous resonance. It reminds us that we have agency and that we can make bad decisions as well as good ones.

In press stories the hero of a tragedy is very often a politician or a celebrity, but it can also be an ordinary person who makes a terrible misjudgement. It is our identification with the protagonist in a tragedy that gives it tension. There is always the sense that we too could be tempted, we too could fall. The story of evil overcome can easily be inverted to become tragedy. One person's monster is another person's tragic hero. If we look, for example, at the coverage of the rape trial of US boxer Mike Tyson (Lule, 2001: 122), we see a man who, for one group, is a monster, unable to master his own appetites, and for another group, a tragic hero who overcame poverty and a difficult start in life to become a heavyweight boxing champion and who was then undone by vanity and greed. Whole groups of people who have been classed as evil in stories in some newspapers can then be re-read as tragic heroes elsewhere.

Tragedy is a very rich narrative because it allows us to examine motivation. In a tragedy no one is a cardboard cut-out. Take the story of Prince Charles and Diana, Princess of Wales. It is almost always told as an unresolved romance (see below), but if we cast Diana in a tragedy, we could conclude that she was blinded by a prince's attention and the thought of the prize that was in her grasp. The rest of the story shows her twisting and turning, trapped in a cage of her own making. As it becomes clear that she is unloved, there are only two possible endings: she must rediscover herself and recouple (romantic – see below) or die (tragic). It is interesting that the story is never told this way (see romance below).

E X E R C I S E

Make a list of prominent people whose careers have ended in tragedy. Look for stories about them before, during and after these events. Note how the narrative frame changes as the events unfold.

4 Romance

This is the story form that perhaps best embodies the human desire for 'wholeness' or completion in human relationships. A romance is always resolved by a happy ending. The form plays with the tension between our fear of loss and our hope for completion so it always involves misunderstanding, or ignorance, which keeps people apart, and then resolution which brings them back together. Tabloid stories about stars or politicians who have affairs, are criticised as trivial, and those who read them are dismissed as voyeuristic, but perhaps one of the reasons why people read them so avidly is that, in a society in which relationships are often short-lived, they reassure us that even people who appear to have it all (fame, wealth and beauty) can suffer and that, even in the midst of pain, there is always the possibility of a happy ending.

Quite often drama is actually created by newspapers looking for gossip and reporting innuendo-filled stories, which are then followed by stories of reconciliation in which the partner who has been betrayed, is forced to deal publicly with humiliation and loss, while the errant partner publicly apologises. When the sought for reconciliation fails to happen, the dumped partner (after a short period of concern) is usually subtly excluded from the story so that an alternative happy ending can be contrived between the protagonist and the new 'true' love. The dumped partner then provides the possibility for a new pairing, which will resolve tensions and allow everyone to live happily ever after. Where the dumpee refuses to disappear and leave the field to the new 'king and queen', the story line stretches on. What keeps it alive is the desire for a final resolution in the minds of the audience. The audience wants the hero to live happily every after.

In the case of Diana, Princess of Wales and Prince Charles, story-telling imposed a particular shape on a stream of life events. It could have been told as the story of a man who falls in love and doesn't marry the girl next door. Instead he marries a very pretty, shallow young woman, whom his family chooses for him and whom he doesn't even like very much. In this version of the story, the death of the young woman and his final coupling with the girl next door should have been a happy ending. But the story was never told that way. We want our heroines to be young, beautiful and innocent. By the time the audience discovered Camilla (Charles's then lover, now wife) she was already middle-aged and Diana was firmly fixed as heroine in the public imagination. According to this version, Charles betrayed her, and she looked for love elsewhere. Sadly, she died before the desired romantic ending. This version did not allow for the happy consummation of the original love match. Charles and Camilla were literally unable to marry for years because that would have provided the wrong ending to the romantic story that we had been fed for so long. In the world of the popular press, Diana is Snow White, just sleeping, her memory kept alive by the continual replaying of her life. This story will never end because it cannot be resolved.

Romance is the stock in trade of celebrity magazines. Read through a couple of them and count up the number of stories which hint at future romance, or revel in recounting the ups and downs of an existing one.

5 Coming of age (rags to riches)

Every reality television show is based on the love for this story line. Stories tracing the lives of sports and film stars regularly use this format as a framework but, unlike the other hero stories, these need not have done anything special to achieve their wealth. The female characters are pretty, and usually docile, and the male ones are characterised by their wit and guile. Jack and the Beanstalk is a classic rags to riches fairytale: a young lad is given his mother's last few pennies and squanders them on some so-called magic beans. When they turn out to be genuinely miraculous he climbs the beanstalk, which grows from them, and proceeds to rob the giant he finds there. At the end he chops down the beanstalk, kills the giant (who has not actually done him any harm – his fear of him is based entirely on hearsay and rumour) and runs off with the loot to live with his mother in luxury. Cinderella is the classic female version. Unlike Jack, she is required to prove herself, not by her wit and guile, but by her inherent goodness.

This is a universal story about growing up. The young pretender overthrows the old guard (or kills the father) and, in most stories, goes on to marry the prince or the princess (rather than the mother – the Oedipal twist in Jack and the Beanstalk). It invokes all the hopefulness of youth that, just by growing up, they will acquire wisdom and riches. Their trials will be small ones and they will, in the end, reign supreme. These stories are perhaps particularly loved in a consumer society in which there is an interest in reassuring people that they too can be lucky and get rich without much effort. In these stories, where there are challenges, they are overcome by ingenuity, charm, luck or innate intelligence. There is no need to journey, no need to slay monsters, riches can be yours – because you are worth it.

The story interest usually lies not in the heroes, who are usually bland, but in the characters alongside: Jack's mother and the giant; Cinderella's wicked step family and the fairy godmother. Similar stories today also rely on a good supporting cast to rise above blandness. An excellent example is a profile of Welsh singer Charlotte Church by Jessica Cartner-Morley (*Guardian*, 8 October 2005). Church rose apparently effortlessly to wealth and fame because of her extraordinary voice. Cartner-Morley peoples this piece with a star cast of characters from the Church family and, what could be deadly, is lively. This quote is typical – Church is trying to give up smoking:

Nana (in Charlotte's pantomime impression) leaned back in her favourite chair, taking exaggerated, Dot Cotton drags on her fag and sighing contentedly. 'I was miserable as fuck and she was just going, "You'll be fine, love." And then, after five minutes she got sick of me looking so fed up, so she said, "Stop moaning and have a fag, you silly cow." So I did and it was lush! I felt so much better.'

E X E R C I S E

Choose a classic fairy story then write out the plot in three short sentences. Now, using existing features and fan sites on the web as a source, construct a 500-word celebrity profile based on this plot structure.

Stories that don't fit

Some stories map clearly on to these underlying narratives. Listening to the radio today I heard news of a high official on the edge of disgrace, a threat of war, an argument between politicians, each a fragment of an ongoing drama. Depending on your point of view, they were, respectively, a tragedy, evil to be overcome or a quest for power (transformation). There are a slew of stories that don't seem to fit into this scheme – at first. People who are murdered, raped or maimed in terrible accidents or natural disasters cannot be constructed as the protagonists of stories in which everything will end happily, nor can we see them as tragic heroes brought down by the flaws in their own personalities.

Life is not the same as stories. Real people are overwhelmed by circumstances over which they have no control. But the purpose of story-making is at least partly to give ourselves a sense that we are in control. So after the initial shock, they are retold as 'transformation' stories in which we look for signs of rebirth or redemption. Someone dies in an industrial accident. We search for someone to blame. Someone is murdered and we expect the police to act and resolve the crime. The victim becomes merely an episode in an ongoing narrative – a search for revenge, or at least for closure. Occasionally the victims may be transformed so that they stand in the public imagination as icons, representing a particular moral value. Steve Biko, a black South African activist, lives on in the public imagination as a symbol of the struggle against apartheid. The memory of Stephen Lawrence, a teenage victim of a racist murder, has been transformed into a symbol of social change in Britain. Often it is the person left behind whose life is transformed and then he or she becomes the hero of the story.

E X E R C I S E

Take a selection of newspapers and magazines and see if you can assign the stories to one of these five story types. Consider whether they could be rewritten so that the story type is clearer. Would that make them more, or less compelling reading? If you were to strengthen the story line, would they be more likely to be printed in a weekly magazine, a 'Red Top' newspaper or a serious daily? Take one story in which you can find traces of one of these story lines and rewrite it so that the narrative is clearer.

Making the facts fit

Whether or not we agree that there are just seven or eight, or five or three basic narratives that work across cultures and across time, they provide a useful organisational template for looking at the way in which writers and editors organise information. It is when the narrative overwhelms the facts. It is in the stories that go wrong that the process of myth-making is most clearly revealed.

Jean Charles de Menezes was a Brazilian electrician, an ordinary man without any power or influence, who was catapulted into the national narrative of the United Kingdom when he was accidentally shot by police in a London tube train on 22 July 2005. It was the day after a group of men had tried, and failed, to bomb the London tube network. Note how the 'facts' were selected to fit a narrative held not only in the minds of editors and journalists but of the eye-witnesses too because these stories are held within the culture – they are not simply dictated from above.

Story 1

To start with, the information emerging came from unofficial 'police sources' and eye-witnesses. The facts chosen suggested that our heroic policemen had saved us from an evil, dark-skinned stranger: 'A man of Asian appearance', as an eye-witness told the BBC news that day. Another eye-witness said that he wore 'a bomb belt with wires coming out' (*BBC News* website, 22 July 2005, http://news.bbc.co.uk/1/hi/uk/47067870stm) and an 'unseasonably warm jacket or overcoat' (*Daily Telegraph* website, 22 July 2005, http://www.telegraph.co.uk). In fact, it gradually emerged that the man was Brazilian, he did not have a bomb or wires, or even a bulky coat. He didn't even have his tools with him as he had left them at work the day before.

Story 2

Very quickly new facts were selected and the story was reconstructed. De Menezes was portrayed as a parasitic, undeserving outsider. The *Daily Telegraph* website reported that: 'It is believed that Mr De Menezes, who is thought to have spoken good English, may have been working illegally in Britain for up to four years'. We were also told that 'Several other witnesses reported seeing the man jump over the ticket barriers', and that he failed to respond to police challenge: 'Sir Ian Blair, the Metropolitan Police Commissioner, said on Friday that the man was "challenged and refused to obey police instructions"' (*Daily Telegraph* website, 23 July 2005). By choosing to focus on his illegal status and refusal to obey police instructions, the newspapers were straining to hold on to the myth of the malevolent stranger. This allowed them to continue to portray the police as heroes upholding the peace. The *Daily Telegraph* adhered to this version of the story even when the De Menezes family and the British Foreign Secretary, Jack Straw, both insisted that he was here legally. They were still pursuing the story three days later in a story about his funeral in Brazil: 'As the body of the Brazilian electrician shot dead by police as a suspected suicide bomber arrived in his home town yesterday, it emerged that his visa had expired more than two years ago' (Steele John, *Daily Telegraph*, 26 July 2005).

Story 3

It gradually emerged that De Menezes had not run away from police, did not 'vault over barriers' and had never been challenged before he was shot. His friends and employer described him as an honest man just going about his business and stories about his immigration status died away when it became obvious that they were in any case irrelevant, had been leaked illegally and were probably wrong. This did not quite fit into the story of an invading alien so a new story was required. For the *Daily Telegraph* the heroic police became the problem – a monster out of control interfering with a vision of England and English tolerance.

'When I was a boy, one of the great boasts of the English was that we had an unarmed police. The sight of gun-toting policemen cluttering up London uselessly fills me with horror,' he says. (David Starkey, interviewed by Damian Thompson, *Daily Telegraph*, 9 September 2005)

In this story the changing facts emerged through leaked information (from the police and other so-called 'authoritative' stories), counterbalanced by the stories told by people who had witnessed the shooting and, finally, by the friends and family of De Menezes himself. As the facts changed the story was retold, but journalists, editors and even eye-witnesses were clearly selecting facts that would work with the idea in their minds of an over-coming evil story: a heroic police force trying desperately to keep people safe from marauding strangers. They selected information in order to tell that particular story. It was a story that 'worked' with the cultural myth of a benign liberal state. When it became clear that the details were not true, the story had to change and this is where the job of a journalist departs from that of a novelist. Journalism must be based on verifiable facts or it ceases to be journalism. When it became clear that De Menezes was not a bomber, had not vaulted over the barriers into the station and was not wearing bulky clothes, editors were faced with a story that did not fit their cultural stereotypes, or the chosen editorial angle, and so the story had to be reshaped. New facts were selected. His family were given the promi-nence that had formerly been given to the police. A more unsettling story emerged which confronted rather than confirmed the nation's view of itself. The death of this electrician led to a national debate about the story of Britain itself: humane and liberal or fearful, fragmented and increasingly authoritarian? (See letters in *The Observer*, 31 July 2005, http://observer. guardian.co.uk/letters/story/0,,1539731,00.htm.)

There is no doubt that the news coverage of this event in some news-papers shamefully distorted the facts. However, it is important to note that the story was first formulated by eye-witnesses who were themselves so imbued with assumptions about what they were seeing that they seem to have invented or at least embellished the facts. Once it became clear that the 'evidence' was wrong, the newspapers did (eventually) change the story. Some newspapers were more circumspect from the start. They tended to be the newspapers that allowed the journalists to go out and find things out rather than deciding on the thrust of the story in advance. In the next chapter we will discuss how to construct stories that use archetypes to chal-lenge readers rather than using them as a kind of cookie cutter for shaping information.

Changing the story

Myth and metaphor are not, by definition, conservative and uncritical. They can also be used to challenge the *status quo* and to breakdown conventions. Transgressive stories are often more arresting than those that operate within conventional normative boundaries. When we read sympathetic stories about people who have, conventionally, been treated as pariahs, they chal-lenge our assumptions. A black journalist working on a conservative daily newspaper in the UK had this to say about how he uses story conventions to challenge attitudes:

Occasionally you have to go to the editor and say 'If these people were white and lived in Cobham would you run this story? Here are the elements of this story: It involves this, it involves that and I can tell you, if this was a middle-class girl from Cobham you would do that story. Actually, using all the thought processes that you use to evaluate any other story, this story still works. Therefore, the only excuse you can have for leaving this story out of the paper is the pigmentation of the people involved. It can't be anything else'. (Phillips, 2003)

The challenge is to understand the power of myth, to know how to use it, but also how to subvert it.

2

CONSTRUCTING STORIES

Where do ideas come from?

Narrative structures may provide a framework for thinking about the world but they don't in themselves provide ideas for stories. Stories are about disruptions to the *status quo*: things that have been hidden and have just come to light, wrongs that should be put right or just changes in the pattern of things. Most stories on the front pages of newspapers are 'managed events': they have been press released or leaked and newspapers have been primed in advance to cover them. Unexpected events have to be big to make it on to a front page – fires, explosions, major accidents, earthquakes, etc.

Go further into your newspaper or magazine and you will come across stories that, while still clearly linked to the news agenda, and the particular moment, owe more to a fresh approach and an ability to spot trends where others might not have noticed them. The more you know about a particular subject (be it trains or politics), the more you will be aware of change. But changes happen around us all the time. They don't have to seem significant and you don't have to be an expert to notice them – just be aware and interested.

Here is an example. A corner shop in a very rundown inner-city area started selling fresh coffee beans. A journalist, living locally, realised that, as small shopkeepers are very sensitive to local needs, this new line could be the sign of a bigger underlying change. She researched a little further and then used her discovery as the lead into a feature on the gentrification of a then rundown working-class district in South London. Ideas are everywhere. If you listen and look you will find them in:

- other media (specialist journals, newsletters, websites, magazines from other countries) – read everything you can lay your hands on,
- chance conversations overheard on a bus,
- unexpected debates on an internet site,
- encounters in the supermarket,
- odd coincidences,
- personal anecdotes or tragedies.

One successful freelance journalist said that after an evening out with friends she makes notes of their conversation. She writes for women's magazines and her friends' concerns are likely to be the concerns of her readers. Ideas are everywhere. None of those below necessarily constitutes a story. They are all threads that could lead to stories. It doesn't take long to find out whether they are just odd 'one offs' that won't really tell us anything of interest, or single examples of a universal story, which is of interest to lots of people.

- A friend of a friend has been wrongly arrested. As well as being a good 'real life' story, this could tell us something about policing.
- A student has survived a freak accident. This would work if it tells us something of universal interest – about health and safety legislation, about the health service, or a personal story of resilience in the face of adversity.
- A friend's neighbour has had six miscarriages. This could tell us something about the state of medical know-how and care. If she then went on to have a baby it could be a 'real life' story for a magazine or newspaper health section.
- A child has been 'abducted' by his estranged father. This is not an uncommon event. It could be used (with other evidence) to shine a light on what happens when divorces go badly wrong. It could make a local newspaper story in its own right.
- A colleague's credit card has been used to buy porn on the internet. This could be part of a civil liberties story about identity theft, or the start of a story about looking after your credit card.
- You cannot find an insurance company who will insure your bike. Is there a problem with bike insurance? Could this be the kernel of a story for a bike magazine? A consumer section of a newspaper?
- You suspect a company is going bust. Find out who would be affected and make sure you have your facts right. Then find out what is causing the problem. If this is part of a trend (rents going up and forcing small business out, a change in buying habits, the end of an iconic brand), then you may have a story. Otherwise, you may not.
- Six friends have had to leave the city because they can't afford to live there. You could have a story about a major demographic change (or just mates who don't earn much).
- Only one person in your friendship group has a driving licence. Is there a downward trend in car use? If so, why? Could it be because of global warming or traffic congestion or just that your friends prefer drinking to driving?

Get used to asking questions. If you want to know how something happens, or why it happens, or why it seems to be happening now when it didn't last year, then the chances are someone else is equally curious. Check newspaper archives to see whether someone else has written about it. If no one has, the field is yours. If there was a piece a year ago, you may be able to do it again with a slightly different spin. If all the papers covered it last weekend, then forget it – you are too late.

If you are stuck for ideas try brainstorming. Write down five random words and then see if you can come up with ideas associated with them: things you would like to find out more about which might amuse, entertain or inform. Look at today's main news stories. What are the questions that come into your mind? They can be closely connected or barely related. Write them all down and see if you can come up with four different feature stories that might arise: comment, newspaper features, special section features, specialist magazines.

E X E R C I S E

Keep a diary for a week. Note the subject of every conversation you have through each day. At the end of the week review them. Choose five topics and then write down every idea, however tenuously connected, that comes to mind.

The hook

An idea is just a starting point. To turn it to good use you need to have a reason why this idea should be written about at this moment. It is the timeliness of a story that provides its hook. Your hook will always be the key part of your story 'pitch' when you suggest a feature to an editor. The timeliness of a story varies according to the publication you are aiming for.

Newspapers and news weeklies

If you write for newspapers you must be immersed in the news.

- A news story may provide a reason to write a piece you have had at the back of your mind for weeks but you will have to work very fast to get your pitch in. A feature based on a news story needs to be written that day, or at the very least by that Friday for publication in a weekend paper.
- A planned event will give you time to research and pitch a piece in advance. Advance notice of publications, new products, research, and so on will give a start on the competition. Always pitch as early as you can. If you don't, someone else will!
- Trends can appear to be newsy. You need to know about the next thing before it happens so that you have the time to research, write about and sell it before everyone else discovers it.
- A personal story can work well if it reflects something that is happening at the time. A particularly poignant story will sell at any time.
- Seasons and anniversaries are predictable and you can plan timely stories to coincide with them.

Trade magazines (business-to-business)

These operate on a slightly longer time frame than newspapers and follow a narrower, deeper seam of news and developments. You really need to be an expert on your subject (and a regular reader) and you should pitch stories at least a week ahead of the day the magazine hits the shelves. But even trade papers are looking for angles and for hooks such as:

- events in the wider world that might have a particular resonance for your market (e.g. demographic changes for a personnel magazine),
- people whose actions could impinge on your specialist area (e.g. animal activists for a science magazine),
- research in a related field (e.g. 'happiness research' for a social work magazine),
- legal cases (e.g. a sexual harassment or unfair dismissal case may provide useful lessons for any magazine aimed at senior management).

Consumer magazines

Monthly consumer magazines are planned months ahead and completed three months before publication so they cannot respond to news. They respond instead to their particular audience, covering a revolving set of concerns presented each month in a different way, with different content, discussed by different people. Weekly consumer magazines are capable of responding to news events in the world of entertainment and celebrity (for most features they have a three-week 'lead time'). In order to write for consumer magazines you must be absolutely immersed in their particular world and hyper-aware of changing fashions. There is only one 'hook' for a consumer magazine feature: you must always write with a sense of the immediate present. As one features editor put it: ideas must be Zietgiesty. The best way to get a start in consumer magazines is with a good 'real life' story (see 'Character as story', page 34) which is clearly relevant to that particular readership.

Missing your hook

Don't worry. You may have to shelve the story this time but hooks are like trains; you just wait for the next one. Your value as a feature writer lies in your ability to think laterally and your willingness to apply that different thinking by going out into the world and bringing back those shining magpie scraps which you can then present to your audience, arranged and polished, and just at the right moment.

Choose a date a few months ahead and find out everything you can about events that have happened on or near that day. They can be seasonal events, anniversaries, holidays, births, deaths or even personal stories. Using these 'hooks', think of five different features ideas, for five different publications.

Gathering facts

The purpose of research is to make sure that you feel absolutely confident that what you are about to write is based on the evidence and that you have fairly weighed the evidence to take into account the views of those people who are interested and/or involved. You may well start out with a pretty clear idea of what you think the story is about. It is tempting then just to go out and find the facts to match your assumptions – resist the temptation. The more certain you are of your 'angle' the more you need to check it out by seeking out opposing views. If you are still sure of your angle when you have finished your research, then go ahead, but always be ready to adapt, change or drop the story if your research proves that you were wrong.

If your story won't stand up on its facts don't prop it up with lies.

Research is not only about collecting facts it is also about collecting atmosphere and emotional temperature and that cannot easily be done by telephone or online. Good stories start with experience – your experience. Writers who rely entirely on second-hand sources are data processors, not journalists. For a start they run the risk of repeating other people's mistakes, but even more important they are missing the point of journalism, which is to go out and verify the facts for yourself – and then to tell your readers what you have found. They are also robbing themselves of the opportunity to inject light, colour and texture into their writing. Mary Hadar, *Washington Post* features editor, says:

Hard news journalists think that feature writers aren't reporters but the best feature writers are the best reporters. Reporting is absolutely key. You can get a lazy writer who has the skill but doesn't go out and really dig – not just ask one neighbour but four neighbours. You have to ask and ask and ask so that you end up understanding the culture you are reporting. You may not show very much of what you have learned but the culture should infuse the whole piece. (Phone interview, May 2005)

There is more about interviewing below. First, you must be sure that you have taken care of the basics. Don't even pitch your story (see below) until you have made sure you understand and have details of:

- the context in which your events take place,
- the characters in your story,
- the details of the story, such as it is, so far.

Online information can be very quickly accessed and is invaluable when you are just trying to get a sense of whether your story will 'fly'. Be very careful not to mis-use data. The commonest mistake is to access foreign data and then apply it to a home story. Make sure the data you use is relevant to the story. Wherever you can, you should use the internet not as an end in itself, but as a way of accessing a person you can speak to. But do the reading first. You will get more information if you are already well informed. If you use online information, documents or other secondary sources make sure:

- you are clear about their authority (or lack of it),
- you know where the originator is located,
- you have a means of making contact to check their bona fides.

You must always verify your facts. Do this by:

- checking with as many different people as it takes to feel confident that you have understood,
- talking to a minimum of two people who are personally involved,
- talking to at least two additional people who might be expected to have differing points of view.

You haven't finished your research until you find that nobody is telling you anything new. Don't skimp and think you can get away with it. You can't – it will always show. Once you have done the basics you are ready to move on to detailed interviews or investigation, adding what you see, hear and deduce from your own observations.

E X E R C I S E

Read two of the longer features in Part II of this book. Go through each and list every different secondary source which is mentioned. Then list every person interviewed. Now make up a speculative list of the kind of information that would have been required as background research. Consider where you would find such information.

Pitching to the slot

A slot is a section or a page of a newspaper or magazine in which a particular kind of subject matter and a particular style and structure of writing has already been decided by the section editor. The editor is responsible for giving that section a special appeal for a particular audience. Your piece must speak directly to this very particular audience. It helps to be able to imagine exactly who the typical reader is. You wouldn't speak to a 14-year-old girl in the same way as you would to a 40-year-old businessman. In the same way, you must always write for a very specific audience. If you don't know who you are speaking to, you are very unlikely to get the subject, or the style right. Study these slots carefully and make sure that when you suggest your story you know that it will fit in terms of its length, structure and style.

Your pitch should be short: a headline and a one-paragraph summary is ideal. You should back this up by some suggestions (ideally in bullet points) as to how you will pursue the research. The subject must be suitable and so should the tone and approach. If there are several different ways in which the particular piece could be tackled to fit in with the section (e.g. a first-person piece or a 'how to' piece), then suggest a couple of alternatives.

Really good editors will always be on the look out for fresh talent, a new way of spinning words and a fresh way of thinking, but they will not be impressed if a writer sends in a 4,000-word thesis (however well written) if the biggest article on the page is only 800 words long. Nor will you get far suggesting articles about social policy in a magazine devoted to clothes and sex.

Marcelle D'Argy Smith wrote for the British *Cosmopolitan* magazine in the 1980s and then went on to edit the magazine in the 1990s. It was the writers, she believes, who were the key to its success. Some people, she found, were good at getting information but the articles had to be rewritten by the subs. However, it's the great writers who 'make' the magazine. Dylan Jones, editor of GQ magazine and four times Magazine Editor of the Year in the UK, agrees, but he looks to newspapers as the seed-bed for talent. Back in the 1980s, quite a lot of good writing migrated the other way, from the magazines into the newspapers.

Editors don't often buy work that has already been written. Dylan Jones says it has happened only twice in the last twenty years on *GQ*. *Marie Claire* features editor, Charlotte Moore, agrees. They would also prefer to work from ideas. *Marie Claire* receives 200 emails every week from freelance writers, news agencies and photographers. Few will be chosen, but they are all read. When uncommissioned work is used it is usually because it is a very well-written personal story – 'Something', says Dylan Jones, 'that would make me fall off my chair'.

Once a story idea is accepted, the features editor will discuss it with the writer. If you are working for a newspaper, you will verbally agree the angle, the length and the people you are going to interview. Magazine editors will draw up a detailed brief. You will be given a word length and asked to provide fact boxes and possibly short interviews to be boxed on the page. If, after you have done your research, the idea changes (see below), discuss those changes and make sure you have agreed a new brief. Don't try to bend the research to fit the old one.

Expect to be asked to rewrite or amend. Even the most experienced writers know to set aside time for revisions. New writers might have to rewrite several times. On consumer magazines features are routinely rewritten to fit the particular formula of the publication. Sometimes people are re-interviewed if the features editor doesn't feel that the right questions have been asked.

The worry is that some magazines are now so proscriptive that writers have learned that they have to fit in to get on. Writing to formula tends to homogenise writing, and the result may be wooden and humourless. If you are working in a less formulaic environment, you will have to learn how to structure your own work. It is probably the most challenging part of feature writing.

E X E R C I S E

Choose four different features: two from newspapers, one from a consumer magazine and one from a specialist magazine. Now write what you imagine the writers' initial pitches might have been.

Finding the characters

One of the major complaints about modern journalism is that too much of it is personal rather than political: '… scandal and sensationalism, too frequently masquerading in perverse guise as "human interest", have become central ingredients of the news diet' (Franklyn, 1997: 3). The fact is that people are interesting. It is the effect of policy on human beings that we care about – not the policy itself. It is the impact of crime on those who have suffered that interests us as much, if not more, than the crime itself. We may be shocked by video of a huge wave engulfing a beach, but after the horror of the initial impact, it is the effect of that wave on the people that we want to hear about. Stories about people help us to understand great events and they help us to understand ourselves too.

This is not to say that newspapers and magazines always tell useful stories, or get the balance right between the personal and the general. Politicians are interesting because of the ways in which they can affect our lives, but they are also interesting for who they are. We need to know about the political – not instead of the personal but as well. When a story about a politician's private life is retold again and again, at the expense of information about his policy and what it might mean for us, then we are certainly being short-changed. But when politicians' lives are picked over and displayed for public consumption one shouldn't assume that stories are trivial.

Personal stories rarely appear in print because a journalist stumbled over them by chance. They are leaked in order to discredit enemies. The success of these strategies usually depends on the way in which the politician in question reacts to the pressure. Politicians seek power and, as seekers, they must expect to withstand trials. They are unlikely to encounter dragons but the way they handle the modern perils put in their paths tells us a great deal about them. Some politicians fail at these trials of strength: perhaps because they are weak, or because they have not been properly supported by their parties. Some fail because they have been shown up as unworthy of trust. I think those are stories worth telling.

Some stories about people are not worth telling. They are often stories about people who are famous for being famous. They are cut and pasted from previous interviews, spiced up with a couple of new quotes and then reheated for public consumption with a few breathless cover lines and headers. These stories are not worth telling because they tell us nothing new and they don't present us with any challenge. Like 'dead metaphors' (Orwell, 1950), their stories (or the stories that are spun about them) have often become so tired and clichéd that they are no longer capable of making us think at all.

Stories about people feature throughout this book. I didn't choose them because they were about people. I chose them because they were good examples of journalism. But in all of them people are important. All of them make the reader stop, think, maybe smile or cry. They are interesting because they are human. Sometimes the character driving the story is the journalist. Sometimes it is the interviewee. In some cases the story is about the character. In others, characters provide evidence, or they are there as metaphors, providing light and colour to a story that would otherwise be hard to understand. Just as it is the character that drives a novel or a film, it is characters who will turn a dull, but worthy, story into something that people want to read. People are endlessly fascinating. Their lives will light up your writing.

Character as story

Pick up any newspaper or magazine any day and you can read profiles, interviews and 'real life' stories that focus exclusively on one person. The subjects of these articles are likely to be:

- famous for something they do: film stars, musicians, authors, directors, athletes, etc. – they are usually interviewed to promote their work,
- famous for their connection with someone who is famous: parents who coach/manage their offspring, partners of famous people, nannies, cleaners, butlers of famous people (privacy agreements make these tougher than they use to be),
- in the news: they have just been promoted to an important job, they have just made an important announcement that will affect lots of people; they have been caught up in a major news event,
- representative of universal human experience: their story can be mapped on to the archetypal narratives described in the previous chapter.

Your interviewee is the 'hero' of your story, so you need evidence of the kinds of challenge he or she has faced in their life. It is their response to these challenges that will provide you with a story. Where a challenge (a tragedy or a scandal) is the whole purpose of the story, this will not be difficult. Indeed, these 'real life' stories, usually told in the first person, are now found in virtually every type of magazine and newspaper. They focus on an 'ordinary' person who has been through a life-changing experience. Usually they follow a 'transformation' narrative with an upbeat ending.

Profiles may also centre around a life-changing event, although these are not told in the first person. They contain comment and observation as well as the story. Sometimes the interview is about the event, sometimes the event is the plum that is plucked out of an otherwise standard interview and then becomes the focus of the article. When you are faced with someone who appears effortlessly to 'have it all', you will have to work harder to find the evidence of 'trials' to demonstrate how your character thinks and behaves. It is the desire to find something interesting to say about apparently factory-produced celebrities that fuels the morbid interest in their love affairs, drug problems and eating disorders. In the absence of any obvious dysfunction, you may find that the companions along the way (parents, siblings, friends, mentors, lovers) will provide you with colourful anecdotes that give you a new view of your subject.

Character as metaphor

A metaphor should stand in place of what it describes in order to help us understand it better, or to make us think more clearly about what we have taken for granted. If people are interviewed to represent trends, opinions or survey results, they too should tell us something new rather than confirming our prejudices.

Sometimes this is done very crudely: a Muslim women is interviewed in order to represent all Muslim women; a teenage mother is a representative of all teenage mothers. Alternatively, celebrities may be interviewed or photographed. Their bodies and their characters will be constructed as representative of a generation and carry with them messages about attitudes towards everything from drug-taking to financial independence and parenthood.

The use of celebrities to comment on subjects that they have no special knowledge of can be irritating but sometimes a famous person really does seem to embody the spirit of the age. The English footballer David Beckham was never popular just because he was good at football. He became a style icon because of his apparent ease with his own beauty. His close relationship with his wife and children seemed to herald a new form of androgynous masculinity. On a less positive note, the conviction of Winston Silcott, for the murder of a policeman in North London in 1985, became a metaphor for black criminality long after the day when he was cleared and freed from prison.

One person's story can also become a metaphor for a disaster. It is almost impossible to take in the thought of 73,000 people dying in an earthquake. By focusing on the living death of just one man, Anthony Loyd makes the impossible comprehensible:

> KHALID HUSSEIN makes no sound; his eyes stare into the distance. Only his emaciated body and the perpetual digging motion of his hands hint at the horror that he has endured.
>
> A few words by a Pakistani doctor on the chart by his hospital bed provide the minimum information: 'Admitted yesterday. Found 27 days after being buried in his house. Tibia fractured. Psychosis.' The report is dated November 11.
>
> Mr Hussein is almost certainly the last person to be recovered alive from the rubble after the October 8 earthquake in northern Pakistan that killed at least 73,000. His survival may be little short of miraculous, but it comes at a terrible price.

The 20-year-old farm worker has not said a word since being pulled into the daylight. He stares drooling into space, clawing at the blankets on his bed at the Al Abbass Medical Institute in Muzaffarabad, in Pakistan-controlled Kashmir, as if trying to tunnel out of a nightmare. Should he recover his senses, reality will reveal that his mother, brother and four sisters died in the landslide that crushed his home in the village of Pahl, in the remote Jhelum valley. (Anthony Loyd, *The Times*, 18 November 2005)

The *Washington Post* writer, Annie Hull, has a particular talent for finding the people whose lives work as metaphors. This is the conclusion of a piece written in the aftermath of 9/11:

At home Mariam goes outside to ride her Razor scooter with a neighbor boy, who by now understands when Mariam is called inside for prayer time. 'Come back in five minutes' she will say.

Her father's car pulls into the garage. In a few hours, he will go to the mosque for prayer. He has a business trip to Las Vegas coming up. ... Diamonds sparkle in his wife's ears. His son prays beside him on the rug and goes to sleep wearing zebra pyjamas. His daughter began wearing *hijab* to school this year. His business is expanding.

'I was born in Jordan', Al-Qudah says. 'But America makes me feel alive.' (Annie Hull, *Washington Post*, 27 October, 2001).

The minor characters

Whereas a metaphor stands in place of a story, minor characters can light up a story, give it depth, pathos and momentum. Take this description from Michael Herr's piece on Vietnam, entitled 'Khesanh':

He was young, nineteen, he later told me, and he was trying to grow a mous-tache. His only luck so far were a few sparse, transparent blond clumps set at odd intervals across his upper lip, and you couldn't see that unless the light was right. (Michael Herr, *Esquire*, September 1969)

Herr could have just said that Mayhew (that was his name) was 19-years-old and left us to fill in the rest. His description, brief though it is, does so much more. It tells us that this is a boy acting the part of a man and not really managing it. We feel for him – his softness in this hard place.

Maggie O'Kane is brilliant at finding and describing the minor characters in her stories. The extract below is from a report she filed from Afghanistan during the war against the Taliban. She was preparing to travel over the border with smugglers acting as guides. She doesn't tell us they are tough men. She shows us:

Meanwhile, the Prince is happy to charge us a king's ransom of $400 per person. 'Everything has a price,' he says, as he carefully peels the skin from the head of a young calf.

One of the smugglers assigned to us is Murbarak Khan. He walks out of the uncovered sheep enclosure where he has spent the night pressed up against a sheer mountain wall. He shakes the ice off his blanket. 'This is not snow,' he says, pointing to the inch-thick hail that has covered the high valley overnight. 'In 20 days it will be impossible to pass – the mountains will be completely frozen.' (Maggie O'kane, *Guardian*, 3 October 2001)

These quotes don't form part of the narrative, as an interview with a central character might do, but they provide light, colour and texture to the story.

Journalist as character

Investigations. If you are doing an investigative piece, then you may find that you are the protagonist in much the same way as the hero of a detective story is the detective. You can use your own experience and reactions to the information you discover, and the people you meet, as the thread holding the piece together. Malcolm Gladwell, writing in the *New Yorker*, takes this approach. He has a strong personal presence in all his pieces, but he is there only to guide the reader through the information, not to proselytise.

Comment and analysis. For those writing opinion or personal pieces, their own character is key. It may not necessarily be the character you would meet if you chanced upon that writer in a bar, as writing may be a way of expressing a character they feel unable to exhibit in life. That doesn't matter a bit. It is the person on the page that is important here. The joy of writing opinion pieces is that you are not expected to strive for balance and objectivity. This is an opportunity to say what you think and the clearer and more opinionated the better. That doesn't mean you should make things up, nor does it mean that you don't need to do any research. A good opinion piece is an argument that challenges the readers and engages them. An opinion column that merely repeats what everyone already thinks is neither engaging nor challenging. That doesn't mean being oppositional for the sake of it either. Readers will quickly pick up on an argument that is not genuinely felt. An opinion strongly expressed needs to be based on evidence just as much as any apparently balanced news story. The better the evidence and the clearer the argument, the more compelling it will be.

Confessional. Personal pieces also rely on the character of the journalist. Very often these are stories of personal trials and tribulations. They may be trivial but funny, or they may be deeply felt and very personal. These pieces are often derided or seen to be not proper journalism and yet they are often the most widely read part of a newspaper. As a colleague of mine pointed out: 'When I come back from Africa with a story that has taken me weeks to research I rarely get any response from the readers. When I write something personal which might have been turned around in a couple of hours I get a massive response.' This may be irksome to those who toil to uncover stories of international importance, but it also needs to be understood. People don't just read newspapers for information about the political world. They also want information about the emotional world. It is unhelpful to see one as more important than the other. We all live in both an emotional and a political world and a story about birth or death that is well written has enormous resonance because it is about a universal experience. Insight into the lives of others helps people to understand and cope with their own lives.

Interviewing

Talking to people is not only the most useful, and fastest, way to get information, it also provides you with quotable material. Judicious use of quotes will drive the story you are trying to tell and provide a sense of immediacy. It tells readers that you are speaking from the 'front line' and it a carries a similar feeling of authenticity as a photograph might. You can, of course, take quotes out of written material but it will never have the spontaneity of a real exchange. Secondary material (from the internet, old cuttings, books, press releases) can be useful for background but it is inert. You cannot ask the follow-up question, the one that would reveal what you (and your readers) really wanted to know. And you cannot see your interviewee, notice his or her reactions, or interpret his or her silences.

Research

Whether this is a report on a local flower show or an investigative piece on defence procurement. Your first step must be to inform yourself. Find out as much as you possibly can about the person you are interviewing and the situation you are going to be investigating. You may have hardly any time to do this but use it as well as you can (see 'Gathering facts', page 29). If this is a well-known person, it is vital to have some background. It is probably better to be five minutes late having read their CV than to arrive on time clueless. Have a list of questions that need answering and keep it in view so that you can refer back to it from time to time during the discussion, but don't be a slave to it. An interview is a conversation.

Recording and note taking.   Tape recorders, in some cases two tape recorders, are standard equipment for interviews of any length. Some people write notes as well as a form of reference to speed up the process of transcription (they only transcribe 'the good bits'). Several accomplished interviewers said they didn't keep notes at all (or only to record 'Status Life'). They simply re-play and transcribe the whole interview. If you are relying entirely on a tape recorder, make sure that it is working. Check at the start and then again at the end of the interview. Personally, I would recommend notes as a back-up.

Be polite, punctual, professional.   Introduce yourself and make it clear how you will record the interview (tape or notes or, preferably, both). Your first job is to put your interviewee at ease. The kind of interviewing we see on television or listen to on the radio is pretty much *useless* to a print journalist. Aggressive questioning doesn't get answers, it frightens your subject away.

Get the basics straight.   Ask for contact details in case you need to ring and confirm anything. Then get details of who, what, where, when and how, and make sure you have spelled names correctly. If there are any numbers involved, repeat them back to your interviewee to check. This 'housekeeping' will break the ice and it is very easy to forget the little questions in the rush to leave.

Ask some open questions to start with.   Even if you know the story, it will allow your interviewee to tell you what has happened in his or her own words, which will be invaluable for constructing the story in print. It also gives you a chance to put your interviewee at ease.

Direct questions.   Don't let your interviewee take over. Once you have got a sense of the story then start directing the discussion. You cannot afford to let your subject ramble on for half an hour and then say that your time is up. Use all the polite tactics at your disposal for getting them to come to the point and answer the questions you need to have answered. But do make sure that you listen carefully and come back with follow-up questions to anything that surprises you or that you don't quite understand. It is always okay to ask someone to repeat a particularly important piece of information so that you are sure you got it right.

Don't guess – ask.   Most people are not hiding terrible secrets. They usually do things because they believe them to be right. If they don't feel that you are trying to attack them, they will probably tell you what they think, or what they know. That is usually what you wanted to find out anyway.

Difficult questions. Establish a rapport and make sure you have some answers written down before you open questions that may make your interviewee clam up. Even if you only have a few minutes, it is better to get some response rather than rush in with the killer question and alienate your interviewee from the off.

Don't be afraid of tears. Someone who has been through a traumatic experience may well cry. Your questioning may also unexpectedly open up buried feelings. Be sympathetic, ask them if they would like to stop for a minute, reassure them (they may feel embarrassed) that you have time to listen and can wait for them to feel better. Don't just rush away thinking you have done something terrible. You haven't caused the tears, you have just provided an occasion for them.

Ask for details. Talking to eye-witnesses can provide the kind of fine detail that allows us to understand what it might feel like to be trapped by rising flood water, or to have your house bulldozed in front of you. Dig for detail. If they say 'it was terrifying, the water was rising', then ask exactly how high it rose: 'Was it up to your knees, your armpits, did it reach the fifth step of the stairs?'

Completing your questions. With any luck all your questions will have been answered during the discussion, but always ask if you can just check your notes before you leave.

Interviewing for character

All the above come first, but then be aware of the following.

Look around you. Make a note of small details that you could use to describe your subject. Look for anything that seems to tell you something about them.

Note reactions. One of the most useful ways of building character is by describing how your subject reacts to events, and to you: a giggle, a sigh, a silence may be more eloquent than words. Don't forget to make a note of them. This is how Lynn Barber describes an encounter with journalist Julie Birchill.

She dashes into the Hotel du Vin, followed by her retinue (she always has a retinue), tears streaming down her face. She hugs me damply and whispers in my ear, but she is squeaking so fast, like a gerbil on speed, I can hardly understand a word. 'I'm so overexcited, Lynn!' she gabbles. 'But why are you crying, Julie?' Between sobs, she explains that she is crying because my husband died a year ago. This is so typically Julie – my husband dies, so she cries all over me and I have to comfort her. Attagirl! (Lynn Barber, *The Observer*, 22 August 2004)

Family background.   Family background is part of the story. It often provides emotional turning points which give you an opportunity to understand your interviewee and could provide the 'trials' you might want to describe when developing the story. Such events may be the death of a close family member, a disappointment such as failing an exam, moving countries or schools, being bullied, etc. How did your interviewee react to such set-backs? Did they strengthen or damage him or her?

E X E R C I S E

Spend some time observing someone in public – perhaps a waitress or bar tender or a teacher in a seminar. Make a note of the dialogue you hear. Try to write down even inconsequential exchanges. Is there a pattern of response that might constitute a characteristic? Does your subject have a 'catch phrase'? Does he/she make a comment that reflects on his/her own personality or temperament? Write a one-paragraph description incorporating the phrase.

Finding your angle

Once you have done your research you have to decide how to arrange these ideas so that they make a coherent story. You may have material for half a dozen stories but you can only tell one at a time, so you have to find a single idea which will hold everything together. I describe it as the coat hanger: the idea from which everything else hangs. If yours is a Vivienne Westwood sort of story, there may be digressions and loops along the way but in the end gravitational pull and clever cutting will ensure that everything fits together and makes a whole piece. I think my coat hanger is quite similar to what 'script guru' or 'script doctor' Robert McKee described as a 'controlling idea'.

McKee says that a controlling idea is composed of 'value plus cause' (McKee, 1999: 115). You might think about the 'value' as the dynamic that underpins a story; it has a great deal in common with the story outlines we discussed in Chapter 1. The value gives it drive but it is the cause that makes us want to read on. For example, loads of stories are about powerful men brought low (tragedies) but we always want to know why this particular man fell from grace. We are fascinated by the details. Very often the cause is hinted at, but not fully revealed until the end. The understanding of cause may provide closure.

Explore the evidence first, allow the controlling idea to flow from it, and then shape the piece so that it continually refers back to this story spine. Of course you need to have an idea to start with, but never assume that your initial hunch will turn out to be right. If you don't leave yourself room at the start to change your mind, then you may charge up blind alleys or produce an article which is misleading or, more likely, hesitant and rambling because you are trying to force the facts to fit your preconceptions. If we return to the coat hanger image, you will find that the information you have gathered doesn't hang easily from your key idea.

> ## You use the evidence to build the argument. You don't use your argument to bend the evidence.

You should be able to summarise your story in one line (often it will become part of the headline or stand-first). If you cannot do this, then you can be sure that it isn't one story, but possibly several stories. Or you do not have a story, but an issue – a rag-bag of ideas vaguely connected to one another with no over-arching dynamic to keep your readers' interest going until the end. Go back to your source material and look again for one single idea which will provide the lead. The rest of the material should be organised so that it supports your major thesis: hanging from it, rather than contradicting it or departing up some different alley. You may find that you cannot use all your material. Never mind. There will be other stories, other opportunities. For this story you need to be disciplined and concentrate on one major theme.

> ## Summarise your idea in one line.

You should have worked through your basic research and worked out your controlling idea before you even pitch a story to an editor. It should be there in your initial proposal. If you find that your idea has changed, then you need to go back to the editor and talk through the changes before you start writing. Mckee suggests that once a scriptwriter has worked out the controlling idea he should stick it to his typewriter (that dates him! But some ideas never grow old) so that he keeps referring back to it as he writes. I suggest that you write a headline and story summary (in other words, a pitch) and keep referring back to it to make sure that you are keeping to the subject, or returning to it from any deliberate digressions. It may stay there as an intro or you may rewrite the intro at the end. But when you have finished the piece you should be able to say to yourself: 'Yes, I have told the story I promised to tell.'

E X E R C I S E

Think about a novel you have read recently. Summarise the key idea in a single headline and then write a short, one-paragraph stand-first.

Structure

You have already collected your information, thought about your controlling idea and considered which kind of narrative you are writing (see Chapter 1). Now go through your notes and find all the plums: the best anecdotes, the most amazing facts, the killer quotes, the telling details – underline or highlight them. This is the treasure trove you will draw on to make your piece lively and readable when you start to write, but first you need to work out a structure. Some people think it through and, once they have a clear sense of where they are going, just start writing, working on the structure as they go. Others write out their structure in detail. The right way is what works for you, but having a sense of how a piece can be structured will certainly help.

The introduction

The Introduction should grab the reader's attention and let them know why they need to read on. Introductions are discussed further below.

The killer fact/inciting incident

This usually comes pretty close to the top – either in the introduction or very shortly afterwards. In a film it would be what McKee (1999) refers to as 'the inciting incident' and what Todorov (1977) would see as the disruption of an equilibrium. It is the event that triggers the action. In journalism it is usually the reason why you are writing the story and it may be the hook.

The background

In most pieces the background will come quite quickly after the 'killer fact'. It will bring the reader up to date with the story or paint details that the reader needs to know in order to understand where the story is going.

The body

Since journalism nearly always starts with what, for a novelist, would be the ending, you are pretty much denied the single most important device in literature – suspense. Operating, as it were, in eternal flashback, a journalist is dependent on small surprises: unexpected evidence of motivation, humour, irony, descriptive power, anecdote. In a long feature these devices are particularly important because they provide interest along the way. We will discuss them in greater detail below. Structurally, pieces fall into four forms (with a fifth, hybrid or combined form):

1 **News form:** The news 'pyramid' starts with the most important facts and then adds information in descending order of importance. This style evolved from the days of 'hot metal' printing presses when stories were often crudely cut from the bottom if they were too long. Most news stories are still structured in this way.

2 **Story form:** If you are using story form, then you will be presenting your material through the eyes of a main protagonist and you will develop the 'plot' by taking your protagonist (perhaps supported by other characters) through a series of trials. They may be internal (the anguish of losing an important game, the joy of falling in love after the pain of a divorce, the fear of losing a job or an important position), or external (war, financial collapse or criminal acts). If it is an investigative piece you will be the protagonist and you will reveal what you have found out chronologically. Once you have initiated the story with the most important fact and then moved back in time to fill in the background, the story unfolds as you describe your protagonist's response to these experiences and will generally proceed chronologically. 'Real life' stories are always told in story form.

3 **Essay form:** This is where you lay out your evidence in the form of a debate. It usually helps to set out the weaker case first and then argue against it. If there are a number of points, you can group them by subject, arguing each one separately. Alternatively, you might organise them in a series of 'scenes', in which case each scene must present evidence that adds to your underlying argument or 'controlling idea'. You should clearly signpost each change of direction, using changes in tempo or emphatic statements to signal each one. Comment pieces are usually in essay form.

4 **Informational form:** You group your information thematically and make sure it is clearly signposted. This form of feature may be broken up into short paragraphs with bullet points or lists (rather like this section) or with a series of short, usually first-person, interviews. The information, in effect, provides the evidence for a short introductory news story or essay. So, for example, a feature on bias in university entrance would ideally start with a summary of the position while

the quotes provide testimony to support it. A piece on lipsticks for the summer would similarly make a pronouncement about the colours which will be 'in', followed by a list of products as evidence. Consumer and health advice is often organised in 'information' form. Increasingly news stories, illustrated with short interviews (vox pops), are also presented in this way.

5   **Hybrid form:** Long features may use a combination of forms. Often story form is combined with essay form. A feature may include a number of short 'real life' stories, each one with its own internal story structure held within an extended essay. In this case, each of the 'stories' must provide evidence to hold up the controlling idea.

The conclusion

There are different concluding techniques depending on the structural form of the piece. In the **news form,** news stories tend to 'tail off', but it is useful to have a good quote or funny anecdote as a final 'kick'. The **story form** nearly always ends with the 'moral of the story'. In magazines it will usually be what the person has learned from their experience. In profiles it may be a warning of trouble ahead. The **essay form** brings the threads of the story together and creates some sort of closure, usually by referring back to the controlling idea. Finally, the **informational form** adds the conclusion to the introduction in a short essay that can be read separately from the 'evidence'.

E X E R C I S E

Take three features and cut them into their component parts. Produce a 'map' of each describing what form the structure takes and how the information is organised.

Getting started

The introduction is the only opportunity you have for grabbing your readers' attention. If they are not stopped in their tracks, they won't read any further and you might as well not have bothered. There are many different ways of introducing a story. Some get straight to the point, others play with their readers, egging them on slowly. American feature writing is much more likely to use a slow, 'delayed drop', teasing introduction. British writers tend to come to the point pretty quickly with a clever sentence, a vivid anecdote, a summary of the story or a contradiction to be resolved. Most introductions will introduce, or at least allude to, the controlling idea of the piece.

Summary

I wrote this introduction to a 'comment' piece in the *Guardian* (30 July 2003). It summarises the issue and introduces the 'inciting incident' (the action which triggered a strike). At the same time it makes clear that this is a story about people standing up against an intransigent force. The cause: concern for their children.

If British Airways had read the latest research on how women make decisions about work, it would not have chosen this particular issue to force a show-down in the middle of the holiday season. Its largely female workforce has accepted massive redundancies and been patient with a snail's-pace wage negotiation; but they will not back down without a struggle over childcare arrangements. (Angela Phillips, *Guardian*, 30 July 2003)

Close-up

Starting with an inciting incident, like a close-up in a television documentary, this introduction catapults the readers into the middle of the action. It is a feature about the abuse suffered by asylum seekers. We have no doubt where this story is taking us and who the villains are.

On the final evening, a brick came through her kitchen and landed on the table. By dark there were four locals prowling with two dogs at the back of the house. At 10.30 a voice started screaming through her letterbox in a lan-guage she did not understand. 'My boy, who's five, was in the kitchen when the man started shouting. He went hysterical.' (Maggie O'Kane, *Guardian*, 3 December 2001)

Extended anecdote

Personal stories are another kind of close-up. They should draw the reader straight into the action. They should be intriguing and give some hint of what the story is to be about (the controlling idea).

Louise Wright set one non-negotiable condition in choosing a man: he must accept her horse as part of the relationship. The 29-year-old blonde from Bristol has been riding since she was six, and with Tigs, her black Irish geld-ing, competes enthusiastically at weekend showjumping trials when not muck-ing out at the stables. Non-horsey boyfriends have generally been dismissive if not downright suspicious of the three hours a day she says that Tigs demands of her. So when she found herself in a romantic rut last winter, she began to despair of ever meeting Mr Right. (David Rowan, *Sunday Times* [magazine], 8 January 2006)

Description

Profiles are most usually written because something has happened (an inciting incident). There is a book, a film or music to be promoted, or perhaps a rumour of a love story. In this profile of Charlotte Church, the controlling idea is a battle between ordinary working-class values and the temptations of fame and wealth. It is this tension that the writer sets up in this descriptive introduction.

> To one side of the stool on which Charlotte Church is perched while she has her make-up done is a shelf piled with very expensive jewellery. Semiprecious gems the size of babies' fists hang from chunky gold chains; a tiny diamanté tiara dangles from a silver necklace. To her other side lies a cardboard box from which peep out a sheepskin waistcoat and a couple of handbags. Just a few of the gifts sent to her by adoring designers since she last came to London. Char – everyone calls her Char – is in her element, with a favourite accessory in each hand: carton of strawberry Ribena in one, cigarette in the other. (Jessica Cartner-Morley, *Guardian*, 8 October 2005)

Scene setting

Where writers of fiction can create tension through withholding information, feature writers have to create interest by the fresh way in which they approach what is often quite familiar territory. David Blunkett was a British cabinet minister who resigned (for the second time) late in 2005. The inciting incident on which the drama hinged was his decision to get a DNA test to prove that his lover's baby was his son. Each new twist in the plot had been followed by news reporters as a separate story, each with its own controlling idea and inciting incident (and there were many), but each one of them (explicitly or implicitly) referred back to the overarching concept: Blunkett as tragic hero or fool. By the time he resigned in November 2005, the inciting incident was already in the readers' heads and feature writers had the task of finding a surprising way into a story that everyone had been talking about for months.

Nick Cohen, in *The Observer*, used the 'delayed drop' first paragraph to set a scene that clearly demonstrates his story line: London and its people are the evil which Labour politicians have tried (and often failed) to tame.

Since coming to power in 1997, Labour politicians have tried to govern Britain from the enemy territory of plutocratic London. All around them have been the City financiers, the CEOs in the corporate headquarters along the Thames, the polished lawyers in the Inns of Court and the media celebs at Wapping, Television Centre and Canary Wharf. Environment determines consciousness, as socialists used to say, and the hostile London environment has produced scandal after scandal.

He doesn't get round to the point of the story (the inciting incident) until the second paragraph:

The otherwise inexplicable decision of a working-class Labour minister from Sheffield to ruin his career for the sake of a devious arriviste from a Tory magazine makes sense only if you grasp the social geography of the capital. (Nick Cohen, *The Observer,* 6 November 2005)

One-liner

One-liners are commonly used for comment and analysis. They can be funny, provocative or just clever, and they usually summarise the controlling idea or the killer fact. *The Economist* magazine specialises in them.

Comparisons to Fascist Italy are rarely flattering, but Britain under Labour seems to be making the trains run on time. (*The Economist,* 2–8 July 2005, p. 30)

Asking a businessman to reform the legal profession is like encouraging a dog to heard salmon: he will be out of his element and liable to get soaked. (*The Economist,* 18–31 December 2004, p. 44)

E X E R C I S E

Keep a note book. Every time you read an introduction that compels you to read on, write it down.

Keep them reading

Good reporting lingers in the memory just as long as the most memorable photographs. It is what will in the end separate the professional writers from the people who just happened to be there at the time. A reporter, unlike a participant or bystander, should have the capacity to stand back and see that captured moment or detail that acts as a metaphor for an event. The moment that, for me, captured the total horror of a serious rail crash was not the details of the tangled wreckage, but the report of mobile phones ringing, unanswered, in the crushed carriages. It translated a visual image into an emotional effect. As I read the words I could feel the fear.

Martha Gelhorn filed this for *Colliers* magazine just after visiting the Dachau concentration camp in 1945:

> ... behind the crematorium the ragged clothing of the dead was neatly stacked, shirts, jackets, trousers, shoes, awaiting sterilisation and further use. The clothing was handled with order, but the bodies were dumped like garbage, rotting in the sun, yellow and nothing but bones, bones grown huge because there was no flesh to cover them, hideous, terrible, agonising bones, and the unendurable smell of death. (Martha Gelhorn, *Colliers*, May 1945)

Small details allow us to take in horrors that are too huge to contemplate in raw detail. Here it is the contrast between the methodical collecting of things and the total lack of concern for people that summarises the atrocity of the concentration camps. Gelhorn also makes use of the cumulative effect of listing the items and then she uses repetition of the key word 'bones', almost like a mantra. James Fenton also described piles of clothes in his account of the fall of Saigon:

> The most dramatic change that had taken place was the complete disappearance of the Saigon army. All around the streets one would come across piles of clothes, boots and weapons. Some of the piles were so complete it looked as if their former occupant had simply melted into his boots. (Fenton, 1989: 88)

These are big events made comprehensible by small detail, but descriptive detail can also work to lift something that might be a routine piece of writing into something memorable. Tom Wolfe, in the introduction to *The New Journalism* (1975), describes what he calls the detailing of 'status life', which is the application of this search for the telling detail to everyday accounts and profiles:

> The recording of everyday gestures, habits, manners, customs, styles of furniture, clothing, decoration, styles of travelling, eating, keeping house, modes of behaving towards children, servants, superiors, inferiors, peers, plus the various looks, glances, poses, styles of walking and other symbolic details that might exist within a scene. (Wolfe, 1975: 7)

You don't need to chuck in the whole lot. Very often just a little detail will be enough to exactly place someone in his or her social context and tell you a great deal about his or her inner state.

It is hard to create the appearance of lying down when sitting on a hard up-right chair. He managed it. Legs sprawled; chin lost in the folds of a hooded sweatshirt; eyes fixed on a point somewhere past my left knee. (AP unpublished note 2005)

Note that it is rarely necessary to use adjectives and where they are used they add detail not vague generalisation. The important thing is to look carefully and record precisely. This is how Joan Didion opens her report on Havana:

Havana vanities come to dust in Miami.
    On the August night in 1933 when General Gerardo Machado, then pres-ident of Cuba, flew out of Havana into exile, he took with him five revolvers, seven bags of gold, and five friends, still in their pyjamas. (Didion, 1987)

Good writing is never padded. Each word is there to do a job. Where adjec-tives are used at all they have a clear purpose: they describe colour, size, number. But there are other stylistic tools being used here. A list adds emphasis, and then the final contrasting banality of the pyjamas as a kind of visual full stop. Such a lot hangs on that detail – its evocation of haste and vulnerability contrasted with gold and guns. The extract below is from a piece by Annie Hull of the *Washington Post*, about the arrival of an upmar-ket grocery store in a poverty-stricken (but gentrifying) part of Washington. This paragraph paints in the background to a grocery worker's past life:

She ... found herself at a notorious cluster of tin-can trailers where drugs were sold and dewy condoms hung on the morning weeds. A door was open and she went to it. The trailers became her blurry encampment. (*Washington Post*, 1 April 2001, also in Woods, 2002)

Libby Brooks wrote this about Kylie Minogue when she had just been diag-nosed with breast cancer:

It may sound strange, but the diagnosis is also a jolting reminder that Minogue is as much blood and bone as the rest of us. She never seemed to have so mundane a component as cells. (*Guardian*, 18 May 2005)

Brooks has an amazing capacity to summarise the way people are feeling in words that nobody but her would have dreamt of using. I don't know where this comes from and I doubt it can be taught, but if you have the knack, you are on your way. Possibly this advice from George Orwell will help:

Probably it is better to put off using words as long as possible and get one's meaning as clear as one can through pictures and sensations. Afterward one can choose – not simply accept – the phrases that will best cover the meaning, and then switch round and decide what impressions one's words are likely to make on another person. (Orwell, 1950: 156)

E X E R C I S E

Go into a shop or café you have never visited, in a part of town where you don't normally go. Look for details that seem to represent what makes this place different. Then write a brief description of them, without using adjectives other than numbers or colours.

What to avoid in writing

Overdoing it

A few gems will light up your prose, but too many and it will look forced and over-elaborate. It is the tiny details that tell the story. Annie Hull, a national reporter on the *Washington Post*, puts it like this: 'If you have a beautiful sentence loaded with three images, its going to drag down the whole sentence. You just need one. Pick one. That takes discipline' (in Woods, 2002: 204).

One way of overdoing it is to mix metaphors, like this: 'Kate Moss ... Sir Philip's latest designer signing ... appears to have been the blockage which has put the snag in the zip of the newest high-street celebrity marrige' (Hilary Alexander, *Daily Telegraph*, 6 October, 2006, p. 5).

Blockage, snag, zip, marriage: three metophors, none of which add anything to the story.

Clichés

Avoid borrowing phrases that have been coined by others. Occasionally, you can turn a cliché to your own use with a subtle shift of emphasis (rather as you can dress up an old pair of jeans if you wear them tight, coupled with an outrageous pair of six-inch heels). But mostly, if a phrase sounds familiar, avoid it. An overused concept is about as interesting as that old pair of jeans (with baggy knees and without the six-inch heels). Here are some phrases to avoid 'like the plague':

- avoid like the plague,
- level playing field,
- gorgeous blonde (or brunette),
- high as a kite,
- passed its sell-by date.

All of them were once new metaphors, which, no doubt, livened up prose and helped the reader to understand what was being discussed. Today we take them in without even noticing what they mean. They have become what George Orwell, in his essay 'Politics and the English Language', referred to as 'empty metaphors' (Orwell, 1950). Metaphors should help us to understand something better by referencing it to another idea, concept or image, but they should also surprise us. It is the slippage between the idea and the metaphor as well as the shock of recognition that makes us sit up. A metaphor which is so well worn that we no longer feel that slight shock of surprise is on the way out.

Clichéd ideas

Topics and ideas can also become clichéd from overuse. This comment appeared in the *Financial Times Weekend* (9 April 2006: 1) the same week that the UK was reconfirmed as having some of the best restaurants in the world. It was in a piece about Americans who chose to live in the UK:

They like Britain's proximity to other countries and the sense of being connected to the rest of the world. Some even like the weather (but not the food – 'bland, tasteless and boiled or fried to death').

This description of British food hails from a stereotype of the 1960s. It's a knee-jerk remark that really shouldn't have been repeated in print.

Repetition

Try not to use the same word twice in one paragraph (never in one sentence). Don't keep using the same word to introduce paragraphs. Only repeat facts for emphasis. If you need to do so for any other reason, it is probably because you have not sorted out your structure.

Long words

Do not use long words where short ones will do or official words where there is a simpler alternative.

If you know something, tell us. Don't tease us.

Rhetorical questions

Don't ask your readers. Tell them. Rhetorical questions are often lazy devices for linking paragraphs that don't quite fit together. So make the paragraphs fit.

Convoluted and overlong sentences

Quite often the problem is that you have used the passive rather than the active voice. 'The man hit the dog', is in the active voice. It is rather more dynamic than the passive construction: 'the dog was hit by the man'. It is also shorter. There may be a very good reason for writing a long sentence. Having broken it up into a sequence of clauses, each of which is internally correct and well organised, your sentence may seem to be serving the purpose for which you designed it and you might feel that it no longer needs to be reorganised, or reconstructed, in the active voice. But it is usually worth the effort.

George Orwell's advice to writers

Orwell's advice (1950) to writers is still as useful as it was half a century ago:

1. Never use a metaphor, simile, or other figure of speech which you are used to seeing in print.
2. Never use a long word where a short one will do.
3. If it is possible to cut a word out, always cut it out.
4. Never use the passive where you can use the active.
5. Never use a foreign phrase, a scientific word, or a jargon word if you can think of an everyday English equivalent.
6. Break any of these rules sooner than say anything outright barbarous.

Rewriting

However talented you are, carefully crafted writing takes time and thought. As ex-editor of British *Cosmopolitan*, Marcelle D'Argy Smith, says: 'its not the writing, its the rewriting that matters'. Always take time to read and re-read everything and never be afraid to cut.

Does your structure work? Go back to your original 'controlling idea' (page 41) and make sure you have stuck to it throughout. If you haven't done so, consider whether you had the idea clear in your mind, and whether it does actually arise from your evidence rather than being imposed on it. If you don't think it works, then you may need to go back to the beginning and start again. If you are still happy with your controlling idea, make sure that the story flows clearly and that you haven't been inadvertently distracted by anecdotes (however fascinating) which don't actually add anything or help the story along? Get rid of anything that interferes with the structure, even if it is a paragraph you have slaved over. If you have slaved over it for too long it clearly isn't working, so out it goes.

Don't let your tape recorder take over. Your interview is there to provide evidence. Decide on your story line and then select the quotes to illustrate it. Don't use the interview as the story. If quotes are confused or over-long, cut them and use reported speech to summarise the points. Short quotes providing colour may be all you need to demonstrate that you 'were there'.

Make sure that every word is the right one. Replace long or jargony words with short simple ones wherever you can. Check each sentence to see whether you can make it tighter and clearer. Cut out any word that is there for effect and doesn't have any other function. Break up, or rephrase, sentences which are too long. You can often improve things just by ensuring that the subject of your sentence is at the beginning and not trailing along passively at the end.

Re-read your introduction, and then read the next paragraph. You may well find that they repeat each other. You will have to drop one of them. This may be tough because introductions are the key to a story and you have probably worked hard on them without noticing that they are both doing the same job.

Read widely and look for really good writing – not to copy it but to recognise it.

PART II

EXAMPLES OF GREAT WRITING

The best way to learn about great writing is to read it. In this section you will find a selection of pieces that I have enjoyed. They are chosen, not because of the moments they record but because of the way they are written. Some are flawed. Journalism is produced fast, to deadline, there may have been little opportunity for considered re-drafting. Many I chose because they had stuck in my mind and I went back to find them. Other emerged from a lot of reading of magazines and collected works. I read a great deal that was dull, published at a length it didn't deserve, so formulaic that the content could be read from the headline, or just plain bad. I also read a lot that was wonderful. I couldn't use everything I chose because I needed a spread of different kinds of writing. Some things I have reluctantly cut out at the last minute for reasons of space. I hope you will enjoy them, and learn from them that great writing is not about forms and formulae, but about zest, enthusiasm and the ability to articulate ideas in ways that make us sit up and see things differently.

3

REPORTAGE

Good reportage is journalism at its best. It makes readers feel as though they have been there and it lingers in the memory long after the newspaper has been recycled into toilet paper. It sounds so simple. You go, you see, you hear and you write it down. Good reportage has its foundations in good research. The research is not necessarily evident but without it your questioning would be rudderless and your story confused. Your knowledge helps you to see, listen and think analytically and then to choose what evidence you need to tell your story. You have at your disposal:

- Dialogue – to give the piece a sense of immediacy, variety and authenticity,
- Description – to provide the 'details of status life' (see page 49) that allows your reader to place the people and events,
- Commentary – which is how you sum up your background knowledge as well as providing interpretation and analysis.

But of course it isn't simple. From all the sights, the sounds, the smells, how do you select the bits to write down? Then how do you arrange them into a compelling story? If you have read the section on narrative you will understand a little about this process. From the mass of information available, you, the writer, have to find a coherent story. You then have to decide how that story can best be told. The very best reportage uses dialogue and description in place of commentary. Having listened to the evidence, you will then select what is necessary to tell the story *as you see it* in the most compelling way you can. It is possible that another journalist will look at the same evidence and find a different story which can then be told via a different selection of the same facts.

 GARY YOUNGE It may seem a bit perverse to start with a story written by a journalist who is at his best on the comment pages (see Chapter 9, pages 196–212). I am using this piece because it demonstrates just how important it is to look beyond the obvious, accepted narrative of events. In spring 2000 Zimbabwe

bounced on to the front pages due to the deaths of white farmers during government-sponsored land disputes. News coverage had focused exclusively on these deaths, reporting within a narrative that concentrated entirely on a fight between good (white) and evil (black). Young arrived in Zimbabwe and, with this piece (published on the front page), changed the framing of the debate. This, like all the other news stories, is a factual account. It is just that he selected different facts and told a hidden story.

This is not racism, it's politics
Guardian, Thursday 20 April 2000

Tichaona Chiminya was a reserved man but when he talked politics he could breathe fire.

His friends describe him as retiring but he knew how to hold a crowd.

'When he was addressing people about democracy he spoke with a certain intensity,' says one of his peers in Zimbabwe's main opposition party, the Movement for Democratic Change (MDC).

This gentle, reflective descriptive delayed-drop introduction, is about as far away from a classic news intro as you can get. It feels like the beginning of a story.

On Saturday evening he was driving with another MDC supporter, Talent Mabika, when his car was stopped by supporters of President Robert Mugabe's ruling Zanu-PF party. They were carrying clubs, sticks and iron bars.

They dragged both him and Ms Mabika into the road, clubbed them to death and then set their bodies alight. His family had planned to bury him yesterday but his body was so charred that the funeral parlour needed an extra day to treat it. They hope to lay him to rest later today.

Now we get the inciting incident. He doesn't tell us how to think about it. There are no adjectives or adverbs. The story needs no embellishment. The details tell it all. We are then brought back to the present and to the grieving family and friends. This choice of story location is deliberate. Front pages of British newspaper had been filled with pictures of Zimbabwean funerals for days. But all the mourners had been white.

In the meantime his father's house in the township of Highfield, near Harare, plays host to displays of defiance and grief. In the front garden MDC supporters toyi-toyi (protest dance) to the chant: 'MDC is for the masses.'

With T-shirts proclaiming 'land to the people, not to the politicians' they shuffle and jive in an apparently endless circle around a drum. They rise and fall with the beat, their open palms – the symbol of the MDC – held high. When they get tired they sit on sofas underneath the lemon tree.

In the back garden family members are grieving: women prepare dinner in tears; others simply sit, in the arms of friends and neighbours, and stare into space. The weeping is sober and persistent.

Chiminya's father-in-law stands by the kitchen door, trying to maintain a dividing line between the personal and political. 'To you this is about politics,' he says. 'To me it is about my daughter's husband.'

That line is occasionally breached. A weeping relative will dry their eyes and shuffle past the vegetable patch to join the demonstrators.

Chiminya was not only a husband and son-in-law but also the father of a daughter of 15 and a son of 11. Once the national organiser of the Chemical Workers Union, he had recently been appointed the driver for the MDC leader, Morgan Tsvangirai.

Few of these details emerged when he was killed. Chiminya was one of at least six black Zimbabweans – five MDC supporters and one policeman – who died in the violence that has engulfed the country over the past two weeks.

He was murdered on the same day as David Stevens, the first white farmer to be killed, but while the Stevens murder triggered headlines of impending civil war, the lives of Chiminya and Mabika earned little more than a footnote in reports of the day's violence.

MDC supporters say that the portrayal of recent events in the country as a racial war is precisely what Mr Mugabe was hoping for. With interest rates, unemployment and inflation all high and only a month before elections are due, opposition leaders regard the land invasions as a bloody sideshow.

'This is not about racism but about politics,' says Remus Makuwaza, an executive member of the MDC. 'The government is trying to divert attention away from its political and economic problems so it has targeted a minority.'

White Zimbabweans make up just 1% of the population but own the vast majority of the best farmland, which was taken from the indigenous people over many decades.

Most Zimbabweans, including many whites, agree that there must be land reform. Few, including most blacks, believe the government is going about it in the right way.

Polls suggest Mr Mugabe's Zanu-PF remains the single most popular party but little of that popularity is rubbing off on Mr Mugabe. The MDC has been gaining ground, holding rallies around the country.

'We have been independent now for 20 years,' says Kitizo, a young man who lives in Harare and refuses to give his full name for fear of reprisal. 'So of course we cannot continue with such a small group of people owning so much land when so many in rural areas have nothing. But we should not be killing them. We need democracy also.'

After the description of the funeral, he reverts to a simple, pyramid news structure but the final quote provides closure and underlines the controlling idea contained in the headline. After this story appeared, the framing of the debate changed, not just in the Guardian, *but in most British newspapers.*

MARTHA GELHORN

It is rare to find a collection of reportage without an example of war reporting. Certainly the framework of war provides drama, tension and pathos but the techniques are not different from those used in the very best of peace reporting: fine attention to detail and judicious use of dialogue. The over-arching plot line here is of good standing up against evil. The angle and the key idea running through the piece is the bravery of the French soldiers. It starts in story form and her hero (the driver) is shown undergoing various trials, but towards the end the structure changes to essay form with a passionate defence of the French against the assumed prejudice of her readers. Carefully chosen descriptive detail is used throughout to build up sympathy for the allies and tap into the readily available dislike of the Germans and Italians. Compare this to the use of similar description to build sympathy, in the piece by George Packer on pages 109–31. This piece, like the first one, clearly has a point of view, and yet both are basically reportage.

Visit Italy
Colliers magazine, February 1944

The French soldier driving the jeep had large dark sad eyes. He was small, thin and dirty and he looked ill. The windshield and the top of the jeep were down and the snow had changed to hail. The road circling up the mountains was narrow and slippery. Wind blew across the grey stone sides of the mountains and over the snow peaks and drove the hail into our faces. The little jeep driver was having a bad time, as was everyone else on the road. From time to time we would pass a completely unnecessary sign: a skull-and-bones painted on a board, with underneath the phrase in French: 'The enemy sees you.' No one needed to be warned. There you were, on a roller-coaster road freezing to death, and if the enemy couldn't see you, he was blind; he was sitting right across there, on that other snow mountain.

> *The introduction is a descriptive passage that takes us right into the middle of the experience. As you read you can feel the physical discomfort: the cold, the wind, the hail and the fear. And you empathise with this sad, thin, sick man. Note how, throughout the piece, images of war are evoked as cold and grey while, by contrast, images of peace are suffused with sunshine and colour.*

The jeep driver spoke with sudden bitter mockery. 'Visitez l'Italie!' he said.

There used to be tourist posters in France, in all the railroad stations, showing a sunstruck and enchanting glimpse of country with a dark-haired girl eating grapes or maybe just laughing, and the posters urged, 'Visit Italy.'

Now we were visiting Italy. It was a small, peculiar and unhealthy piece of Italy – the French front. It was a bulge of mountains; the French held these mountains, and opposite them, on higher mountains, were the Germans. The mountains to the right were occupied by the Poles, and to the left, around Cassino, were the Americans. The Italian front is very curious anyhow. One day we figured there were twenty races and nationalities stretched across Italy from the Mediterranean to the Adriatic, all fighting the Germans. The French held the highest mountains of all: this front. It was colder here than anywhere else though it was cold enough everywhere and no one believed this wind would ever blow at less than gale force, and just when you began to hope that spring might come it would snow again.

Before he came to this naked road, the jeep driver had been a barman in Casablanca. Now he said, through stiff, cold lips: 'Have you ever had an Alexander cocktail, Mademoiselle?'

We passed a burned American tank, rounded a curve and saw two trucks which had plunged down a ravine and were hanging almost perpendicularly against the side of the mountain. An Alexander is a horrible, sweet drink made with *crème de cacao*.

'Yes, indeed,' I said, holding a tin hat in front of my face as a shield against the hail.

'I do not mean to brag,' the Frenchman said, 'but I made the best Alexanders in Casablanca.' Then we were silent because it was too hard to talk. Perhaps he was thinking of his bar, or the small café he hoped to have in France after the war. I was thinking about that wonderful phrase, 'Visit Italy.'

Coming north from Naples, you drive in a steady stream of khaki-colored traffic: trucks and jeeps, command cars and ambulances, wrecking cars and trucks and tank destroyers and munitions carriers. There is no end to the traffic, and if you are unlucky you will find yourself behind a convoy which rumbles along like marching elephants, and, since the roads are narrow and the traffic is thick both ways, you are forced to learn patience.

Along the sides of the road are endless tent camps pitched in the mud lakes that form under olive trees or in the deep gluey mud of open fields. One soldier is always shaving under the forbidding sky, with care and a comic solemnity and quite alone. Naked to the waist in the cold, he wages the losing battle to keep clean. Acres of cars are parked, with men working on broken motors in a misery of mud. There never was so much wheeled transport, you think; all Italy seems to be moving.

When you first pass through the villages they are incredible; it is not possible that once these places stood up foursquare and people lived in them. No cyclone could have done as thorough a job as high explosive has. After a while you do not even notice the sliced houses, the landslides of rubble, the torn roofs. The roads are bordered with telephone wires, looking like thick, twisted vines in the jungle; dozens of wires, draped and hung over what trees remain, or simply trailing on the ground. Then there are the neatly placed tent hospitals, and suddenly out of a side road tanks appear, loud, blind and waiting for nothing.

As you get nearer the front, Italy becomes an even stranger country to visit. Three Italian children take turns swinging on a piece of old telephone wire hung from a tree in an ammunition dump. Blown bridges rest like boxcars in the river beds. Jeeps pass, with their names painted on them: Calamity II, Death Dodger, Betty Ann.

In a hollow below the climbing road, Italian women are washing clothes at an old stone trough, and six-wheeled trucks plough somehow up the hill through mud that looks like churned brown cement. The echo of shell explosions bangs crazily against the mountains. You pass through a mud flat, where nothing grows except guns, and two French batteries of 155s open up against the Germans, who are on a mountain you cannot see, and everyone on the road is briefly deafened. If you are right under the guns, you open your mouth and breathe hard.

The road keeps climbing and now there are soldiers' camps on the upright sides of the mountain. They are French native troops wearing American uniforms. Suddenly the road turns and before you there is a wilderness of mountains, crushed against one another, rolling higher and higher to the north, with the snow very clean on them. It is the most beautiful view of all – so beautiful that everyone notices it, though everyone dislikes it, for the Germans are there.

> Note the use of contrasts: cold air against warm naked bodies; a sea of mud and men trying to keep clean in spite of it; children swinging over a munitions dump; women washing as guns roar; the beautiful view, and the hated Germans. And throughout the rhythm of endless, slow ponderous movement.

At the turning, a French colonial soldier wearing a long, striped robe and a turban is standing on the roof of a pillbox, inspecting the German mountain range. He stands like a statue, as if he had just found this nice place to rest when he had some free time to himself. From now on, you circle down to the Rapido, and the war gets smaller and you see fewer people and less transport. You begin to hear and see with fierce concentration, holding your body tight together.

Now a change of direction – we are moving on to more detailed description of the French soldiers and how our heroes have been tested. We are also moving away from 'objective' reportage into passionate debate. A series of rhetorical questions signal the change in tone. The next few paragraphs are full of anger. Again notice the use of contrasting details: the French provide first aid and the Germans send shells.

Visit Italy, indeed! It is all this and so much more. It would take a rare kind of guidebook to tell you the sights of Italy alone. And how about the new tourists, the soldiery? How will you ever know about the twenty races and nationalities who fight as allies in Italy? How will you ever know all they have done and seen and felt and survived? Some of them will write about this campaign after the war, and that will be the good writing. But perhaps it is impossible to understand anything unless it happened to you yourself.

The jeep driver and I were going to San Elia, which used to be a town and is now a mass of blown-up masonry. Two French first-aid posts operate here. They are stationed in dirty basements that have beautiful thick walls. Otherwise there is no use for the town; it is only a place that troops and transport pass through, a place to be shelled whenever the Germans think it profitable.

Across the Rapido from the town is the Belvedere, a bleak grey stone mountain that the French took. What the French take they stay on, and it is quiet on the mountains now. A sizable unit went into the attack and hardly more than twenty per cent were able to walk off the mountain, but the French hold it, and that is what they want. Because each mountain they take, at whatever cost, is a mountain nearer home.

The French are earning their way home and they do not complain. They know exactly what they are doing and they are doing it superbly. They are fighting for the honor of France, which is not just a phrase, as you might think, but the personal, undying pride of every one of them. And they are fighting to get home to a country cleansed of Germans. Home means a street, a house, a face that has not been seen for too many years. Home means the lovely sky and the lovely land of France.

One group is described only in terms of their finest points and the other is described only in terms of their collective guilt. The fact that she is travelling with a medical unit (there to pick up the wounded) helps us to build up a picture of the French as human and vulnerable and the Germans as casually brutal. This selective use of detail helps to build the particular narrative she has chosen to use.

The mountains of Italy are horrible; to attack always against heights held by well-entrenched and well-trained enemy troops is surely the worst sort of war. Nothing can help the infantry much in mountains: Germans dug into the stone sides of these cliffs can survive the heaviest shelling. Tanks cannot operate. So at last it is the courage and determination of a Frenchman against the courage and determination of a German. The French have been taking their objectives.

The jeep driver belonged to a *compagnie de ramassage*, which means literally a pick-up company. His outfit has to collect the wounded from the sides of these mountains, carry them down on stretchers and drive them back to base hospitals over roads which would be dangerous even if no one shelled them. In these mountains it is not unusual for a wounded man to be carried for ten hours before he reaches a road and a waiting ambulance. The present headquarters of his company was one of the basements in San Elia. We drove rapidly past the two known evil points at the entry of the town – there are always the places that are certain to be shelled, and then there are the surprise places.

An ambulance was parked inside the front door of the first-aid station. The stretcher-bearers slept on straw on the floor next to the ambulances. Down a dark, stony passageway was the room where the doctor worked. A fine-faced, cocoa-colored soldier from Martinique lay on the improvised operating table. He had very bright eyes and he was quite silent but there was this odd, birdlike curiosity in his eyes. Across the room a white soldier sat on a chair, not moving, but looking at his friend. Under the blanket you could see that the Martiniquan had only one leg. They had just been brought in.

These two were repairing a telephone line beside the Rapido when a shell landed near them. A sliver of the shell pierced the left eye of the Frenchman, another fragment almost severed the leg of the Martiniquan. The blinded man made a tourniquet of telephone wire to stop his friend's hemorrhage, and then, because the torn leg was hanging by skin and tendons only, he cut the leg off with his clasp knife. After this he carried his comrade to the road and went for help.

The Martiniquan kept saying in his soft, old-fashioned French, 'I love my friend very much but he should not have cut off my leg.'

The soldier who had only one eye refused treatment until he was sure his comrade was well cared for, then he accepted a shot of morphine. Nothing could be done for his eye; it would have to be taken out at the base hospital.

It is worth noting that many of the French soldiers were black. She makes much of the rapport between black and white perhaps to contrast the humanity of the French troops with the racism of the Fascists.

There were no more wounded, so the doctor, the transport officer and I went down to their living quarters, a very cold room in another cellar. Half the dirt floor had been covered with old doors to keep the damp from the mattresses they slept on. There was a table with a marble top, an iron stove that barely worked, two kerosene lamps, four uncertain chairs, an upright piano with planks for legs, a radio, some mice, a pervading odor of damp and good thick walls.

We sat with a bottle of Italian cognac, which tastes like perfume and gasoline, and waited for dinner. An American AMG (Allied Military Government) major was in town with his aide. They had evacuated the entire civil population and were leaving for another village in the morning, but tonight they were coming to dine. They would presumably arrive before the evening shelling started.

We got Switzerland on the radio in order to learn what was happening in Cassino, seven kilometers away. We also tuned in on Berlin to hear what they were giving out, and they announced that they would now play the music of a grenadier regiment fighting on the Italian front. These were the German troops two kilometers away from our cellar. 'It is not bad music,' the transport officer said, 'except for all that boom-boom they always have.'

> Note that even the German's music is described only to increase our sense of them as loud and brutish. The Italians are dismissed as less than human in contrast with the humane French and Americans who share their food, their drinks and their culture.

The two Americans arrived and were warmly greeted. The evening shelling started while we ate our C rations. The French doctor told the American major that there were three civilian corpses in the church, and the American said, 'My God! Are they still there? It's too awful the way the Italians won't take the trouble to bury one another.' The twenty-year-old soldier who was the major's aide said he was going to write a book entitled *My Life on a Bull's-eye*. This reminded the French of a wonderful American book they had once read, called *Gentlemen Prefer Blondes*, and they rocked with laughter as they retold each other all the jokes.

Then a soldier came in and said someone was wounded by a mine in a field near the Rapido, so the transport officer went out to get the wounded man. The Americans went home after a while. They lived in a house that always seemed to get shells in the garden but never in the building, and they were counting on this.

The doctor said it was terrible about the mine fields; they no longer allowed anyone to walk into a field to pull out wounded men, because one day seven men were killed trying to get one man out. The mines were perhaps the worst of all. Now one just threw a rope to the wounded man and dragged him back to the swept, safe ground.

'Think of it,' he said, 'for years after this war, people will be killed all over Europe in such fields; men will be killed sowing their wheat and children will be killed playing. It is horrible. Everything about war is too horrible to consider.'

The transport officer came back after a while and said the man was dead.

That night I lay in my cot and listened to the mice and the shells, and thought about the French in Italy. It is impossible to describe the hardships of their life; it would take too long, and the words wouldn't mean anything. They eat the same food all the time, the universally loathed C and K rations; they are never warm; they are never sure to be dry; they have no possible relaxation. They watch their comrades die and know how entirely expendable they are, and that they have no replacements.

I remember the dead girl ambulance driver, lying on a bed in a tent hospital, with her hands crossed on a sad bunch of flowers, and her hair very neat and blond, and her face simply asleep. She had been killed on the road below San Elia, and her friends, the other French girls who drove ambulances, were coming to pay their last respects. They were tired and awkward in their bulky, muddy clothes. They passed slowly before the dead girl and looked with pity and great quietness at her face, and went back to their ambulances.

I remember the troops on the roads, tough and hard, watching the Italian refugees pass by with their usual bundles, the usual blank eyes and the usual slow, weary walk. There was no kindness in the French soldiers. One man said to himself but speaking for everyone, 'There were refugees on all the roads in France. Each one in his turn.'

I remembered the snow-topped mountain called La Mainarde, and the deep, beautifully placed German machine-gun posts, and I thought of the Frenchmen who had taken this mountain. They are dying very fast, but they always go on to the higher and higher mountains.

You hear a lot of rot, traveling around the world. You hear people say France is finished, the French are no good, look at their politics, look at the collapse of France, they will never be a great people again. So I lay in my cot and thought that anyone who speaks or thinks like that is a fool, and if he wants to know how foolish he is, he'd better visit Italy.

© Estate of Martha Gellhorn

ANTHONY LOYD Reporters in a war zone are only seeing fragments of the action. Loyd seeks out people to stand as metaphors. In doing so he allows us to see the human beings behind the rhetoric and the statistics of war. He makes judicious use of dialogue to tell the story and keeps his own comments to a minimum. Unusually for a piece that was published on the news pages, this is written in story form, starting with an extended anecdote, moving on to provide background and returning to the chronology. It is a transformation narrative – from child to killer. The key idea is the mother who murders.

Kalashnikov matriarch emerges to tell of her life as an Afghan warlord
The Times (London), 21 October 2004

CODENAMED Kaftar – 'the Pigeon' – the veteran Afghan commander pulls a Kalashnikov from the folds of a coat and loads a round as our vehicle nears the valley's last village.

The inciting incident: note the theatrical way this gesture is described and the use of status life (the coat and guns and the relationship with the people around the main figure) to build character. We are already expecting trouble.

'I have a problem with some of the people here – old enemies,' Kaftar says quietly, huddled in the back seat cradling the assault rifle. But the vehicle passes through the narrow muddy streets without incident, and Kaftar hails a traveller and passes him the Kalashnikov. 'Take my rifle back up the valley to my sons in the house,' the man is told. 'We need all the weapons we have.'

Blood feud and gun law: familiar syndromes in Afghanistan's remote valleys where families can battle for generations over zar, zan, zamin – money, women, land. But Kaftar's case is unique. A killer of many men, and the former commander of a 1,200-strong column of Mujahidin, Kaftar is a woman.

He keeps this 'killer fact' back for three paragraphs, building up tension and then surprising us. Note also the structure of the last phrase. The key information is dropped at the end of the sentence in four words. The change in pace adds to the surprise.

The legend of Kaftar had long persisted, with tales reaching Kabul of a woman based in a remote valley in the country's northern Baghlan province who fought against the Soviet Union and then the Taleban.

It was not until April this year, as a UN programme to disarm Afghanistan's child soldiers was put into effect, that the rumours were confirmed. UN officials returned to the capital saying they had discovered Kaftar, living in the Darisujan valley with an entourage of Mujahidin, including children and female bodyguards.

Denuded of her command by a subsequent demilitarisation programme, she now lives on her own except for her horse, her guns and her sons. She is haunted by memories of a lifetime's fighting, embroiled in blood feuds and troubled by an abstract concept of peace.

> *The use of a alliterative three-part list gives the sentences a rhythmic quality.*

'We Mujahidin have not been given our rights,' she complains, her face framed by thick braids beneath an open scarf. 'We fought for so long but this Karzai Government has given us nothing.'

> *The background to the story makes it clear that we are privileged to meet this remarkable person. Then we return to the chronology of her life.*

Kaftar, whose real name is Bibi Aisha, is unable to read or write and puts her age at between 50 and 55. Her ascent to military command was made possible by violent tribal infighting and the power of her father Haji Dawlat.

The eldest of ten children by the second of Dawlat's seven wives, Kaftar was his favourite. She was carrying a gun by the age of 14, defending her home against rival families, and had killed her first man long before the Soviet invasion of 1979.

> *The use of dialogue adds the 'Wild West' feeling. It is terse and to the point – perhaps because it is being translated – but these word bullets add to the sensation of toughness.*

'I can't remember how many I have killed since,' she says. 'I remember getting my first Russian though. It was early in the occupation and he was a commando. He was close. A young man. I shot him. Later at the Battle of Kelagai we were killing so many we just threw their bodies in the river.'

She married a businessman named Shad Muhammad, the same year she took up arms. He bankrolled her gunslinging family. They later divorced.

Her seven sons, two of whom were killed on operations under her command, became the mainstay of her power after her father died in 1981. Of the 1,200 fighters Kaftar led, mounted on a horse and dressed in US-style combats, 400 were family members including two step sisters who were her bodyguards. 'But I never had a problem giving orders to men,' she insists. 'My father was head of a powerful tribe.'

The death of two of her boys along with one of her brothers, slain in combat with the Taleban, appears not to trouble her. It was the death of her commander, the iconic Ahmad Shah Masood, assassinated by a suicide bomber in September 2001, that now shadows her days.

He selects three pieces of information: all of them counterpoint death and motherhood. This, it becomes clear, is the controlling idea of the piece and it is returned to in the final sentence.

'Oh, Masood!' she sighs. 'I smiled as I buried my sons, because they died in the way of God fighting a jihad, and I was proud of them. But Masood was my leader and was murdered. It was the saddest day of my life.'

As the chill of an autumn afternoon settles around her home, she kills a chicken for her foreign guests, even though it is Ramadan and she cannot eat until sunset. Her reputation for cruelty seems unfounded.

But after we leave her cousin Abdul Ghaffur, a former Mujahid whose legs were blown off by a mine on the last day of the war, speaks. 'You saw the blood of the chicken in the yard,' he says. 'But you didn't see the blood in the stables.'

'Two of Kaftar's sons cut the throat of a 20-year-old man from another family there three weeks ago on her orders. There have been killings in this valley as long as anyone can remember, and there will be killings for a long time to come. And Kaftar's family are always involved. Don't mistake her. Tough, yes. But very cruel.'

© The Times

MARTIN WAINWRIGHT

It was only a little flood by the standards of 2005 but this report, which appeared in the news pages of the *Guardian*, demonstrates that observation, description, use of metaphor and judicious use of dialogue, in addition to good research, is just as important in home news as it Is in war reporting. Check online for other reports of this event. Most have similar details but lack the vivid immediacy of this one.

Villagers clean up after flash floods
Guardian, 21 June 2005

As an 80mph wall of water hits an area once seen as safe, minister warns that climate change means many more homes are vulnerable.

The stand-first neatly encapsulates both the controlling idea and the inciting incident. Then, unusually for a news story, this one starts with an extended, descriptive introduction, which includes the kind of detail of status life that helps the reader to imagine exactly what it might feel like to have been here but also who these people are. It also includes a great deal of information: from the age of the stones, so suddenly up-ended, to the exact wind speed.

Ruth Mitchell's garden wall had stood for probably 200 years between her picturebook cottage and Thirlby Road, but yesterday its huge, hand-carved stones were tumbled across her flower borders like broken dominoes.

In less than 10 minutes a welter of water travelling at 80mph sucked the soil from the foundations and left the great slabs on Miss Mitchell's lawn as the 87-year-old fled upstairs with the Sutton Beck's water only inches behind.

It stopped at the ninth of her 11 stair treads, after metal rollerdoors at her neighbours' double garage caved in, releasing enough of the swollen torrent – along with their car and caravan – into a paddock and fields beyond. Thirlby Road, meanwhile, curled up in whole sections as the water forced its way under the tarmac, rolling it away from stone and rubble underlay as old as Ms Mitchell's vanished wall.

Then we have the background detail, which places this flood among others in the region.

She had never seen anything like it, she said yesterday as shocked neighbours in Sutton-under-Whitestonecliffe – once the home of the Yorkshire vet and author James Herriot – took stock of the narrow but devastating path which flash floods cut through the hamlet's heart. Unlike the slow ponderous floods which have engulfed York, Selby and Carlisle in the last three years, this one was focused, furious and very fast.

Now the evidence is gathered together. Note the freshness of the description. These are not stock phrases, they are eye-witness accounts from those who were there but also from the journalist himself. This is not the sort of reporting which can be done behind a computer terminal. Note also how background details (gathered by phone or via agency reports) are tucked into the account.

'All we could hear was raging, crashing, thudding and smashing,' said Shelagh Smith, whose garden was one of half-a-dozen still smeared in a thick film of grey Yorkshire mud. A few yards away, close to the village's steel bus shelter which was the only thing still upright close to the beck, another garden wall was sticking at an acute angle out of a hole gouged in the ground.

Miss Mitchell's ruined wall shared her flowerbeds with a tall wooden cupboard, a fridge, two pink armchairs and a matching sofa – part of a mountain of damage which is expected to cost insurers at least £40m.

Now we move into a more conventional news story in which the details of the events have been gleaned from a number of sources and worked into a standard news triangle with information simply ordered in descending importance.

The damage followed an equally focused deluge on Sunday night. One of a band of heatwave cloudbursts, accurately forecast by the Met Office, drenched the catchments of the Sutton beck and river Rye with the area's entire average rainfall for June – some three inches (7.6cm) – in less than three hours.

The rivers rose instantly, at a rate not seen in the rich farmland below Sutton Bank for some four lifetimes, while sheets of surface water streamed down bone-dry fields on the steep escarpment of the Cleveland Hills to add to the torrent. Part of the A170 disappeared under a landslide, one bridge was carried away, two buckled and a third, the ancient main road crossing below Helmsley castle, remains closed and may need major structural repairs.

More than 2,500 houses were still without power last night after a day which saw Helmsley, one of North Yorkshire's busiest summer tourist centres, look like a Middle Eastern souk with pungent carpets drying in the sun on pavements and roads. Twenty houses and shops were inundated and several suffered structural damage.

The flooding was described as an 'extreme event' by the minister for flood defence, Elliot Morley, who thanked rescuers, including RAF helicopter crews who lifted about nine people from trees and roofs in the worst-hit areas.

But both he and the Environment Agency warned that the effects of climate change might increase the likelihood of freak weather damage in places which had not previously been seen as vulnerable.

'This is a reminder that flooding may now happen at any time and in unexpected places,' said Mr Morley. 'People have to think more about what they can do to adapt their homes to mitigate the impacts.'

Bewildered residents in Hawnby, a village above the medieval ruins of Rievaulx abbey which were cut off by a new lake at the height of the deluge, said that they had never imagined that flooding could affect their hilly perch.

Other victims included biking enthusiasts clearing up after a 10,000-strong rally at Duncombe Park, just outside Helmsley, where caravans were swept away and big touring motorbikes dragged downstream. Lord and Lady Feversham, who live at Duncombe, served teas to 50 bikers in the mansion, while a helicopter from RAF Leconfield hauled others from the flooded ruins of the campsite.

Two flood warnings and two lower status flood watches still covered most of the North York Moors and Vale of York river system last night. North Yorkshire police and volunteers were searching isolated areas, but all nine people initially reported missing had been located.

All but one of 25 dogs at a kennels in Hawnby which briefly became a land-locked Noah's Ark were rescued, but 350 sheep are feared drowned.

> *A neat ending with a humorous detail which is only possible because, though this might be a harbinger of worse trouble to come, nobody died in these floods.*

The floods also hit the centre of the large market town of Thirsk, where household belongings were washed into the streets and a lavatory seat ended up incongruously round a pavement bollard like a hoopla ring.

Guardian Unlimited © Guardian Newspapers Limited 2005

4

GENERAL NEWS FEATURES

There is increasingly little difference between news deadlines and feature deadlines. Some features are planned in advance to fit in with an anticipated release of information but many will be turned around in hours or days. These are where newspapers and weekly magazines have a real strength. They have the space to analyse news, bring together background information and relevant research and to go behind a news report to provide depth and context. They can be more detailed, more speculative and more reflective than news bulletins, and they can be researched, written and published in a fraction of the time (and at a fraction of the cost) needed for similar depth in television or radio. The information they contain can be read at speed and then browsed at leisure so there is no worry that you might be packing in more information than a viewer, or listener, can absorb. These are the 'work-horse' of weekend newspapers and feature sections. The writing is rarely flashy. They are produced quickly and depend on good research and interviewing skills. The skill is in analysis, clarity and structure.

There is very rarely time to interview people in person. Most of the interviews will have been done over the phone and, where there are descriptions, they are reconstructions from the accounts of witnesses. Compare these pieces with the reportage or profile examples and see how much harder the words need to work to make up for the lack of descriptive detail.

OLIVER BURKEMAN

This is an unusual feature for a British newspaper because it looks in depth at a crime that has no political resonance. However, for men brought up in the inner cities, it has a universal quality – it is just one step beyond everyday life. It is a metaphor for a particular kind of urban life. It was written and published within a week of the trial. Had it been a high-profile trial it would have appeared earlier, probably the day after.

The fatal step
Guardian, Thursday 5 August, 2004

On May 2, Sri Lankan Vipula Prasanna accidentally trod on Michael John-Charles's son's foot at Wembley Park station in north London. It was a mistake that would cost him his life. Oliver Burkeman reports on a random encounter that led to tragedy.

> *The inciting incident is in the stand-first. The piece then goes on in story form as the jour-nalist seeks to unravel what happened in the lead up to this apparently casual encounter. The narrative is a tragedy in which John-Charles, the killer, is the protagonist. It has a very simple structure: two stories, told one after the other, with a brief summary.*

In Wembley Park, where the suburbs of north-west London finally surrender to the trunk roads and exhaust fumes, the day that Vipula Prasanna died was an otherwise unremarkable one – a quiet Sunday in May that started foggy and never got much brighter. As almost everyone involved in the case would remark at some point over the following weeks, a few seconds' difference and it would have stayed unremarkable. Prasanna, a 40-year-old Sri Lankan, wouldn't have reached the tube station exit barrier at precisely the same time as Michael John-Charles and John-Charles's five-year-old son. And the fine boundary that separates a general atmosphere of aggression from outright vio-lence on the London Underground might never have been breached at all.

> *A slow summary introduction weaves together fact and description in a way that is absolutely characteristic of the Guardian. Here the controlling idea is introduced. We live on a knife-edge of random aggression – and could die tomorrow. Then we launch straight into a chronological description of what happened, using witness statements from the court.*

Instead, this is what happened: a few minutes before 11am, Prasanna, who was planning to visit a cashpoint before attending a Buddhist temple, reached the barrier a few footsteps ahead of John-Charles, a former dancer on his way to see his mother, who was visiting from the Dominican Republic. Then Prasanna stopped, realising that the gates immediately ahead of him were for passengers entering the station. He turned to his left, scanning for the exit gates, found them, and changed direction. John-Charles and his son had been heading directly for the correct gates; in the few seconds it took Prasanna to cross several feet of yellowed floor tiles, they had caught up with him, and the three converged at the barrier.

In the next moment, a 15-year-old girl on a school trip heard someone shout something about a shoe. A Nigerian woman, on her way to church, remembered John-Charles telling Prasanna that if he didn't apologise, he would get hurt. James McShane, a station attendant, turned towards the noise and saw a confrontation at the ticket barrier. John-Charles's face was inches from Prasanna's, one witness recalled, and John-Charles was screaming, 'Do you think you can step on my son and get away with it, you fucking cunt?' McShane remembered that Prasanna 'might have sworn back', but mainly his impression was that the Sri Lankan was 'trying to defuse the situation'.

This is detailed reconstruction of the events, almost in the manner of a magazine 'true life' story, but the sourcing of each detail gives it both immediacy and a feeling of authenticity.

By now, the three had made it through the barrier, and CCTV footage shows Prasanna extending his arm as if imploring John-Charles to see reason. On the narrow, cracked pavement outside the station, no longer in view of the cameras, Prasanna turned to the five-year-old, witnesses said, and 'leant forward and touched the young boy ... in a gentle and reassuring manner'.

'Don't you fucking touch my child,' John-Charles shouted, and clenched his right hand into a fist.

We are left hanging as the writer stops, partly to create a moment of tension, and partly to fill in some background evidence.

Two hundred and thirty-eight people were violently killed in London in the year to June, some for reasons just as trifling as stepping on somebody's foot – like the 15-year-old knifed to death in Fulham in June, apparently for his mobile phone. But something about Vipula Prasanna's death on May 2 seemed to shake even seasoned police detectives and lawyers. It wasn't just the sense that anyone could have been the victim, but a troubling flicker of a thought that it wasn't all that hard to imagine being the perpetrator, either. 'It's just sad, really sad,' says one veteran official connected with the case, before adding bluntly that there have been times on the tube when he has felt like punching people, too.

Note how the writer chooses evidence (both statistical and in a quote) to back up his controlling idea: this is something that could have happened to anyone. He then returns to the story, continuing with a chronicle of the events as they unfolded.

Not that the official would want you to believe that he might have done what John-Charles did in the moments after he delivered an upper-cut to Prasanna's jaw. The blow, though not fatal in itself, pushed one of Prasanna's teeth through his lip, and sent him reeling backwards. He hit his head on the pavement, where he lay motionless. More than one witness said they saw 'the life go out of [Prasanna's] eyes'. But John-Charles apparently ignored him, striding off with his son down the road, past the Food King and the funeral directors' towards a nearby council estate. Prasanna was carried by air ambulance to the Royal London Hospital, in Whitechapel, and attached to a life-support machine. Three days later it was switched off.

A day after that, according to John-Charles's legal team, the 38-year-old was driving past Wembley Park station when he saw the police boards requesting help in finding a suspected murderer. He recognised himself in the CCTV photos, called a solicitor, and made arrangements to surrender the following morning. Police say he told them little, though it did emerge that the foot-stepping incident might have happened earlier in their journeys, at a different station.

> *This detail is important because it establishes the killer as a reasonable man – someone who had acted on impulse and regretted what he had done. Note that the writer has chosen not to tell this as a single chronological story, but to tell each story separately. This structure allows him to build up a sympathetic portrait of the killer, before we meet the family of the victim. Try weaving the stories together. You will find that it is much harder to build up sympathy for the perpetrator.*

Last Friday, John-Charles was jailed for manslaughter at the Old Bailey, and the curious details that emerged about him then seemed somehow to intensify the poignant randomness of the two trajectories that crossed at Wembley Park. John-Charles had worked as a professional dancer, appearing, his defence counsel said, with 'several major singers' on *Top Of The Pops*. He had apparently trained for the ballet, and was described – in a detail the newspapers jumped on – as the 'first black student to enrol in the Royal College of Ballet'. (This was also, however, one of the many details of the case that seemed to collapse at the slightest prodding: there is no Royal College of Ballet, and John-Charles was not a student at the Royal Ballet School or the Royal Academy of Dance. His lawyers declined to clarify the matter.) After dancing – and before giving up on the arts altogether, and moving into computers – he had tried singing, even recording his own album. A single called 'No Chorus', by a Michael John-Charles, was released in January 1998, in the same month as Catatonia's hit 'Mulder and Scully', and 'Under The Bridge', by All Saints.

> *Note how the writer selects information to build up a picture to elicit sympathy. We understand this man is also a victim – someone who had really tried to live a successful life. We see that the aggression was a flaw, but not a defining characteristic. Now we go on to a second story which looks at things from Prasanna's point of view.*

News of Prasanna's death made a forceful impact in Sri Lanka – not so much because of its randomness, but because of the way it seemed to strike at the foundations of some long-held Sri Lankan ideas about the British character. 'The British are known as gentlemen,' says Prasad Gunewardene, who covered the story for Colombo's *Sunday Observer*. 'Maybe it was unintentional, but it has brought down the standards of the Britishers among the people of Sri Lanka. They don't expect British people to assault a person who is already pardoning himself.'

This story also starts with an introduction establishing context. It then goes back in time and unfolds chronologically using testimony from a reporter in Colombo and Prasanna's landlady. Note the reference to standards of behaviour which will recur later.

Prasanna's family heard the news on his wife's birthday. At their modest home in Colombo, Sudanthika Prasanna answered a phone call she expected to be from her husband - but the voice at the other end was that of Irene Fernando, his former London landlady and a fellow Sri Lankan immigrant. 'I was sitting there, and the police inspector was over there,' Fernando recalls, speaking this week, after John-Charles's sentencing, and gesturing around the small front room of her semi-detached house 10 minutes' drive from the spot where Prasanna was attacked. 'They don't speak English, and the police didn't speak their language. So it was down to me to tell them he was on life support.' Soon after, at the Royal London, Fernando held a mobile phone to Prasanna's ear so that his four children, aged between four-and-a-half and 20, could talk to their unresponding father. 'Oh my God, they were screaming,' Fernando remembers. '"Don't turn off the machine!' Don't turn off the machine!" But the doctors decided they had to, and who am I to argue?'

By the time he died, Prasanna had been living in the UK for four years, working mainly in a souvenir shop on the Edgware Road and a discount store in Brixton, sending a portion of his wages back to Colombo each month. 'And perfume and makeup,' Fernando says. 'His daughter [20-year-old Sashika] would say, "Send me this, send me this". I told him, "You can buy them in Sri Lanka – what do you want to send them from here for?" But he'd say they liked British things.'

The basic information is summarised quickly leaving space for quotes to provide atmospheric detail. This was a man with a loving family who depended on him. He was a father just as his killer is. We then get a small detail that adds to the poignancy and the randomness of his death.

Prasanna had arrived as an asylum-seeker, but his application had been refused twice by the Home Office. His friends say that he had no interest in staying illegally any longer, and planned to return home in July.

'And now the problem is for the children,' says Anura Medagadara, sitting in an office at Willesden Community Hospital, the broken down NHS establishment where he works as an orderly. Medagadara, a small, jowly man in his 30s, barely knew Prasanna, but is active at the Buddhist temple he sometimes attended, in the London suburb of Kingsbury. After the attack, Medagadara raised about £5,000 for Prasanna's family through the London tabloid *Newslanka*. Much of it was spent bringing Sudanthika and her youngest son, Divyanjali, to London in June, to co-ordinate the return of Prasanna's body to Colombo. 'In our culture system, they always need the body.' Sri Lankan Airlines gave them discounts, but now little of the money is left.

According to Gunewardene, at the *Sunday Observer*, Prasanna's funeral in Colombo on June 26 drew almost 1,000 mourners, and took nearly three hours to process four kilometres from the family home to the cemetery. In the family's only interview, Sashika told Gunewardene she thought that her father had been phoning to wish her well in an imminent exam. 'He had hope in me and wanted me to study well,' she said. 'Who will assault a man who tenders an apology for an error that he had made? Do British people behave in such a dastardly manner?' For her part, Sudanthika seemed as angry as she was upset. 'We want prime minister Tony Blair to ensure justice,' Gunewardene quoted her as saying. 'Englishmen are known to be people with manners.'

> *This is the third time we have heard this. People were not just shocked by the death but were even more shocked by the context: the lack of respect for a man who has apologised. Why the repetition of this detail? Perhaps to hint at the cultural misunderstandings which add to the general tension? It is worth considering what the controlling idea might have been if this story had been told not in the liberal Guardian newspaper, but in a newspaper with a different agenda.*

In the end, the fate of John-Charles was decided by a turn of events as random as the encounter that killed Prasanna. The night before he gave his plea, the judge who had been scheduled to hear it, Michael Hyam – who might well have ended up deciding his sentence – suffered a heart attack and died. The next morning, every judge in the Old Bailey crowded into Court Number Four to pay their respects. Shortly afterwards, in an adjoining courtroom, John-Charles's defence lawyer announced that he would be pleading guilty to manslaughter. Last Friday, he received a sentence of three years, half of which was suspended; given the time he has already served in custody, he should be free by September next year.

> *This detail about the judge is presumably intended to reflect back to the controlling idea and the randomness of events. I am not sure it works.*

The sentence reflects the clear lack of homicidal intent on John-Charles's part, but Prasanna's friends in Britain are understandably furious. 'I never heard of anything like this in my country,' says Medagadara, who expresses his anger with bursts of nervous laughter. 'In Sri Lanka, the killer would get real punishment. A lifetime sentence. He's getting three years, he comes back. Yeah, it's manslaughter, but if he didn't attack, Prasanna would never have fallen down. Prasanna would never have gone to the hospital, and never died.' He sighs. 'But it doesn't matter now.'

On the grey day of Prasanna's death, Wembley Park station was closed until after 6 pm, but things have long since moved on. The ticket barrier where the confrontation occurred is closed as part of extensive renovation works; passengers are currently diverted through a side passage. Most of the surrounding area, in fact, feels like a construction site – from the cranes along the side of the railway tracks to the giant swooping arc of the new Wembley Stadium nearby. On the street outside the station, the spot where Vipula Prasanna's head hit the pavement is unmarked.

A gentle conclusion which takes us back to the spot and reminds us, once again, that we are all just specks of dust, blown about by circumstances beyond our control.

News Focus

Almost every week, Sunday newspapers publish long features focusing on a piece of research that has just been published. These features use the research (which may already have been reported in the newspapers the week before) as a jumping off point for an in-depth analysis of the trend or issue on which the research has focused. Compare this feature with the piece by Emma Brockes (Chapter 5). Here the interview material is chosen to provide evidence for a controlling idea that will have emerged from research, whereas Brockes teases the controlling idea out of her material. Note also how the interviews are used to provide the emotional content of the piece. These are mainly telephone interviews so the writer cannot use 'status life' detail to build character. She has instead used details of their background and interviewed them about their feelings.

YVONNE ROBERTS
Yvonne Roberts is a prolific, freelance journalist. She has worked as a features editor and also writes fiction. The stories she prefers take her out to interview ordinary people. She had already been in contact with one of the key interviewees for a story on Aspergers syndrome when the features editor asked her to re-angle the piece to focus on

cannabis. 'I did five days of talking to people and then stayed up all night to write it,' she said. This is the result.

Focus: Cannabis psychosis – off your head?
The Observer, 19 February 2006

Daniel Hrekow is 23, articulate, musically talented and academically bright. In the past five years he has dropped out of two universities and experienced two breakdowns. At the age of 19, after several years of feeling depressed, anxious and increasingly disconnected, he was diagnosed as having Asperger's syndrome, a form of autism.

Signs of Asperger's include an inability to empathise or understand other people's emotions, difficulty in tolerating change and obsessional behaviour. In Daniel's case, this obsessional behaviour can mean periods of smoking cannabis for several days and nights at a time. Since his teens, out of fear and frustration, Daniel has tried to control every aspect of his mother Mary's life. He has also become extremely violent to her, his father, Peter, and younger brother, Ben.

> *An extended anecdote introduction (briefly interrupted) is much favoured by* The Observer. *It brings the reader face to face with someone who is directly affected by the issue under discussion. The structure of the piece is a hybrid: a mixture of story and essay structure. Most of the interviews are presented as part of the evidence. Daniel's story is extended to provide a narrative thread, with whom we can identify. He helps us to read on because we want to know how his story ends.*

Daniel is the human face of a disturbing statistic revealed last week – an alarming 40 per cent rise in hospital admissions for mental ill-health prompted by cannabis use since 2001, when it was first proposed to downgrade it from a Class B to Class C drug.

A new study demonstrating the link between psychosis and cannabis – written by Professor Tom Barnes – will be published in the *Journal of Psychiatry* next month, adding yet more pressure on the government to take a fresh look at the price paid by increasing numbers of young people dependent on cannabis.

> *Now we get the hook: a study out last week and another one due next week. There is the additional spin of a possible political connection giving it more relevance. Then back to the story with the most shocking detail of Daniel's condition.*

Daniel is just one example of this growing problem. 'When he's violent, he bangs his head against the wall, punches and shakes me, smashes furniture and cuts himself with kitchen knives,' says Mary. His parents have had to ask the police to remove their son from the family home several times – and again this weekend, Daniel has been abusive and threatening. Meanwhile, he and his mother are waiting to hear if a place will be funded for him at the Rookery, in Somerset, one of the few residential settings in the UK offering education for young people with Asperger's.

Still in story form but now we move in to hear the background. Most of the story is retold in indirect speech. Quotes are used to highlight the critical points of the case. In Daniel's case, the quotes are used to tell us how he feels – in his own words, so that we identify with him in spite of his behaviour. It is the interviewing skill which makes this feature work. These short interviews are the anchor points which keep us reading. We care about these people and want to know what should be done.

Mary has fought hard to acquire support for Daniel from the South West London and St George's Mental Health NHS Trust, often with little success. At one point the Hrekows, both education consultants, remortgaged their home to raise more than £30,000 to pay for Daniel's care.

Last September, after 18 months in a residential unit, Daniel decided to return to university. He was supposed to receive support but none was forthcoming from the trust. After several weeks at Goldsmiths College in London, he began to do what he has always done, since the age of 15, to ease the pain of alienation – he began to smoke cannabis excessively.

'When you're trying to live life as a normal person, and you're stoned, you disguise yourself because you're pretty much out of it,' Daniel says.

He gives a long and moving account of life with a cannabis addiction. 'At first, with cannabis, it becomes so much easier to float by unnoticed. But then you become paranoid. You're quick to assume the world isn't going to make a place for you. Through drugs, I've come close to destroying myself, but sometimes the only option is to be in this oblivious state, trying to get a break from the pressure. But it's no break at all really.

'In my teens I used to champion cannabis but once you've taken yourself to places I've taken myself to, you can't hide from what your brain felt. Now, I don't get a high at all. Instead, my brain hurts so much, and I don't sleep for days. It goes wrong so quickly that what's going on internally becomes visible to everyone and that's frightening for me. No one at 23 who's been into cannabis for years can get away with saying it doesn't mess your head up. If you're smart and have potential and you do drugs for too long, it takes you further away from a healthy balanced way of living which is what you secretly wanted in the first place – with that first joint.'

Now we move into three paragraphs of background detail taken from research. Note the emphasis on numbers. Editors and readers feel reassured by research based on numbers. Numbers, like 'being there', seem to suggest thoroughness and authenticity. The statistics provide the glue holding together a series of case histories and quotes.

In 2001, 490 patients were admitted to hospital as a result of excessive use of cannabis. There were 710 admissions in each of the past two years. Several recent studies have demonstrated the links between cannabis and schizophrenia. Professor Robin Murray, a consultant psychiatrist at the Maudsley Hospital in south London and one of the leading researchers in the field, estimates that 25,000 of the 250,000 people with schizophrenia in the UK could have avoided the illness if they had not used of cannabis.

In addition, the Advisory Council on the Misuse of Drugs (ACMD), in a report to Home Secretary Charles Clarke arguing against reclassification, suggested for the first time that cannabis may not only cause schizophrenia in those with pre-existing mental conditions, but could also exacerbate a range of other mental health problems.

In the UK, 250,000 people experience psychosis – a term that refers to symptoms including delusions and hallucinations, rather than a specific diagnosis. 'Five years ago, 95 per cent of psychiatrists would have said cannabis doesn't cause psychosis,' says Murray. 'Now, I would estimate 95 per cent say it does. It's a quiet epidemic.'

A second story provides additional anecdotal evidence supporting the expert evidence we have already been offered and adds emotional depth. Note the recurrent emphasis on what these young people could have achieved. These are not monsters but are people just like us the readers, our friends or our sons.

Steve Hammond, the 27-year-old son of mental health worker, Terry, began smoking cannabis at 16, graduated to smoking up to 10 joints a night over weekends, then, in his twenties, was diagnosed as schizophrenic.

'Steve was a brilliant sportsman: a gifted footballer, a superb runner, a natural athlete,' says his father. 'Now, he is just a shadow, a recluse. This is definitely an emerging issue. Everyone knows a "dope head" who has used cannabis, the "safe" drug. It's not just the number of cases of schizophrenia and psychosis that's a concern, it's the thousands upon thousands who have lost a future.'

The ACMD report says that 'the mental-health effects of cannabis are real and significant'. While it is true to say that many millions of people have used cannabis moderately without impairment to their daily lives, can we afford to ignore the hike in hospital admissions?

This is the beginning of the debate and we move clearly into essay form. Now the anecdotes, are being used as evidence. The first piece of evidence demonstrates the seriousness of the issue and sets up the argument in favour of greater intervention.

And have a number of recent court cases dealing with horrifically violent crimes involving cannabis raised us from years of torpor about the use of cannabis? Earlier this month, Peter Thomas, aged 21, was given an indefinite jail sentence after beating Lisa Voice, the mother of his former girlfriend, so severely that she needed 11 operations. 'He smashed my skull, my nose was a pulp … he smashed my eye sockets and my eye was hanging out,' Voice said. Medical experts said Thomas had been suffering from 'cannabis-induced psychosis'.

Now we are told the kinds of intervention that are already in train – and why they are inadequate. The vigour with which these interventions are dismissed makes it clear that there is a point of view guiding us but we are not being given an opinion – we are being persuaded by use of evidence.

Charles Clarke promised last month to 'implement energetically' the three main recommendations of ACMD – a 'substantial' education campaign, strengthened medical services for those dependent on cannabis and further research into the implications of cannabis use – although whether there will be sufficient funding is extremely doubtful. In 2005, France spent £2 million to educate young people about cannabis. In comparison, a recent British public health campaign on the same issue received £230,000.

Next month, the National Treatment Agency for Substance Misuse is launching its Young People's Effectiveness Strategy for under 18s. Professionals say it is impossible for the strategy to encompass excessive cannabis use because so little is known about it – who is using it, how often, why some individuals appear more vulnerable than others to its effects and how many are seriously impaired. Nor do we know enough about what works in terms of 'education'. What is certain is that, in many parts of Britain, a young person with a cannabis problem would be very fortunate indeed to find effective help. Heroin, cocaine and crack cocaine have a more established link to crime and death, so receive a far higher priority in public policy. Cannabis may lay waste to lives, but often the casualties suffer a lifetime of delusion and reclusiveness while their families privately mourn their loss.

Using the evidence of experts in the field, we are told why it is urgent to change the nature of the debate. We don't yet know where exactly she is leading us so we have to read on.

For years, the debate on cannabis has progressed little. 'The issue has been polarised between those who argue that if everyone smokes it, it will lead to world peace and those who believe that a few spliffs may send you psychotic,' says Dr Luke Mitcheson, a clinical psychologist. 'That shows a deep immaturity in the face of increasing evidence that we need a far more sensitive dialogue.'

Cannabis is the most widely used illicit substance around the world, particularly among young adults. Users are smoking it from a younger age and in larger quantities for longer, not least because young people today have more ready cash than their Sixties counterparts did and a small quantity of cannabis is now cheaper than a packet of cigarettes or a couple of pints.

There has been a staggering 70 per cent increase in teenage mental-health problems since 1974, according to the Institute of Psychiatry. Young people in the UK use more cannabis than their peers on the continent. In the UK, latest statistics reveal that 1 per cent of all 11-year-olds, 17 per cent of 14-year-olds and 26 per cent of 15-year-olds used cannabis last year.

Cannabis, or marijuana, comes in different forms. Hash, the resin of the plant, is less expensive than grass or weed, which is the plant's dried leaves. 'Skunk', at around £200 an ounce, is herbal cannabis grown from selected seeds by intensive indoor methods. Skunk is twice as potent, on average, than hash or weed.

Some say the increase in psychosis and schizophrenia is because skunk is more readily available and easier to obtain than hash or grass, but other professionals believe that the market is simply responding to demand for the more 'mind-blowing' version. The ACMD said that the evidence on whether 'skunk' was playing a major part in the apparent increase in psychosis was 'unclear' because there was 'too little information about the potency and pattern of use of cannabis by consumers'.

Cannabis, often mixed with tobacco, is either smoked in a joint or in a water pipe, or cooked into food and eaten. The plant contains more than 400 chemicals including delta-nine-tetrahydrocannabinol (THC), its main psychoactive component. Interactions between THC and specific proteins on the surface of the brain cells, known as cannabinoid receptors, produce the laid-back, pleasure-enhancing awareness after smoking cannabis and is sometimes accompanied by an urge to eat.

This background paragraph sits oddly here. Perhaps the sub-editors felt that readers needed more detailed information. It is the next paragraph that contains the 'killer fact'. It is the key reason why we need to act to prevent young people using cannabis. It would have been difficult to use it earlier (in spite of its importance) because it requires the sort of complex explanation which would turn readers off at the start of a piece but which they will accept once they have been pulled along this far.

Recent breakthroughs in neuroscience show, contrary to earlier research, that even in adolescence the brain is still developing. A paper to be published soon, as part of a campaign by the charity YoungMinds, explains how the frontal cortex – where this development takes place – is essential for functions such as response inhibition, emotional regulation, analysing problems and planning.

Research also shows that sustained use of cannabis over several years may result in cognitive impairment, affecting memory, attention and the organisation and integration of complex information.

Several controversial key studies have recently shown the impact of juvenile cannabis use. One, carried out by Murray and the University of Otago in New Zealand, followed a group of 750 adolescents over 15 years and found that those who had smoked cannabis at age 15 were four and half times more likely to be schizophrenic at age 26.

A third story is used, not as evidence in itself, but to illustrate the expert evidence and give us a brief relief from complexity so that we keep reading on.

Two weeks ago in Portsmouth at the inquest of 23-year-old Roy Jackson, who died after bingeing on methadone and cough medicine, coroner David Horsley underlined the tragic downhill spiral that cannabis dependency can produce in a mentally ill person. Roy had begun to smoke joints at age 14 and eventually moved on to skunk. He was diagnosed as schizophrenic at 19. 'The use of cannabis exacerbated his mental health problems,' Horsley said. 'It predisposed him to smoking more regularly than was good for him.'

Roy's sister, Lisa Male, said: 'It was horrible. He was sectioned at 19 when it should have been the best time of his life. He had been a bright boy at school. One doctor told my mother that the increasing use of skunk had created a ticking time bomb.'

Roy's family, understandably, want the laws on cannabis tightened. But reclassification will not stop young people rolling a joint – nor will it encourage them to put a brake on excessive use.

Roberts, for the first time, steps out of 'reporter' mode and makes a very clear statement of her own belief that changing the law is not the answer. She now uses the rest of the piece to tell us what she thinks is the better solution. She starts the section with an anecdote which changes the direction of the piece. This is not a man to be pitied but to be admired.

Three months ago, J-Rock, an actor and a member of R&B group Big Brovaz, decided to give up 'the weed'. Now 27, he had smoked up to 10 spliffs a day from the age of 13. 'Everything in my life had weed around it,' he says. 'I was paranoid, I couldn't handle my life any more, I had to stop.'

But he was helped by an early-intervention counsellor, using motivational techniques which have proved successful in Australia and the USA. Contrary to myth, coming off cannabis can cause withdrawal symptoms – including insomnia, irritability and physical discomfort.

'I suddenly got my dreams back and they were really vivid. That was strange, but my counsellor had prepared me for that.'

J-Rock and the counsellor worked together three times a week. He was instructed to keep a diary, to look at when he smoked and why; he was encouraged to develop activities to distract himself from smoking and to establish goals for the future. Thirty-one days after giving up, a test showed THC was still inside his body. Yet now, he is drug-free.

'So many young people grow up seeing Snoop Doggy Dog smoking weed and they think you have to do that to achieve, to be creative through weed,' he says. I'm successful beyond some people's dreams but I was doing it under the influence of drugs. Now, I'm acting, recording and it's a whole lot easier. This is me.'

Now evidence from authoritative voices who can back up the anecdotal evidence with their broader experience. They make the personal political.

'Given the right help, people can change surprisingly quickly,' says Mitcheson, who works as a clinical psychologist in Lambeth, south London. 'Just setting up a service for cannabis users isn't going to work. Young people don't identify with "I have a problem and yes the problem is cannabis". Often that's only part of a range of difficulties and adolescence is a time of change anyway when some become unstuck.'

The government has established 109 Early Intervention projects around the country. The concept is good but, in practice, some projects consist of a single worker covering many hundreds of miles. 'What we still have too often is a service open five hours on a Monday, Wednesday and Friday,' says Kathryn Pugh of Young Minds. 'What a young person needs is help on a Sunday night when he's alone in his bedsitter.'

This section could stand as a short feature on its own for a specialist magazine. By incorporating it in a longer piece with a lot of anecdotal evidence it will be read by a much wider audience.

Another problem is that a young person has to reach a crisis and experience a psychotic episode before help is given. Little exists for the heavy smoker who wants to cut back before it gets out of hand. Early Intervention projects may also suffer because of the financial crisis faced across the NHS. Government money allocated for young people's mental health budgets, however generous, is often siphoned off for other uses.

In-volve, a charity set up by Colin Cripps, runs 15 services for young people around the country. 'We've never tailored intervention in any way that made sense,' says Cripps. 'Now, following Danish research, we wait for a couple of weeks until a young person has got enough cannabis out of his or her system, then we work with them as a person not as a drug user. Most of the problems are about identity. Heavy users have often grown up feeling failures.

It takes weeks and weeks of intensive counselling of the right kind and opportunities for education, training and employment to persuade a young person they can make something of their lives. Only then is cannabis recognised as the problem.

'In-volve uses texting, flyers, chat rooms, events and word of mouth to spread its message. So much of drugs education in this country ignores the changes in communication and leaves young people cold.'

The work of Dr Jim McCambridge, of the National Addiction Centre, and his colleagues, is beginning to demonstrate how young people are capable of helping themselves given the right opportunity. For the centre's ongoing study, students in colleges across London were randomly picked. Of those, 50 per cent subsequently said they had difficulties with cannabis. They were then interviewed for half an hour and, using motivational techniques, encouraged to evaluate their own lives and goals.

A few months later, the students were reassessed and it was discovered that the interview had had a positive impact on their behaviour. Studies are now taking place to test whether training in motivational techniques, for professionals such as teachers who come into contact with young people every day, might have a long-term impact on reducing drug use.

'Given the prevalence of cannabis, there's so much we don't know,' McCambridge said. 'Who's using heavily? Why? How best can they be helped? The tragedy is that with no overarching strategic direction, we have pockets of good practice and waste lands where there is no help at all.'

Having established what ought to be done, Roberts reminds us of what will happen if we do nothing. Once again she uses as an example, a young man who had aspirations and a clear chance of achieving them. This is not only to engage with her audience but also to undermine stereotypes of the kind of people who get hooked.

James, in his twenties, began smoking cannabis at 15. 'The reason I never did any other drugs was because their dangers were well known. I was a sensible person,' he said, aware of the irony. 'Even when I went to two GPs, saying I was having problems with anxiety and paranoia, they gave me antidepressants and said if the cannabis helped me to relax, I should carry on.'

At 19, he had a breakdown and was hospitalised with drug-induced psychosis. At school, he achieved seven A stars in his GCSEs. Now he is unable to hold down a job. 'My brain works but I don't do well in social situations. If only I'd known about the risk.'

What's required now, experts in the field say, is for Charles Clarke to put his money where his mouth is. However large or small the issue of cannabis dependency, it needs ring-fenced sustained funding, more research, the right support available across the country and improved universal drug education given earlier in schools and to professionals such as GPs.

> *The ending takes us neatly back to the beginning and to Daniel. It is an optimistic ending worthy of the transformation narrative that underlies this piece.*

In the meantime, Daniel Hrekow is optimistic that if he receives the right kind of help, he will be able to build a life for himself. But his mother, Mary, is angry.

'Everyone on the ground will tell you there's a big problem with young people and cannabis,' she said. 'But where do they or their families go for help? Mental health services are at the bottom of the spending list, and cannabis is even lower.' Mary knows it will be a long and hard road, but she wants her son back.

© Yvonne Roberts

5

TOPICAL FEATURES

Why now? Features are often published just because they grab something of the moment. They may be seasonal, they may be timed to coincide with an election, or they may deal with a theme that is rumbling along just under the radar: changing patterns of immigration, political unrest in another country, concerns about crime or policing, trends in social behaviour. These sorts of subject come in and out of fashion in cycles. Consumer magazines are particularly sensitive to trends that are just breaking. They have to know what is happening at least four months ahead of the rest of the world just so that they don't look dated. The result is often safe and bland. Newspapers and weeklies, on the other hand, can catch the crest of the wave and publish pieces in-depth which go behind the issues that trouble, concern or amuse us.

RACHEL CUSK Magazines love events that are predictable and what could be more so than Christmas. This piece shows that, with a little bit of imagination and lateral thinking, it is possible to find a completely original angle on a very old theme. This is a beautifully written piece. A real 'curl-up-by-the-fire and enjoy' experience. Rachel Cusk is a novelist who has also written about new motherhood in grimly ambivalent detail. This is entirely autobiographical and yet Cusk's writing about motherhood clearly speaks to many people. Is this journalism? I think it brings us news of who we are, or how we might be. I wouldn't advise trying to emulate it. It is here mainly because it breaks most of the rules – and still works.

Sweetness and light
Vogue, January 2005

I remember my mother mixing Christmas cake one year in a baby's bathtub. The bathtub sat on the kitchen floor. I watched her stir the vast, brown, spoon, with insane exertion, through this substance that appeared to me somehow primordial, like clay, or the contents of a volcano. There was no bowl big enough for it: the bathtub was a good idea. It contributed to my impression that something out of the ordinary was occurring in our kitchen – creation itself, in a blue plastic crucible. Something was being made to exist that had not existed before.

> *This piece is warm, evocative, involving, mysterious. It clearly has a hook (Christmas), the introduction is an extended anecdote (which includes an inciting incident: the cake in the bath) but it uses structure like a trapeze rather than a strait-jacket.*

I had watched raisins and currants spill out over the batter from a measuring bowl like little black landslides and seconds later be folded in as though to the earth. The spoon churned up glace cherries and nuts and candied peel from the depths. Occasionally the mixture would thickly belch out pockets of air. I was aware that to the unsuspecting visitor its presence in the baby's bathtub could be perceived as vaguely monstrous. Nevertheless there would be awe, at this ceremonial display of viscera; for everything had to have its genesis somewhere and while sometimes Christmas seemed to be summoned by magic out of the black hat of winter, on this occasion I felt a party to its appearance. I saw how it was made; or rather, I saw, in this painstaking expression of the season, this giant cake, a form of human aspiration, and I wondered whether or not it was necessary to life.

> *'What is it about?' I bark at my students. 'What is the story?' Well I think this is an allegory of procreation, motherhood and food. About how mothers don't eat the cake – they are the cake. I think it is a coming of age narrative, but I want to read it for the way it sounds and feels.*

I had a book called *The Duchess Bakes A Cake*, in which an aristocratic lady demonstrates precisely this aspiration, with pleasingly ambiguous consequences. She is seized by the desire to make a cake: she blunders her way through inappropriate areas of her castle in pursuit of the kitchen, and while her aproned staff look on in alarm she rolls up her sleeves. In a purposive ecstasy she measures and mixes. Flour leaps in arabesques about her bowl; sugar cascades from its bag; she breaks eggs, wearing her tiara the whole while. Finally she puts the mixture in its tin and slams the oven door with a satisfying crash. I can't remember how the cake first escapes from the oven – I think the duchess opens the door to take a look and out it comes, steadily expanding, moving out and upwards with irresistible force. The duchess throws herself on top of it but still it rises, up and up, through the ceiling, until it has broken the fastnesses of the castle and is heading for the sky with the duchess still clinging on. By the time it stops rising, the duchess is sitting in the clouds, out of sight. I found this an arresting image. There was an illustration of it, in which it is made clear that the duchess, while not realising quite what she was getting herself into, nevertheless regards the whole situation as a sort of manifestation of personal exuberance. In a way she's quite proud of her cake. There's her husband, the duke, down below, squeaking imprecations up at her with all his staff and courtiers and declaring a state of emergency, while she sits there high in the airy heavens. Presently she tears a chunk from her cake and eats it. Quite delicious.

A flight of fancy that equates cake-making with the lightness and freedom of an American childhood. And then comes back to earth. Literally.

I have always thought of cake as indigenous to the idea of Englishness; an idea that, to me, represented the world – particularly the world of food – in a 'real', almost ancestral, form. In America, where I grew up, cake was a powdered substance that came in Betty Crocker packets emblazoned with mysterious claims: 'Pudding in the mix!' or 'Whole Extra Egg!' Betty Crocker, the Ronald McDonald of home baking, was a chief representative of the new religion of convenience, to which the English had not yet been converted. Like Cheez Whiz and Twinkles and Oreo cookies, cake-mix cakes were almost unbearably pleasurable to eat; or rather, they caused sensations of pleasure that were unrelated to even the most superfluous forms of nourishment. My childhood memories are of food as both delicious and deracinated; as something you could eat and eat without locating its living texture. When we returned to live in England, our meals sat before us in a sort of ominous three-dimensionality, emanating rich fumes. Everything seemed brown, and imperfect. The food in England was heavy, as if to stop you going anywhere. The heaviest thing of all was cake.

This second literary allusion tells a very different story. American cakes are not all lightness and frosting. Women have paid a price for them. In choosing this passage she opens the door to maternal ambivalence: the fear of not matching up to expectations. This is a theme that she develops later on.

In America, cake was merely an occasion for 'frosting', a thick, pastel-coloured casing of it, bland and abundant as fake snow; the principal aim being, as I remember it, to create a brilliant, blinding mirage of professionalism. In Michael Cunningham's novel *The Hours*, a suburban housewife in Fifties America spends a morning with her small son trying to make her husband a birthday cake. Her faltering progress through the recipe, her disastrous icing, her shameful consignment of the whole thing to the rubbish bin and her equally shameful preparation of a second cake to disguise the failure of the first, are the elaboration of her feelings of ambivalence about love, marriage, domesticity. From those tortured hours at the mixing bowl, Cunningham cleverly draws an analogy of female consciousness bending itself to a pre-ordained condition. Yet it is the superfluity, the extraneousness of the cake-making that undoes her, for if she were contented, would she not be able to give more, offer more than what was merely necessary? And also; if her life were tolerable, would the first, faulty cake not be sufficient?

As Cusk moves from America (childhood and fairy dust) to England (growing up, context, memory, mud) we feel her ambivalence again, the tug of childhood against the seriousness business of adulthood.

The English concept of cake was different: it was not about perfection. It was about memory: the words 'Victoria sponge cake' suggested a confection whose roots lay mysteriously in the past. And 'fruit cake'! A slice of fruit cake was like a slice of earth, old and black and full of rubble. It caused the adult to fall silent, or to reminisce. It appeared to contain no sugar whatever and frequently emanated the smell of alcohol, which confirmed what I had already begun to suspect, which was that in England cakes weren't baked for children; or at least, they failed to adhere to the terms of the known alliance between children and sugar. The world of the Twinkle – shrink-wrapped, thoroughly sweet, as soft and unresisting as dust – lay far behind me. I saw that I had entered a sphere of great and impenetrable artistry, where a cake was something that existed in the context of other cakes, in the context of cake history: It was a form, like poetry: It was difficult and unnecessary and it made people sigh, or emit great groans of feeling.

I made a cake as a psychological experiment. My intention was to make something that tasted delicious but looked inedible. I believed that this would demonstrate to those who ate it their prejudices about the world around them. Perhaps if I'd been a boy I'd have done it the other way around. But diligently I creamed the butter and the sugar and added the eggs and the flour and then I put a teaspoon of blue food dye into the mixture. (I did not do this recently: it was when I was about 10 years old.) When I took it out of the oven the cake was the colour of a swimming pool. I made some icing and dyed it green. At the time I thought the effect was hideous; in fact it would now be regarded as *comme il faut* at any five year-old's birthday party. The problem was that it tasted disgusting because I'd put in the wrong proportions of everything, though everyone insisted it was because it was blue and green. There was a moral there too, but I wasn't sure what it was.

Later, as an adult, I started to make cakes in earnest. To me, it seemed rather like writing books, only quicker. There you were, all alone, deeply subsumed in a procedure that, while requiring its complete co-operation, seemed to effect a suspension of the body; a procedure that was practical and personal and widely viewed as inessential and hence appeared to me as a sort of art. There was no situation to which making a cake could be seen as the correct response. It belonged safely within the sphere of counter-cultural activity.

It becomes clearer that cakebaking is a metaphor for her own feelings about femininity and motherhood.

To the end product – the cake itself – I maintained an ambivalent attitude. My early aversion to 'adult ' cakes survived the standard evolution of my taste in food to more sophisticated things. It still got me every time. Once, I made a Madeira cake flavoured with rosemary and watched as people fell around in ecstasy. What was it all about? I didn't know. The fruit cake, being the gold standard in this area, could provoke a sort of methodological frenzy, particularly in people over the age of 50, of which, like an errant post-structuralist, I occasionally fell foul by tampering with the recipe. I went through a polenta phase that seemed to cause considerable distress. My American roots surfaced in an irresistible desire to put cinnamon in everything. I turned against icing and thought that everything should be plain. Then I turned against plainness and thought that everything should have fruit on top.

Then something else happened, which was that people – women – started to remark on my cake-making. It usually began as a conversation about their cake-making. They had to make a cake and they didn't know how. It's really very easy, I'd say. But I can't, they'd say. You can, I'd say. No, no, they'd say, you don't understand – I can't. I really can't. I'm just going to, you know – buy one. I was never entirely clear what these conversations were about. They seemed to be about the fact that making cakes was not a particularly normal thing to do. It was a Women's Institute thing to do. It was a pre-feminist, housewifely thing to do. It was old-fashioned.

There is something extraordinarily anxious about this. Cake-making is a refuge, a place where specific rules apply. A place where she is not asked to compete because what she is doing is outside the accepted realm of the possible for women of her age. And then her cakes lead her in the opposite direction. She finds herself at the centre of feminine competitiveness. The very place she sought to avoid.

I sometimes felt that I might have preferred it if cake-making didn't result in … a cake. Then there would have been nothing to explain. The truth was that what I liked was the act itself. I liked the curt, conspiratorial language of the recipes – 'Cream the butter and sugar'; 'fold in the flour with a metal spoon' – and the precision of the measures. I liked the way the hands of the clock turned in the silence of the kitchen. I liked the fact that of all the things you could choose to cook, a cake exceeds the sum of its parts the furthest. It bears no relation to the things it came from.

> *This is so clearly about procreation. A baby is the thing that most of all exceeds the sum of its parts. But, like the cakes that refuse to rise evenly, babies defy the instructions. They demand the cake, and the cake is mother. And Cusk is not yet ready to take her own mother's place.*

I don't make so many cakes now. I started burning them, or they came out wrong. For a while they all sloped at the same angle, as though the kitchen were subsiding. As a cakemaker I am no longer, as people say of writers, at the height of my powers. Perhaps all I ever wanted to do was recapture the day we mixed the Christmas cake in the baby's bath, though I've never tried to make a Christmas cake. I wouldn't dare: when it comes to Christmas cake, I'm like those adults I remember as a child, eating the earth, their mouth full of memories. I'm definitely a spectator.

© Rachel Cusk

EMMA BROCKES

Emma Brockes is a consummate feature writer. This is the second part of a three-day series behind the scenes at a London police station (you can find the rest on the GuardianUnlimited website). She uses a straightforward story structure with the pace and the choppy movement of a television cop series. The case of the 'road-rage suspect' provides a spine that holds the piece together. She then uses the other cases as sub-plots, each one helping to provide evidence for her key idea about the arbitrary use of power. Her observations are used as evidence, teasing out the relationships between the officers and the 'clients', between the officers and the solicitors and among the police themselves. She manages also to reflect on the vexed question of racism in the police force (both institutional and personal) and the question of police morale that had been a recurrent feature of debate in the aftermath of the Macpherson report, an enquiry into the death of black teenager Stephen Lawrence in February 1999. Everything is conveyed through the use of dialogue, carefully chosen and constructed into a story. She never once moves out of her role as observer, or overtly takes sides in the debate, nevertheless she is directing us, by her choice of information, towards a particular conclusion.

Call me sergeant
Guardian (G2), Thursday 13 December, 2001

'How are you today?' asks Sergeant Hudson. 'Are you aggressive? I'm not going to take off the cuffs if you're aggressive. It doesn't cost anything to be polite.' The man standing before him is 6ft tall and furious. He has been arrested following a road-rage incident. He alleges that another driver called him a 'black bastard'. She alleges he punched her on the nose and dragged her out of the car unprovoked.

Here we have our 'inciting incident'.

'She called me a black bastard,' says the man. 'This is a racial motive. She called me a black bastard. Then she got her friends over – they hit me and they arrested me 'cause I am black'.

'Please stop sucking your teeth,' says Hudson. 'It's bad manners.'

'My teeth are ACHING, my face is ACHING. I am in pain. I am in pain.'

'What is your postcode please? And do you pronounce the 'g' in your surname?'

'No.'

'Now, isn't it better when we talk calmly?'

'Yes, sir.'

'Don't call me sir. Anyone can be a sir. Call me sergeant.'

'Yes, sergeant.'

'Are you calm?'

'Yes.'

'You're a bit mercurial, aren't you.'

'What are you calling me?'

'Mercurial. Up and down. Like a thermometer.'

'I'm not a thermometer! I'm a human being like you are!'

'Do you want a drug referral?'

'I don't take drugs! I am a Muslim! I don't take drugs! I don't eat pork!'

'OK, don't get out of your pram. As for your accusation of institutional racism, I refute that.'

'How come I was the only one arrested?'

'We treat black people just like we treat everybody else.'

He takes off the man's handcuffs.

'Do you read and write English?'

'Yes,' says the man, igniting again. 'Why would I not? Am I not speaking the same language as you?'

'I can speak a bit of German, but I can't read or write it. There's a difference.'

'My girlfriend is a lawyer. I'm afraid of nothing. Nothing!'

'Stop raising your voice, please.'

'Sorry, sergeant. You are all racists! I pay for you! I work hard, I pay for you! Sorry, sergeant. I'm going to take this to court myself.'

They remove him for a body search. 'I don't have NOTHING on me. You can check my bollocks if you like.'

'We'd rather not,' says the sergeant. 'Officer? Cell number seven is beckoning.'

> *This uninterrupted stretch of dialogue (an extended anecdote intro) takes us straight into the scene – as witnesses. The choice of this particular fragment of conversation provides us with a sense of the 'controlling idea'. We are witnessing the exercise of power in its most banal form and the road-rage victim, not the officer, is our chief protagonist. It is his tragedy which is unfolding before us.*

At the back of Kentish Town police station are 11 cells and two juvenile detention rooms. Prisoners are held here for up to 36 hours. Since something as simple as arresting a shoplifter can take six hours to process (including one hour in the queue to book them in), officers spend a lot of time here, too. There is dirty light from a single window; a wooden bench; a height chart, a panic strip and a poster illustrating how to restrain a prisoner without asphyxiating him. 'Remember your training,' it reads. 'Prone restraint will need to be justified.'

Besides the road-rage suspect, there are three people in custody today. Two were caught stealing buns from a hotel's buffet breakfast (they weren't staying at the hotel) and the other is an alleged housebreaker. The bun-stealers are subdued and say they 'can't be arsed' to come to the phone when their solicitor rings. 'There's no audience for them to perform to,' says Hudson cheerfully. He is a veteran cop with a grey moustache and the girth of a bull seal. 'They're just a little voice in space.'

> *Note how, even while she portrays his jocular responses she is also making it clear that he (and the other police officers) holds the power. She uses physical description to build this impression. The choice of details to describe the prisoners makes them seem powerless even when they talk back and the pay off quote in this paragraph encapsulates this relationship.*

The duty jailer is a young officer seconded to the job for three months. PC O'Shea escorts prisoners to and from cells. He is affectionately mocked by colleagues for reading the *Guardian* and holding progressive views on the licensing laws.

'Camden has always been an arty-farty neighbourhood,' says Hudson, indicating his colleague. 'I suppose they call them the chattering classes. Kentish Town is more solidly working class. We have famous people living in the borough: Joan Bakewell; that Oasis fella – Liam is it? And Harry Enfield. There's houses up by Regent's Park you couldn't afford to lease even if you won the double rollover.'

The use of this quote provides background, context and also contrast. Note the triviality of the crimes: stealing two buns from a hotel buffet in a place where even most millionaires cannot afford to rent a house. It is a detail that works as a comment without requiring interpretation.

At lunchtime, a teenage boy is brought in by two plain-clothes officers and charged with causing damage to property. Hudson reads him his rights and gives him a date to attend Camden youth court.

'I'll go if I can be bothered,' says the boy.

'You'll go unless you want to come back and see me,' says Hudson. The boy picks up a broken stapler on the sergeant's desk. 'I can fix it if you like,' he says. 'I know where the spring goes.'

A touching well-observed moment – the boy reaching out for a second from his tough shell.

'Flash little git,' says Hudson after the boy has gone. 'You'll get some clever-bugger solicitor advising him not to comment and of course you can't let him off on a caution if he denies it, so a kid with no previous convictions goes to court because a solicitor is trying to be clever.'

4pm

Two policemen seek me out and ask to speak anonymously about the culture of despair in which they say they work. 'Everyone's keeping their heads down and trying to get to the end of their 30 years,' says one urgently. 'There's no way my son is going to be a police officer. It would kill me. It's shit money for shit work. We deal with the people that the rest of society wishes didn't exist.'

'There's a culture of portfolio-building,' whispers his colleague. 'In order to get promotion, you must be seen to have changed things. So the people upstairs make bullshit changes for the sake of it and we're the ones who suffer. You risk losing your job every time you come into work. You hear the word race and you think, "shit". People are demoralised, pissed off and burnt out'.

'I have a black colleague,' says his friend. 'After the Macpherson report I'm looking at him thinking, "Does he think I'm racist?"'

Later, one of their colleagues comes over and says: 'Ignore Tweedledum and Tweedledee. They're always bloody moaning.'

> *Again she uses fragments of dialogue to tell the story of demoralisation – and leaves it hanging without comment.*

6pm

An almighty row is emanating from cell seven. The road-rage suspect has used his belt buckle to smash up the ceramic toilet bowl in his cell. 'That old thing, the race card,' says Hudson, shaking his head. 'It mitigates all evils.' He settles down to fill in the paperwork. 'Once everyone has calmed down, we'll get to the truth.'

The arresting officer exhales. 'I don't know if we'll ever get to the truth,' he says wistfully.

> *Note how the passing of time is recorded. We are made aware that this man has been sitting in a cell for many hours.*

7pm

Through the hatch, the road-rage suspect yells that he's going to take the Metropolitan police to court for wrongful imprisonment. 'We don't have the wisdom of Solomon,' says Hudson. 'We have to make a call in the heat of the moment. The lawyers can sit there and ponder, but you're faced with a violent situation and you have to decide what's going on. It may be that we end up arresting the other driver. If we are wrong, all we can do is put up our hands and say sorry. But people always think it's a conspiracy when we get it wrong.'

7.30pm

One of the bun-stealers is brought out for questioning. She is four months pregnant and replies to everything with a roll of her eyes. Records show that she has failed to turn up for several previous court dates. Hudson decides to keep her in overnight. 'Do you have anyone to bring you in extra goodies?' he asks. She shakes her head sadly.

> *Brockes uses adverbs fairly liberally but they always have a purpose. They nearly always contradict the impression given by the words alone.*

8.50pm

'I use Nivea facial for men,' confides Hudson. 'It's got vitamin E in it.'

Why this very personal piece of 'status life' detail? It just hangs there allowing the reader to invest it with importance. Does it signify that he is not quite the tough man he appears? Or is it just here to evoke the banality of his life, the ordinariness of a day in which he holds power over the lives of a clutch of other, mostly pathetic, human beings? Or is it a mean little dig that she knows will be used against him by his colleagues? Just one line but it comes freighted with a multiplicity of different possible meanings.

The solicitor for the road-rage suspect runs in carrying an overstuffed leather briefcase. Hudson eyes him suspiciously and, when the lawyer is out of earshot, says: 'Solicitors really get up my nose. We had one here the other night, a young lady. I said to her, "You're here late," and she said, "Oh, I don't mind. I'm earning £40 an hour." "You're lucky," I said. She said, "I'm a graduate," smug as anything. They speak to us as if we're halfwits. But one-third of police officers are graduates.'

When the solicitor returns, Hudson says testily: 'If your client destroys any more police property, I'm going to charge him.' Hudson turns his back and the solicitor rolls his eyes. 'Old school,' he says. 'People like him make life as difficult as possible for us.'

The solicitor, the suspect and the arresting officer go into an interview room.

'Not one independent witness supports your statement,' says the officer.

'You did not have grounds to arrest me,' says the suspect. 'It's because I was a black man and everyone else was white.'

'What made you push her?'

'She was saying abusive words. You're not listening to me.'

'You seemed annoyed that she wanted to reverse park.'

'What? So I was in the sin?'

11.06pm

The man is charged with common assault and released pending a bail hearing. 'What a nice, friendly chap he was,' says Hudson. They are going to 'refer him' – that is, let the superintendent decide if the case is worth pursuing. The man has a couple of previous cautions, but none for violence. 'It feels like a bit of a cop-out – all that work then a caution,' says the arresting officer dejectedly.

'That's what the CPS [crown prosecution service] will want,' says Hudson. 'Anything to avoid going to court.'

Our hero has been defeated by his own anger and a system that has reduced him to insignificance. He may not be charged but we are left in no doubt that he has been the loser in this unequal encounter.

Midnight

Hudson has been relieved. A new team clocks on. One of them is rooting about in the fridge, searching for a lost DNA sample. Over the next six hours a man will come in after stabbing his best friend with a kitchen knife, a heroin addict will be held for credit-card fraud at a supermarket, and a 24-hour plumber will fix the toilet bowl. 'Don't touch the gate on cell one,' warns the night sergeant before handing around some rubber gloves. A teenage girl, brought in for calling a kebab-shop owner a 'Turkish bastard', has been maliciously dribbling saliva through the hatch.

© The *Guardian*

WENDELL STEAVENSON

This piece is clearly topical but it is not tied to the news agenda. It was originally published in *Granta* magazine, then it was picked up by the *Sunday Times*. It goes behind the scenes of a war zone and tells us about the people. It is not about bombs and manoeuvres (although they are there); it is about human emotion and motivation. Steavenson sets out to try to understand what motivates a terrorist. She sees Osama as a tragic hero, deluded but likeable and certainly doomed. It is his adherence to Islam and lack of interest in American culture that she sees as his fatal flaw. The very traits he clearly sees as his motivation. It is written in story structure.

Osama's war: on getting to know an Iraqi terrorist
Jubilee, *Granta*, No. 87, September 2004
(This is an edited version which was also published in the *Sunday Times*, 26 September 2004)

Osama was slightly built and wore checked shirts and pressed trousers, always clean and neat. His eyes were large and roamed the places in which we met – hotel cafés, mainly – like sweeping radar, picking up on the blond man with a Walkman who didn't look like a journalist, the table of South African security mercenaries with guns and walkie-talkies strapped to their thighs, and, on one occasion, two American GIs, helmets and M-16s clattering, buying some chicken to take away.

This is a filmic, close-up introduction. She uses 'status life' detail as a film-maker would use images. We meet our main protagonist and the camera lingers on him so that we learn that he is important to the story.

Osama would note these threats and I would ask him if he was okay. He would tut at my worry and assure me that he was not afraid of such things; fear and jihad were incompatible.

We talked many times between the end of April and the beginning of June, the months the insurgency took hold. Osama had begun fighting the Americans in a mujaheddin cell in Baghdad a few months after the invasion in 2003. We met through a mutual friend who we both trusted; because of this, because I eventually met nearly all his family, including cousins, because I cross-questioned him and because I found what I could check of what he told me to be true, I believed him.

This background paragraph, which also provides the hook, is an opportunity to establish the credentials of the interviewee and, incidentally, the journalist.

His manner was always polite and modest, usually serious. He was a sort of Everyman template for a set of beliefs and opinions and actions that has enveloped his generation of Arabs. In the end I liked him. I told him I'd be upset if he was killed. He smiled at me and said that was because I had no belief. He, of course, had nothing to be frightened of; if he died as a muja-hed he was going to paradise.

Osama may be a real person but he is also a metaphor. He was chosen because of what he represents. Through understanding this man we are promised the chance of under-standing terrorism. This is the 'controlling idea'. Indeed the Sunday Times entitled it: 'Inside The Mind of a Terrorist'.

Shut in, circumscribed, lied to, bitter, proud and angry: Osama was an Iraqi. He'd had 12 years – half his life – of sanctions and UN handouts of bad-quality flour, which baked tough bread that ground grit into the cavities of your molars. He was the married elder son of a kebab restaurant owner on a street full of mechanics, the child of a poorish mixed Shi'ite and Sunni neighbourhood.

He was a Sunni and he kept his belief wrapped tight around him. It was a blanket wall I could not penetrate. No matter how much he tried to explain the logic of morality the Koran provided for him, I could not sympathise with his beliefs – I did not believe in them. His outraged disaffection, how-ever, I empathised with. Baghdad was a shithole.

She quickly paints in the background to his life and makes clear the limits of her own sympathies. Then she goes on to describe, again in restrained, deft strokes, the reality of living under occupation.

Rubble had bred rubble. Green lakes of sewage spread through dark unelectrified rubbish-strewn neighbourhoods. Government was only men in ministries interviewing their relatives for the few new jobs.

In the midst of this mess there was the everyday reminder of an occupying army, faces with sunglasses for eyes, alien invaders driving around in armour.

The pictures of the Abu Ghraib atrocities released all pent-up indignation. All anyone talked about were the hard-knock night raids and missing sons, missing husbands, missing fathers, missing brothers, American snipers, spies, contractors. There were a lot of stories about Iraqi girls being raped by American soldiers and plenty of cheap CDs full of porn stills showing uniformed actors ganging some dark-haired girl to prove it.

> *Note how she invokes the kinds of image that we all remember from movies about aliens – images that lock into our own stock of stories. She then goes on to mention a small detail (the dress) which locates Osama as an ordinary, struggling man, pitted against these aliens.*

Osama, absorbing all of this, was not so very different from many run-of-the-mill, unemployed urban Iraqis – perhaps the only difference was that he was fighting. Poverty and war had hemmed his life. He longed to buy his young wife a dress, he wanted to visit the famous mosques throughout Iraq, he thought vaguely about being an ambulance driver.

His brother Duraid, five years younger, felt these losses and gaps and injustices too. 'I want to live like the world lives,' Duraid once told me. Unlike Osama, he was able to imagine his own future; he found solace in a job, in kidding about with friends, in thinking about getting enough money together to buy a car.

> *This short passage is key to understanding this article. All Iraqis live under terrible conditions. They don't all become fighters. What makes this person different? She is suggesting that, in understanding him, she will help us to understand why young men are ready to blow themselves up for a cause. From here we move into a simple story structure in which the events of Osama's life are told chronologically and we learn about his character, from the incidents that he recounts, and the way in which he reacts and handles them.*

When the Americans had first arrived, Osama said, his feelings were scattered, he didn't know what to think. He had been beaten by Ba'ath party members for attending mosque and for neglecting to join the Ba'ath party; he was not a supporter of Saddam Hussein's regime. But it was difficult for him to feel liberated by a foreign army. He told me his heart had soared with happiness when he'd seen pictures of the World Trade Center collapse in 2001. 'This great superpower was hurt in its heart,' he said, amazed that someone could have managed such a bold swipe. 'Those that did it were very courageous. I felt that day they gave us back a bit of our rights. America wants to control the whole world's economy. When they want to impose sanctions on a country they don't care about the UN. They want to lead the whole world and make everything according to their tune, to impose their way on the world.'

> *The American occupation is the inciting incident. Everything proceeds from here. We are taken through his development into a fighter. The quotes she chooses illustrate how he felt, not what he did.*

After Baghdad fell, in the interim of looting, Osama and some friends from the mosque gathered the weapons left behind in abandoned barracks and police stations and buried them.

'We had the idea to fight for our country, not to protect any regime, but to protect our land and our mosques and our families. We talked about fighting but we didn't yet have any idea of holding a gun; we didn't have a single bullet at home.'

They went to an abandoned Iraqi army base and practised. Osama and his group had little or no military experience; sometimes ex-soldiers were drafted in to show them what to do.

'At first I was worried and afraid. I never expected that I would have the ability to do such things. When we were first hitting the Americans I considered myself a true mujahed. I feel it has strengthened my character and given me more trust in myself, and, of course, pride.'

His first operation was planting an improvised explosive device, an IED, in August after the invasion. It exploded and flipped a Humvee.

Osama's group operated along the Qanat Road, which began near the sprawling Rashid military base and ran north through the eastern suburbs to its outskirts. One baked May afternoon Osama and I drove down the Qanat Road listening to the American forces' Radio Freedom. The underpasses were pocked with spattered blast marks, chunks of asphalt were bitten away with explosives. The day before, Osama and his friends had exploded an IED in the middle of one of the rusty iron footbridges blocked up with bales of razor wire to prevent the resistance from using them to explode IEDs. Osama pointed out the hole: a ragged metal gap, and the torn roadbed below.

Did it hit? 'Yes. Part of these bushes caught fire.' In the broken-down mess of Baghdad the hole and the scratched road surface and the bit of burnt shrub didn't amount to much.

How do you know it hit the convoy? 'We don't know,' he admitted. They could not afford to hang around to survey the damage. A week before, a mujahed from another group had been shot in the returning hail when he had fired a rocket-propelled grenade at a midnight checkpoint.

We can't really use an RPG on the Qanat Road,' complained Osama. 'There isn't a place you can shoot it from where you can't be seen. Mostly it's IEDs.'

The IEDs were jerry-rigged electronic appliances packed into explosives hidden in a hollowed bit of breeze block or kerbstone, the cavity covered with a piece of painted polystyrene. Groups like Osama's tried to plant the IEDs at night, when the electricity was off and everything was dark. The Americans would drive by and miss them hiding in the undergrowth. Sometimes they were spotted by the Iraqi police, sometimes they were shot at and had to run off, abandoning the device.

Once, one of Osama's group was caught planting an IED by the Iraqi police and arrested. They had to pay a Kalashnikov to the custody officer to get him out of the police station.

Homespun, improvised, hit-and-run. I once watched a resistance propaganda video that included a 20-minute segment of grainy night shot as five separate hands tried to light a succession of matches to set off a mortar. One after another, matches flared and blew out in the wind. Hushed urgent voices could be heard marshalling the mortar's aim: 'Move it, move it, just a little, just a little.'

Finally the fire caught and flamed and lit and the rocket flashed and whooshed like a flare and hit nothing. Sometimes it was on the tip of my tongue to ask Osama: why is the resistance so crap? Anything to make a blast, a point, blow off some limbs, kill one or two Americans. The most successful operation Osama's group managed was when they blew up a Humvee and killed four Americans.

'We did not celebrate,' he said severely, 'but we felt very very happy.'

The deaths of four people is not a small thing, but in the context of this story it is brushed aside as evidence of their ineffectiveness. We are being asked to sympathise with him and his inexperience.

We drove past a cigarette kiosk. Osama said the cigarette-seller was a spy working for the Americans; his group had information from someone who knew. They were discussing what to do about him. There were lots of spies, the Americans paid for them, they were everywhere.

'Here,' Osama said, pointing out the car window at a lump of nondescript concrete lying in the dust at the side of the road. A single nugget amid a city of lumps of concrete, infrastructure rotted to rubble or pickaxed or blown up. 'That one didn't go off, we don't know why. We want to come and get it, but we have to wait for the battery on the timer to run out before we can retrieve it.'

During the week the group had twice planted IEDs that failed to detonate and a third time had planted an IED that exploded against a Humvee but wounded no soldiers. The fourth time Osama found himself among a group of Americans soldiers, trashing through the piles of roadside garbage with their carbines in search of hidden IEDs. Osama had the detonator strapped around his ankle; the IED they'd planted was a few metres away. The Americans didn't find it and Osama walked right past them. But the detonator didn't work. He was frustrated. 'And there were eight of them! We missed an opportunity.'

IEDs, RPG hit-and-runs; Osama was stuck in small-scale stuff against superpower armour. To be so much the underdog made him sad and defiant.

'You can't stand in front of an American tank, it'll just blow you up.' He stopped and looked grim for a moment. 'And when we hit them,' he said dully, 'it doesn't seem to make any difference.' It was an unguarded moment, but he soon recovered from it.

'It does make a difference,' he said to counter himself. 'They are sending more soldiers. But we are happy the Americans are staying because we can attack them more. This place will be their graveyard and their end will come at our hands.'

Now we move on to Osama's brother. He is here, not in his own right, but to throw light on Osama. Note the use of 'status life' detail to demonstrate how different the brothers are.

Osama's brother Duraid sold cans of Pepsi out of a Styrofoam cooler just outside an American base a couple of hours from Baghdad. We went to visit. If he sold Pepsi to the Americans in Baghdad, someone would shoot him for it. Here it was just a job, he was making some money. He was surprised at how nice and polite the Americans soldiers were and at the short shorts the women soldiers wore. 'Our eyes are out of our heads, with their sexy legs.' Duraid was a teenager, with a Chicago Bulls T-shirt and a baseball cap and an American accent. He liked Metallica and movies with Julia Roberts. He was curious, he was looking for nothing more than fun, he wanted to visit America.

'The way Osama thinks is different to the way I think,' he explained. 'I have girlfriends.' He giggled a little. 'I drink, I smoke.' Osama had no music at his wedding for religious reasons – although he had once admitted to me, laughing, that he'd liked Michael Jackson when he was younger. Osama had come to see his brother for a few days, to relax and regain some energy.

The brothers played Juventus versus Inter Milan on Duraid's PlayStation. Duraid told Osama that he had been offered a translating job with the Americans, $600 a month, and that he was thinking of taking it. Osama was not happy: he told Duraid it would be a sin, he didn't approve of his working with the Americans and anyway it was dangerous; the local mujaheddin might learn about Duraid's job and kill him.

> Everything in this passage has been chosen to demonstrate the differences between them. It is not just a question of ideology but a question of attitude. Duraid wants what America has to offer; Osama resents it.

Their mother worried about them both. 'I don't want Osama to be fighting them and I don't want Duraid working for them,' she said. She had only learnt of Osama's resistance activities when she was cleaning under his bed and found a box of RPG rockets, two Kalashnikovs and some grenades. She confronted him and he did not respond. She didn't tell his father; she knew he would only worry.

> Their mother worries about them. A detail chosen to 'normalise' these young men, bring them within the map of common meanings. But now, having established that Osama is worthy of sympathy, she goes on to debate with him. She has chosen the ground for this debate and it is her values that he is asked to consider – not his own. Though she quotes him liberally it is clear that she is completely in control of the agenda. Every argument ends with him, apparently contradicting himself. He may be a sympathetic character, she is telling us, but he doesn't understand what he is doing.

Once, in the car, the radio was on and Sheryl Crow was singing. Out of deference to Osama, I asked the driver to turn it off. Osama told me, laughing, no he didn't mind, he didn't need to impose his religion on a song. Oh yes,

I remember, I teased him, you like Michael Jackson! He nodded. 'And I have been following his trial. I think the American government created this trial to distract people from the war in Iraq.'

Baghdad was full of twisted conspiracy theories; I think most Iraqis assumed all governments behaved more or less as nefariously as Saddam did – and since western governments do try to manoeuvre public events such as trials or media campaigns, these conspiracy theories were often hard to dislodge in argument.

Osama would just sit there and grin at my naivety. He knew very well the reality close to him. He had no time for the nuances of democracy. I told him once that his world seemed narrow; he shrugged. It was very clear to him what he should do when he woke up in the morning. 'We only think about today, because today we might be killed. Tomorrow we think about tomorrow.' Once I asked him what kind of Iraq he wanted to live in. 'I want Islamic rule. But there would be conditions. All the other religions would be given their rights and allowed their traditions. But the Koran should rule in this region like it did in the time of the Prophet, the first Islamic state where Jews and Christians lived and had their rights respected.'

What about freedom of speech?

'That is something very good, excellent. Everyone should have the right to say what they want openly, without pressure.' So there can be criticism of religion, of imams and of sharia? Can I write in a newspaper saying that, for example, Islam controls women and subverts their independent rights? He knew the answer. 'But that is not true. Islam does give its rights to women,' he said confidently. 'Everything has its limits. I saw there was a cartoon in a newspaper in Beirut of a shoe with the words Allahu akbar written on the sole. This is not respectful. This is not freedom. This is not criticism. It is insulting religion. Can I insult Christ in this way?' I told him of course you could insult Christ any way you liked. He smiled and shook his head and said quietly: 'I don't understand your freedom.'

My conversations with Osama went in circles. What's the biggest problem in Iraq now? 'Security.'

Is blowing things up contributing to that security? 'We're doing it to hit Americans; not to make security.'

So you hitting Americans is more important than security? 'Yes.' I asked Osama about the wider world, about Al-Qaeda, Islam versus the West, suicide bombs and kidnappings.

'To be honest,' he said, 'when you use the word terrorist, I get angry.'

But what about the bombs in Spain, I asked him, what's your position on the targeting of civilians? 'Yes, I supported them.' But the majority of Spaniards were against the war. 'Really?' said Osama doubtfully. 'I didn't know that, but the bombs in Spain changed something. People saw there was a threat, so they bought their safety. They kicked out the prime minister and brought their troops home.'

That's terrorism, I said definitively. 'No, it's not. You don't live here. You don't feel how we're boiling now. When each day passes and it feels like your soul is leaving your body. Killings in the street, our oil is being stolen, there's no electricity.'

What's your definition of terrorism? Osama looked at me coyly. 'You'll be angry.'

No, tell me.

'Israel and America.'

No, tell me the definition, like it would be in a dictionary.

'Terrorism as I see it is when a person with money and power goes into a neighbourhood and starts shooting randomly. I think that is terrorism.'

> *The climax of this tragedy is under-stated. Is this the end of an episode or the end of the story? We are left with the suggestion of a sequel. The young man whom events have turned into an amateur soldier will now go on, severed from family and friends, to become a much more dangerous person.*

A week after my last meeting with Osama, three American Humvees and a tank surrounded a house in his neighbourhood at four in the morning. Five of his resistance group were arrested. He was the only one not there and not caught. The next morning he emptied his house of weapons and got ready to leave.

Will they talk? Will they give your name? Osama was worried and frightened and his eyes darted around. 'It all depends on the beating they get.'

His mother came into the room, with tears in her eyes. 'They will come here, to this house, and they will arrest all of us!' She sat on the sofa paralysed by fear. Osama left within the hour, first for his cousins' place out of Baghdad, and then, probably, for Syria.

© Granta

GEORGE PACKER

This is a masterly piece of writing which demonstrates how important it is to have a very clear 'controlling idea' to keep together all the elements of a story. In a feature of this length (8,000 words) it would be easy to meander, and for the reader to get lost. The controlling idea provides a spine to which all the elements are firmly attached. The basic structure is quite simple. There is a long introduction and then three sections of debate (each evidenced by observation, interviews and comments) followed by a summary. This feature is evidence-based but very clearly opinion-driven. However, the opinions are not expressed directly, they are there in the selection of the evidence and the way it is structured. This is 'showing' not 'telling'. Look at the way in which 'status life' detail is employed to build up sympathy or antipathy.

Gangsta war
New Yorker, 3 November 2003

From my balcony on the eighth floor of the Hotel Ivoire, I could see down-town Abidjan across the lagoon in the mist. Skyscrapers rose along the waterfront, a blue neon sign blinked 'NISSAN,' and the plate glass of the commercial banks reflected the silver afternoon light. At this distance, it was easy to pretend that these skyscrapers weren't emptying out; that the African Development Bank hadn't abandoned the city; that the shipping traffic at the port, on which all West Africa depended for an economic pulse, hadn't dropped by: fifty per cent. From the balcony, it still looked like the glamorous capital of twenty years ago, before decline and civil war, when young men and women from all over French-speaking Africa came to Abidjan to seek their future in the city of success.

A descriptive introduction that manages also to be a summary using those emblems of Modernism: skyscrapers and neon signs, to signify progress – and decline.

I was living in a small village in Togo then, two countries east of Ivory Coast; in the evenings, I would listen to the mother of the family in my compound describe the time she had spent in Abidjan as a kind of dream. There was abundant work in Ivory Coast, and foreigners like her were thrilled to find themselves in a truly cosmopolitan city, one where everyone spoke the same Abidjanaise French. The ambitious students in the village school where I taught knew that, short of Paris, Abidjan was the best place to be. An African privileged class of bureaucrats and professionals ate in fine restaurants downtown and kept the night clubs open till all hours. A robust economy based on coffee and cocoa exports employed several million African immigrants to do the manual labor and forty thousand French expatriates to run businesses and advise the government. The French, some of them third- or fourth-generation, enjoyed a slightly updated version of the colonial life. In the eighties, a French teenager in Abidjan could celebrate his birthday by racing his moped around town and then jumping off a bridge into the lagoon, to the cheers of an Ivorian crowd. The French who have remained in Abidjan now call that time *la belle epoque*.

In Togo, I was a Peace Corps volunteer, living in a village without electricity, and one detail I learned about Abidjan struck me as miraculous. The Hotel Ivoire, I was told, had a large skating rink with ice that kept a perfectly glazed surface even when the temperature outside topped a hundred degrees. The capital also had world-class golf courses, because President Felix Houphouët-Boigny, the relatively benign dictator who had led Ivory Coast since its nominal independence from France, in 1960, considered the sport to be a mark of civilization. He had turned his home village of Yamoussoukro, a hundred and twenty-five miles north of Abidjan, into a grand political capital of wide boulevards lined with street lamps. He built a Catholic basilica there that rises out of the palm forests like a hallucination of St. Peter's, of which it is an actual-size replica. He also erected a vast Presidential palace, and surrounded it with man-made lakes that were filled with crocodiles. (Houphouët-Boigny, who died in 1993, is buried in a mausoleum near the cathedral.) While the rest of the region 'was becoming mired in coups and wars and deepening poverty, social scientists talked about the "Ivorian miracle." The country was one of the most prosperous in Attica, and Ivorians weren't killing one another. The residents of Abidjan said that their country was "blessed by the gods."'

> *Two paragraphs of back story, which places the Ivory Coast economically and politically and, incidentally, establishes the credentials of the writer as a person with a right to describe this tragedy and to try to analyse it. It is the country itself, and its people, which is the central 'character'. What we are about to read is a study of its rise to riches (the envy of Africa) and its collapse into poverty. The central theme (the cause of the collapse), we gradually discover, is the destructive impact of globalisation and in particular global media. There is a secondary theme of betrayal. Young people, of whatever faction, are portrayed as railing against the failures of their parents.*

As soon as I went down to the hotel's lobby, my vision of old Abidjan began to fade. The skating rink, on the grounds behind the hotel, was closed. An artificial lake that once was dotted with paddleboats had been drained because of chronic scum, and blue paint was peeling off its concrete walls. In the restaurant, a Liberian lounge singer was belting out 'Yesterday' and the theme from 'Fame' for a handful of lonely white mercenaries and West African peacekeepers and their prostitutes; she had the desperate brio of a resort performer in the off-season. I hailed a taxi, and as I sat in back, listening to my driver – who was garrulous with rage, like most men in Abidjan – complain about the traffic, the heat, the economy, the government death squads, and the ongoing civil war, it was hard to believe that the ovens of the Patisserie Abidjanaise, across the Charles de Gaulle Bridge, were still disgorging sheets of warm, perfect baguettes. But so they were.

A descriptive paragraph in which each detail effectively acts as a visual metaphor for change and decay and for the violence that accompanies it. There is one deliberately written simile that probably should have been cut as it only serves to slow down the passage.

Abidjan valiantly clings to the idea that it remains the refined city it was twenty years ago. The University of Abidjan, once an impressive institution, now decrepit, continues to turn out thousands of graduates every term for government jobs or foreign scholarships that no longer exist. In the nineties, the French began to restrict immigration and opportunities to study abroad, just after a catastrophic drop in commodity prices plunged Ivory Coast, the world's largest cocoa producer, into deep debt. Today, Abidjan is populated with educated young men and women who have no outlet for their ambitions. 'All the generations until 1985 found work – state work, private work,' Ousmane Dembelé, a social geographer at the university, told me. 'All goals were satisfied. But after '85, '90, '95, all these generations of youth in Abidjan could find nothing. Nothing.'

This is the kernel of the story, the inciting incident. It lacks any information about why commodity prices dropped, or what prompted France to restrict immigration but it does make clear that the catastrophe was not of its own making. Ivory Coast was a victim of global trading conditions. Packer has chosen to leap forward to examine the ways in which the country has responded to this change in its fortunes. What he finds is a country tearing itself apart and it is the details of this destruction on which he now focuses. From here on he uses a loose essay structure to hold the piece together. We start with background to the current situation.

These days, Abidjan looks less like Paris and more like a decaying Third World city. Residents encounter symptoms of decline on every street, from collapsing infrastructure to violent crime. 'It's not Lagos yet,' the financial manager of an architecture firm told me. 'But we're headed straight there.' The northern part of Ivory Coast is largely Muslim, and poorer than the mostly Christian south, with its cocoa plantations and Abidjan. On September 19, 2002, rebel soldiers from the north mutinied against the government. The civil war has regional, religious, and economic dimensions, but its basic cause is political. The mutiny was a violent reaction to several years of anti-northern and anti-immigrant policies pursued by the series of southern Presidents who succeeded Houphouët-Boigny. During the 2000 election, the Presidential candidate from the north, a former International Monetary Fund official named Alassane Ouattara, was disqualified on the dubious ground that he was not of Ivorian parentage. The winner, a history professor named Laurent Gbagbo, from the cocoa region, took office amid riots, during which his supporters killed hundreds of Ouattara's primarily Muslim followers. Since the civil war broke out, at least three thousand people have been killed and more than a million have been displaced from their homes. Throughout the conflict, one of the government's favored weapons has been the rhetoric of xenophobia.

> *Now we move onto the body of the piece in which Packer collects evidence into four main sections. Most of the evidence comes from observation and from interviewing people whom he regards as representative of the various factions. He uses authoritative voices and secondary evidence to back up their testimony. The first section fleshes out the government (Young Patriot) position. Note that he starts by telling us that the Young Patriots are in the pay of the government. Already he is establishing his 'preferred reading' (Hall, 1996) of the situation. He gives us the least favoured position first and will then go on to stack up the evidence against it.*

The taxi was taking me to a rally of Ivory Coast's Young Patriots, a coterie of young men paid by the government to stir up nationalistic feelings against the rebels, who, soon after starting the civil war, occupied the north of the country. The Young Patriots railed with equal intensity against immigrants, blaming them for the country's soaring unemployment rate.

At the Young Patriots' rally, I wanted to get a glimpse of their leader, Charles Blé Goudé. The drive to the rally took me near the Place de la Republique, a public square of cracked concrete, where, in late January, Blé Goudé had spoken to tens of thousands, denouncing the French government for failing to rescue Ivory Coast from the rebels. (France, refusing to take sides, had pushed Gbagbo's government to reconcile with the insurgent forces.) The iconography of those demonstrations was remarkable. It was virulently anti-French and desperately pro-American. 'USA WE NEED YOU AGAINST THE "OLD EUROPE,"' one sign pleaded, just a few days after Donald Rumsfeld coined the term. Blé Goudé waved an American flag and delighted the crowd by refusing to speak French. 'Are you ready for English?' he yelled, and the crowd roared as he spoke a few clumsy sentences in the tongue of the superpower, which, in Ivory Coast, is the language of youthful resistance. The January demonstrations had led to anti-French riots, and thousands of French expatriates fled the country while young Ivorians spat upon them, attacked their businesses and schools, and tried to block the departure of Air France jets from the airport.

The rally this afternoon was in a slum called Port-Bouët, on a waterfront strip near the airport. My driver got lost in Port-Bouët's labyrinthine streets, which were choked with the blue taxis known as woro-woro. About fifteen years ago, the city government of Paris sent Abidjan a fleet of used green-and-white municipal buses, which grew filthy, broke down, and were never replaced or repaired, even as the city's population exploded. The 'woro-woro' run local routes to fill in the gaps, but their drivers are notoriously reckless. We passed clogged roads, shantytowns, and entire neighborhoods without decent water, power, or sewage systems.

The taxi turned a corner, and suddenly there were hundreds of people crowding around the perimeter of a dirt rectangle the size of a football field. This was Place Laurent Gbagbo.

Port-Bouët is a government stronghold. High-rise housing projects in advanced states of decay ringed the field, and residents hung out from the windows, their arms dangling beside their laundry. A young m.c. was warming up the crowd with a call-and-response that always ended in the word bête, or 'stupid.' The rebels who held the northern half of the country were bête. The neighboring countries suspected of arming them, Burkina Faso and Liberia, were bête. The immigrants in Abidjan with Muslim names, who supposedly sympathized and even conspired with the rebels, were bête. And the French, who had failed to defend their Ivorian brothers and sisters in the hour of crisis – the French were more bête than anyone.

For all the hostility in the slogans, the crowd was cheerful, like spectators awaiting the main act of a show they'd seen before. Almost everyone in the crowd was young; most of them clearly had nothing better to do. Boy vendors were selling hats in the national colors, orange and green, with the warning 'Don't Touch Our Country' and T-shirts declaring 'Xenophobe-So What?'

In the front row of a tented seating area were the Young Patriot leaders, local stars in their twenties who were dressed like American hip-hop singers: gold chains, tracksuits, floppy hats. Their scowling bodyguards sat behind them, wearing muscle shirts and mirror glasses; a few were armed with Kalashnikov rifles. Sitting quietly and pathetically in the back rows were the neighborhood elders. In the traditional hierarchy of African villages, the old are elaborately deferred to by the young. Here the elders had no role other than to applaud while the Young Patriots took turns swaggering and jigging out on the speaker's platform and the loudspeakers blasted reggae or zouglou, the home grown pop music of the movement. A favorite anthem, by a zouglou group called the Bastards, was 'Sacrificed Generation':

> *Each detail is used to provide evidence for the 'controlling idea' that American values are taking over and eroding traditional African values. The elders sit 'pathetically' while the young 'swagger'.*

They say students make too much trouble
They say students go on strike too much
At the start they took away our
scholarships
They made us pay for rooms and meal
tickets
Students are poor ...
When we present our demands
They answer us with tear gas ...
The big brothers are angry
The old fathers don't want to get out of
the way!

Each speaker tried to outdo the last in scabrous wit and extremist views, before boogying back to the tent to touch fists with the others, like an N.B.A. star returning to the bench. At another Young Patriot event, I had heard a heavyset demagogue pronounce the true 'axis of evil' to be Liberia, Burkina Faso, and France, and then declare, with malicious irony, 'Yeah, I'm Jean-Marie Le Pen!' Meanwhile, at night, immigrants were being hounded from their homes. Under the pretext that they were supporting the rebels, entire shantytowns had been bulldozed, and the corpses of opposition politicians were turning up at dawn in remote corners of the city. Everyone knew that paramilitary death squads were at work, though no one could prove the rumor that they were directed by the President's wife, Simone, an evangelical Christian with a taste for inflammatory rhetoric against Muslims, immigrants, and whites.

This spring, President Gbagbo, under pressure from France, agreed to include rebel ministers in a new cabinet. In July, the civil war was declared to be over. But late last month rebels started boycotting meetings of the unity government, and threatened to resume the war. This was fine with the leaders of the Young Patriots, who had thrived during the civil war, making regular appearances on television; many had become national celebrities. These young men have no desire to return to the ranks of the eternal students and the jobless street-corner orators.

Blé Goudé arrived very late, in a convoy. 'They're coming! They're coming! I see Charles!' the m.c. informed the crowd. By the time Blé Goudé, his figure lean and tense, made his way with an armed bodyguard to the tent, and then out across the open dirt to the speaker's stand, the moon was rising over Port-Bouët.

Blé Goudé, the son of a peasant from President Gbagbo's region, rose to prominence in the nineties, when he became a leader of the national student movement. The group clashed frequently with police during the chaotic years following Houphouët-Boigny's death, and Blé Goudé was sent to prison many times. At the end of that decade, when the student movement split into two factions, the university campus became the scene of a small war. Blé Goudé, whose side won, earned the nickname Machete. (He never received a degree, however, though for years he pretended that he had.) The leader of the losing side was Guillaume Soro, an overweight, soft spoken student from the north. Soro is now the political leader of a major rebel group, the Patriotic Movement of Ivory Coast. The country's destiny is being shaped by former students who have never held a job.

Blé Goudé took the speaker's platform. He was wearing baggy green army pants, a tank top, an Adidas pullover tied around his waist, and a black baseball cap with the bill turned up in the imitation-gangsta style of the Young Patriots. But he didn't strut; his hungry, liquid eyes and knowing smile projected the self-containment of a leader. As he spoke, darkness fell, and gradually he became a disembodied voice. He didn't shout, unlike the others; his was a deep, calm voice.

Blé Goudé denied press reports that he was getting rich off his leadership of the Young Patriot movement. 'They don't understand that some people fight for their beliefs,' he said. 'They think everyone can be bought. They say my belly is getting bigger.' Shrieks of laughter rose from the crowd as he patted his flat stomach. 'All this stuff about xenophobia and exclusion is just a cover,' he said. 'The Ivorian youth is showing the whole world its attachment to democratic principles. I'm not just talking about the Ivory Coast of today. I'm talking about the generation that will rule Ivory Coast. Because the little kids of ten or eight all say France is no good.'

Note that very little of what Goudé said is actually reported. Only the 'sound bites' that provide evidence for the story which Packer is shaping.

Other Young Patriots had been funnier and nastier. But when Blé Goudé finished speaking and the music started up, the crowd swarmed around him. For a moment, he had actually made them feel that the future was theirs.

The Young Patriots represent a new kind of African success story. They're celebrated by many young people in Abidjan for beating and cheating a system gone rancid. With the corrupt 'old fathers' refusing to get out of the way, and with all the old channels to success – emigration, foreign study, state employment, family connections – blocked, the new hero is a young trickster with a talent for self-promotion. The model is no longer the formal bureaucratic style of the French colonizer; it's the loud, unrestrained style that everyone in Ivory Coast calls American.

When Blé Goudé drives around Abidjan in his armed two-car convoy – Renault in front, four-by-four behind – he's saluted as 'the General of the Youth.' According to one well-connected Frenchman I spoke with, the government, at the height of the demonstrations in January, was giving Blé Goudé eighty thousand dollars a week to distribute to his fellow Young Patriots and their crowds of followers. I was told by a Western diplomat that he runs a Mob style racket in the campus dorms, taking a cut off the illegal lodging of students, who sleep two to a cot or on the floor. Blé Goudé has become a sort of urban warlord.

It is not easy to verify facts in a place like this and Packer's 'authoritative sources' are both Westerners who perhaps have a vested interest in making this young man seem as evil as possible. The view that he is in the pay of the government is then softened by the observation in the following passage that he is far from living in luxury. Note how 'status life' detail is employed to build up a sense of the man and his relationship to other people.

He hasn't completely grown into his success, however. When I sat down to talk with him over lunch, it was in his mother's under-furnished cinder-block house, across a rutted dirt road from a small shantytown. Blé Goudé was wearing grey socks monogrammed with his initials, 'CBG' (a friend had made him ten pairs), and, along with half a dozen hangers-on, he was eating the peasant dish of rice and sauce.

'Our elders deceived us,' he told me. 'Our predecessors, the political leaders and others, have shown us clearly that our future doesn't matter. That's why I've organized the Ivorian youth. To give it a political arm.'

Note the reference to betrayal by the elders. Note also (in the next paragraph) the suggestion that Goudé might be older than he says.

Blé Goudé says he is thirty-one; others claim he is older. In his mother's living room, without the charmer's smile I had seen in Port-Bouët, he looked hard-featured and edgy. He said that he was tired from his work, but he mustered the energy to urge an American intervention in his country along the lines of the Iraq invasion – a request that his followers had presented to an American official outside the United States Embassy. Blé Goudé hoped to exploit the Franco-American rift over Iraq, and he explained that Ivory Coast's struggle was the same as America's: for democracy and against terrorism. The rebellion of September 19 2002, splintered Ivory Coast, and to him the connection with 9/11 was obvious. 'There's only eight days' difference,' he pointed out.

'And a year.'

'And a year. That's all. It's the same thing. Only it wasn't helicopters here. That's all. It wasn't the World Trade Center, that's all. So, voila – the connection.'

I asked whether he thought Americans even knew what was going on in Ivory Coast. He didn't respond, but it was clear that the youth of Ivory Coast thought they knew what was going on in America.

'Even if the United States didn't colonize our country, they should come to our assistance,' he said. 'Ivory Coast is a land to be taken. Above all, the generation today has been educated in the American spirit. The American spirit is freedom. The American spirit is integrity in action.' Blé Goudé extended his arm in front of him. 'When the U.S. says what they'll do, they do it. They don't say one thing at night and the opposite the next day, like the French.' It was just as true, he said, of the American celebrities worshipped in Ivory Coast, like Mike Tyson and Jay-Z. 'Boxing has no tricks in it. When someone hits you, he hits you. Basketball – it's all straight up and down. Rap comes out of the ghetto, to convey the suffering of the young people there. When they sing, you listen, and the message comes straight at you.'

Now the feature changes direction. We have heard the story from the government, or Blé Goudé angle, now we hear the other side. Once again we start with a background paragraph which moves us from one scene to the next. Look at the way his relationship with others is described to help us build up a picture of him.

In the eyes of Blé Goudé and the Young Patriots, Amadou Guindo is the enemy. Guindo, an immigrant's son, lives in Koumassi, another Abidjan slum, separated from Port-Bouët by a land bridge across the lagoon. It smells of oranges and sewage. Because there is a high concentration of northerners and foreigners in Koumassi, the government regards it as a hotbed of rebel sympathy. One morning, a month after the war began, several gendarmes stormed down an alleyway, entered a cinder-block compound where the landlady was washing clothes, and broke down Guindo's door. (He happened to be out.) The landlady convinced the gendarmes that it was a case of mistaken identity, but not before they had rifled through all his belongings.

Guindo, thirty-three years old and unemployed, is known as Cool B, for Cool Boy. On the wall above his bed hung a large American flag; overhead, taped to the low ceiling panels, were posters for B movies like 'War Dog' and 'The Arrival.' A Richard Wright novel was on his bedside table, next to CDs by Stevie Wonder and R. Kelly. Outdoors, when he cruised the crowded dirt roads of the neighborhood he calls *mon ghetto*, where someone yelled out his name every few yards and the teenage prostitutes approached to flirt and the guys sitting in doorways exchanged fist-to-chest salutations with him, Cool B, his head shaved and his eyes concealed behind a pair of Ray-Bans, carried himself in a manner that he called 'the American style.' It bore a close resemblance to the style of the young men on the other side of the conflict. Cool B told me that ninety per cent of the young people in Abidjan imitate the American style, which he defined as 'total independence. Liberty to express yourself, Economic independence, too. A way of talking and walking.' And he demonstrated by sauntering up the road with a novel combination of the pimp roll and the keep-on truckin' stride.

> *This young man also mimics American style but Packer picks out attributes which make Guindo sound endearing: he listens to softy singers Stevie Wonder and R. Kelly and is sufficiently accommodating to demonstrate his 'pimp roll'. Blé Goudé, on the other hand, is coupled with boxer Mike Tyson and rapper Jay-Z and described as 'edgy'. Now Packer tells Guindo's story, starting with an inciting incident, then moving on to fill in the background before moving into chronological story form to offer the highlights of his life.*

Though he has spent his entire life in Ivory Coast, Cool B is technically a citizen of Mali, to the north, where his father comes from. This is how he acquired Malian citizenship: One night in 1996, Cool B was walking through his ghetto in the company of his German girlfriend, Petra, when a group of policemen approached and demanded his papers. He produced his Ivorian identity card (his father had had him naturalized when he was sixteen), but this only enraged the police. 'Amadou Guindo,' one of them said, seeing that the name was foreign. 'What name is that?'

'It's *my* name.'

The police pocketed Cool B's card and told him to come with them to the station. When he asked why, they fell on him and handcuffed him. His white girlfriend's presence seemed to provoke them to ridicule, Cool B recalled. 'I said, "It's because of my name you arrest me, you humiliate me. O.K., you don't have to be Ivorian to be happy in life. Go shit with my card, I don't give a fuck. From now on, I'll keep the nationality of my parents."' Instead of going to the police station to ask for his card back and suffer more abuse, he took citizenship from the Malian Embassy. 'I'm proud of it,' he said. 'I know nothing of Mali. But if I try to get Ivorian nationality they'll humiliate me every time.'

Cool B speaks with a slight stutter, and as he told me this story, in the privacy of his sweltering ten-foot-square room, the stutter grew more pronounced, his crossed leg jiggled, and the lines deepened in his face, which, with the Ray-Bans off, looked older than his years. Stripped of the American style, he seemed vulnerable, as if he were trying to ward off disappointment.

> Interesting that Cool B 'looks older than his years' while of Blé Goudé he remarks 'he says he is thirty-one; others claim he is older'.

In 1996, the same year Cool B became a 'foreigner,' a new word emerged on the political scene in Abidjan: *ivoirité*. The English equivalent that best captures the word's absurdity might be 'Ivoryness.' In practice, *ivoirité* meant that immigrants were subjected to harassment and shakedowns and restrictive new laws. Ivorians from the north, who tend to share family names and the Muslim faith with immigrants from Mali, Guinea, and Burkina Faso, came in for similar treatment. If a single word can be said to have started a war, *ivoirité* started Ivory Coast's.

Cool B's father worked as a nurse in Abidjan for thirty years before retiring and returning to Mali, in 1991. Cool B didn't go beyond high school – instead, he pursued an early career in what he calls voyousie, or the hoodlum life. The scale of his activities was small, but he made it a habit to insult pretty much everyone who crossed his path. 'The troublemaker doesn't know why he makes trouble,' he said. 'He's just proud of himself. He has a certain pride.' One day in 1990, when Cool B was in high school, a Frenchman came to his drawing class and asked the students to do illustrations showing the proper use of condoms. Cool B found the assignment foolish, and at the end of the class he stood in the doorway to block the Frenchman's exit.

'You're going around the world showing people pictures of how to use condoms?' Cool B asked mockingly. 'I'll show you what to do.' He snatched away the man's prospectus and, reading from the text, improvised an anti-AIDS rap on the spot, in the manner of LL Cool J.

The Frenchman was impressed. Within a couple of days, he had arranged for Cool B to record the rap at a downtown night club, and the song made him a momentary celebrity among Abidjan youth. It also began his long association with white people – among them Petra, his girlfriend, who eventually went back to Germany, and Eliane de Latour, a French filmmaker who employed him for a while as a researcher on a feature about Abidjan youth. Cool B keeps pictures of them on his wall, and he tries to figure out why, in spite of these connections, he remains stuck in Koumassi. He spends his ample free time and his limited funds at a local Internet café, surfing international dating sites and chat rooms where people he knows have found marriage opportunities that got them out of Africa. Or he visits a green-card lottery Web site. His ambition, short of leaving Africa, is to open his own Internet café.

'I don't understand my situation,' he said. 'I'm still blocked. I want to get out of my problems one day. I don't have the totality of independence.' Cool B's residence permit expired last year, making him an illegal alien in the only country in which he has ever lived.

When the room grew too hot for us to stay inside, even with a fan blowing, we went around the corner to pay a visit to Cool B's gang. A dozen young men were seated on facing benches under a ramshackle tin roof; they spent twelve hours a day there, like a conclave of village elders, except that Cool B was the oldest person in the group. The others regarded him with respect and sought his advice. They were all immigrants or northerners, keeping an eye out for the police. They wore gold chains, tank tops, and Nike caps. When I asked what kind of work they did, most of them replied, 'Tent rental,' which began to seem like a euphemism for unemployment, though some of them had part-time work fencing stolen goods.

At noon, a communal basin of rice and sauce appeared, and the young men plunged their right hands into it. The gang argot of Abidjan, which combines French, profane English, and the language of Ivory Coast's north, is called Nushi, or 'mustache,' a reference to the way bad guys look in Hollywood movies. The inferior type of rice that Cool B and his friends had to eat is derisively referred to in Nushi as *deni kasha*, or 'lots of children.' The young men all came from poor and enormous polygamous families in which there were as many as thirty-five siblings. 'That's what spoiled our future,' a surly fellow with a shaved head told me. 'When our parents worked, they didn't think of us first. In Europe, they set up an account to help the kids when they grow up, right?'

Once again he lingers on the details which demonstrate similarity – here is another group of young men, dressed in American style clothing eating rice from a communal pot. Note also a return to the theme of betrayal of the youth by their parents. These running metaphors help to provide direction and to weave disparate elements into the story.

This was the story they all told: fathers who did nothing for their sons, extended families that might have made sense in a rural village but crushed the life out of them here in the city. Cool B's closest friend in the group was a rangy twenty-five-year-old, wearing wire-rim glasses, who introduced himself as McKenzie. He'd taken the name from a character in an action movie. Growing up in a northern town called Odienné, McKenzie (whose real name is Morifère Bamba) used to watch American Westerns on a communal TV. John Wayne made a particularly strong impression. These movies lit a desire to live in his 'dream country' which remains McKenzie's sole ambition.

At twelve, he quit school – his mother was dead, his father too poor to support him – and the next year, 1990, he came alone to Abidjan. I asked how he had imagined the city then. 'It was the city of success,' McKenzie said. 'The city that would give me the ability to realize my dream.' Abidjan was a way station on his escape route to America. This, I thought, was the difference between Cool B's gang and the Young Patriots: they all copied the American style, but the Young Patriots had found a way to make it work for them in Abidjan.

Again, global media brands are invoked to demonstrate just how much these young people are influenced by American culture.

After a few years in the city of success, McKenzie realized that he was entirely alone. 'Succeed how?' he said. 'You have to have lots of connections and acquaintances. Guys go into banditry to realize their success.' McKenzie joined a gang, began smoking cocaine, fought, stole, and saw a friend die at the hands of the police. Movies like 'Menace II Society,' which seemed to glamorize the gangster life, finally convinced him that it was a dead end.

McKenzie left the gang and learned the electrician's trade, at which he worked irregularly, trying to save money for the trip to America, until the war started and jobs disappeared altogether.

Now we change direction again. A new scene is introduced with these two short, linking paragraphs as we move into the war zones.

The war was out there somewhere. In Abidjan, a ten-o'clock curfew enforced by gendarmes at roadblocks had shut down night life, but the city was no longer a conflict zone. It was hard to believe that a couple of hundred miles away, in the interior, teenage militias were machine-gunning children and cutting old men's throats. Like so many African wars, Ivory Coast's had degenerated into looting and massacres by bands of loosely controlled, generally underage fighters; it became part of a larger conflict that had been spreading through the region for years – ever since the outbreak of Liberia's civil war, in 1989 – producing hundreds of thousands of corpses and millions of refugees.

Seen from a distance, Africa's man-made disasters look senseless. But to the participants, who tend to be young and poor, these wars have meaning. The war in Ivory Coast began as a struggle over identity – over the question that haunted Cool B, the question of who gets to be considered Ivorian. The country's decline made identity a political issue, but it also extends to the larger, almost existential question of what it means to be a young African living in the modern world.

After a week in Abidjan, I drove north, to Bouaké, Ivory Coast's second largest city and the main rebel command center. Behind the ceasefire line patrolled by French and West African peacekeeping troops, the town hadn't seen fighting in months. At rebel headquarters, in a former nursing school, a polite, bored young official was doing a Yahoo search for Uzis and grenades. Out on the half-empty streets, every civilian vehicle had been commandeered, license plates had been removed, doors had been ripped off, and young rebels had painted the sides of the vehicles with Spider-Man logos and self-styled unit names: Delta Force, Highway of Death. Without a war to fight, they were turning into gangsters.

At the hospital, the staff of Doctors Without Borders reported that the most serious injuries were sustained by the young rebels who routinely smashed up cars or accidentally shot themselves in the foot. One night while I was in Bouaké, a notoriously violent young commander named Wattao threw himself a lavish birthday party, with a fawning m.c., cameramen, hundreds of guests who watched themselves live on video screens, and gate-crashers who ended up exchanging gunfire.

Notice again the references to globalised media, for example, to Yahoo, the logos painted on the vehicles and the party videos. We move on to a fourth scene, starting with a linking paragraph which takes us to where the action is – in the west.

The rebel military leadership, which had maintained fairly good discipline since the outbreak of hostilities, was turning to a local priest called Abbé Moïse to rehabilitate the restless underage recruits. 'They haven't killed a lot,' the Abbé told me. 'They're recoverable here. The children of Bouaké aren't as traumatized as those in the west.'

That was where the real war was taking place. In November, 2002, two new rebel groups had suddenly appeared near the Liberian border. The western groups claimed an alliance with the northern rebels, but they had no clear political motivation, and their rebellion quickly took on the violent, anarchic quality of Liberia's and Sierra Leone's civil wars. In fact, some experts have concluded that the western rebellion was the inspiration of Liberia's President, Charles Taylor, who has had a hand in all the region's murderous and intertwined wars, organizing and arming rebels in Sierra Leone and Guinea as well as terrorizing his own country for a decade and a half, until his forced departure this past August. Although Taylor is out of power, the widespread instability he fomented won't dissipate in West Africa anytime soon. The region is now populated with young fighters who float from country to country, looking for war.

The conflict in the west was a catastrophe. Both the rebels and the government were recruiting Liberian mercenaries to do their fighting. The Ivory Coast government also used MI-24 helicopter gunships with Eastern European or South African mercenary crews; the rebels used the feared Sierra Leonean warlord Sam (Mosquito) Bockarie and his battle-hardened teenage fighters. (Bockarie was killed in Liberia in early May; most likely on the orders of Taylor, against whom he might have testified at the war-crimes court in Sierra Leone, which had indicted him in March.) Hundreds of civilians were being slaughtered in western Ivory Coast, and entire villages had been looted and left empty. It was in the west that the 'Ivorian miracle' met its final demise and Ivory Coast became just another West African nightmare.

The scene set, he moves on with an anecdote about travelling. This helps us to locate the action but also provides an opportunity to pick out details which then act as metaphors. In this case we are shown the contrast between the past (the fetish figurines, the gifts of fruit) and the present (guns).

Before the civil war broke out, the journey from Bouaké to Man, the biggest town in the west, took eight or nine hours. It took me two days, because

I had to pass through at least fifty roadblocks. In some places, there was a roadblock every quarter mile. They were makeshift affairs: a tree limb, pieces of junked machinery, concrete blocks. The boys on guard roused themselves from the shade of a tree. When they noticed a white face in the car, they put on angry expressions and went back to grab their AK-47s. Glowering behind sunglasses, they stalked over to the car, fingers on triggers. Around their necks hung leather thongs with polished wooden or stone amulets, which they believed made them bulletproof. Carved fetish figurines stood guard alongside the roadblock. The boys ordered me to open the trunk, they pretended to search inside, they demanded to see my travel permit. A standoff: everything was in order, but they hadn't given the signal to go, and they had the guns. This last detail made all the difference, yet I found it hard to accept the obvious power relation. Most of them looked the age of the middle-school village boys I had taught twenty years ago in Togo. Those boys had called me Monsieur and left presents of papaya at my door. It was as if I had come back to the region to find all my students armed and snarling, ordering me to get out of the car.

I tried to talk my way through the roadblocks in the old jokey Peace Corps way. And it usually worked: the boys' faces softened, the barked orders turned into requests for cigarettes or money or aspirin, which were only half serious and then even a bit sheepish, and, as the car started rolling forward, we exchanged a thumbs-up, and a boy began giving me breezy compliments – 'If you Americans were here, we'd already be in Abidjan!' – as if the guns had just been props and everything were friendly between us.

The farther west I drove – past the ripe anacard-fruit trees that no one was tending and the storehouses of cotton that couldn't be sold and the carcasses of vehicles that the rebels had wrecked and abandoned – the less useful my Peace Corps skills became. In Man itself, picturesquely nestled in a ring of steep green mountains with waterfalls, the boys at the roadblocks, drunk or high, muttered about stealing the car. Pickup trucks bristling with Liberians carrying rocket-propelled grenade launchers slalomed wildly through the rebel army's obstacle courses. The walls of government buildings were bullet-riddled, and the freshly turned mass graves gave off a sharp smell. It was hard to tell who was in charge of Man – the rebel commanders or their underage Ivorian and Liberian recruits, who, according to townspeople, were becoming indistinguishable.

In the middle of town, the young rebels hung out at a maquis, or open-air eatery, called the Tirbo, which smelled of porcupine stew. The youngest I saw, toting his AK-47, was no more than nine. I ordered a plate of rice and looked around. A boy with a red checked kaffiyeh on his head was staring straight ahead: filled with some private rage. Draped around the necks of other boys were leather dubs or sheathed knives or bandoliers. There was no one over thirty in sight.

Look back at all the references to age. Here is more evidence that this war is a sort of oedipal conflict in which the young men are seeking to overthrow their fathers.

At midday, a group of four Liberians arrived and sat down at a table. The young men, who propped their weapons between their legs, began making their way through a bottle of Mangoustan's rum. Their names were Sha, Shala, Johnson, and Romeo. Shala wore an American flag bandanna, Rambo style. Sha, the most intoxicated of the group, lifted his shirt to show me his wounds.

I asked how much he was paid for his services to the rebels.

'The cause is much more important than pay,' Sha said. 'I don't appreciate pay.'

What was the cause?

'Peace and unity in Africa,' he said. After the war, Sha said, he wanted to go to New York and become an American marine and learn to fly helicopters and use heavy weapons. 'I love America,' he slurred, making an effort to lean forward. 'America is my culture.' He waved his glass at the others. 'All of them love America.'

Note once more the references to American images and culture, but also, confusingly, the red-checked kaffiyeh – with its Arabic connotations – which are then fleshed out below.

Romeo's glass fell to the floor and shattered. He stared at the fragments without moving. Johnson told the waitress that they would pay for it. Romeo slouched, sunk in a dark mood.

A few months earlier, a recruiter had come to a refugee camp along the Liberian border and persuaded Romeo to join the rebels. There was no better offer on the horizon. 'I want something because I don't want to be suffering, I don't have nowhere to go,' he said. 'Someone say, "Take money, go to war. You will not go there? You will go."' He turned his dead-eyed stare on me. 'If you can't pay the young stuff, the war will go all over the world. The war will enter America – let me tell you today. Because you don't give them money. The man we want to see is bin Laden. We want to see him, to join him. Because he can pay revolutionaries. You think you can get pay for this?"' Romeo held up his left calf to show me a bullet wound. 'You can't. Bin Laden can pay it.'

I had seen bin Laden's face painted on the side of a rebel vehicle. Some fighters wore T-shirts with bin Laden's face and Bush's face side by side. In this part of the world, there was no ideological contradiction. Both men stood for power.

At a hospital in a town not far from Man, an Italian doctor named Albert Brizio described the imagery of this war as 'a perverse effect of globalization,' adding, 'It's what I call the Liberianization of war.' Brizio had seen the effect in other African countries: young fighters styling themselves after performances, often brutal ones, that they'd seen on TV or in movies. 'It allows people to see events or situations they would never have thought of, and they imitate them. These situations have always been contagious, but then you had contagion by contact. Now you have contagion by media.'

Here is the kernel of the argument. He uses a quote from another source to give his view a greater weight but it is clear that this is what he has been building up to all along.

But contagion by media can go in both directions, as I discovered when I met a young woman in Man named Jeanette Badouel. She was moving around town in the company of rebels, but, unlike the handful of girl recruits in their ranks, she carried herself with an air of blithe authority and pop stylishness. Jeanette was impossible to miss, decked out in sparkly gold jeans labelled 'Pussy' and rolled to the calf, six-inch platform shoes, and a pink frilly blouse; her hair was dyed blond and done in short braids. She shopped for her Liberian made American-style T-shirts and shoes at Saturday markets along the border, which was one of the most dangerous places on earth. She was born in a village twenty miles south of Man but had been living with her French husband and their children in Rennes, where she directed a non-profit group called Association Métissage, whose Web site says that it 'realizes projects favoring cultural diversity and solidarity among peoples.' When the western rebellion broke out, just as Jeanette was visiting her parents in Man, she refused the French government's offer of evacuation and decided to set up a rebel television station, using the digital equipment she happened to have brought. Though she claimed to operate free of political interference, it was clear that TV Grand Ouest served up pro-rebel propaganda to the region, if anyone was watching.

I sat in the station's bug-filled studio with Jeanette and watched programming. There was a traditional dance, performed to express villagers' happiness with rebel rule, the voice-over explained. There were Eddie Murphy movies. And there was footage of the aftermath of a recent massacre by government and Liberian forces – the hacked and bullet-ridden bodies of peasants lying in houses and on roads just south of Man – with Jeanette conducting breathless interviews.

I had trouble figuring Jeanette out. She loved fashion and reading *Paris Match*, yet rebel-held Man seemed to suit her fine. The rebellion looked to her like a wonderful example of cultural diversity and solidarity among peoples. It was almost like America. 'For me, it's democracy,' she gushed.

'Everyone is here – the Liberians are everywhere. You'll see a lot on the way to the border. Guineans, Malians. For me, it's the people.'

This portrait of a young woman caught up in the struggle and mindlessly enjoying it is probably the most damning of all of them. Her enjoyment of fashion is no different from the young men's and yet she is picked out for vilification in a way that they are not. It is hard to see what she represents in this story and she is the only young character who is viewed in an entirely negative light. I have trouble working out what she is doing here. This is the one discordant note in the whole piece.

Twenty years ago, V. S. Naipaul published an essay in this magazine called 'The Crocodiles of Yamoussoukro,' an account of life in Ivory Coast at the height of the 'miracle' under Houphouët-Boigny. Toward the end of the piece, Naipaul has a dream: the bridge on which he is standing starts to melt away: The concrete and steel of Abidjan turn out to be perishable. 'The new world existed in the minds of other men,' he writes. 'Remove those men, and their ideas – which, after all, had no finality – would disappear.'

Now we move into the summary and conclusion, in which the various threads are brought together. The missing thread is the one that was thrown away at the start – the question of world commodity prices. Packer suggests that it is the other globalisation – the globalisation of the media and the spread of American values – that is mainly to blame for this revolt of the young.

Naipaul's prophecy that Ivory Coast would slip back into a primordial past seemed comforting compared with the new reality that was taking hold. Cool B and his gang, and the Young Patriots, and the rebels in the north and the west are severed irrevocably from the traditional sources of meaning – the village, the elders, the extended family that I found in West Africa two decades ago. Their heroes are American celebrities, local warlords, gangsters, and demagogues. In the cities and the ragtag armies, they live in a society consisting of only the young. Tempted and tormented by images and words from elsewhere, trapped in a money economy with nothing to sell, they have no ready way of realizing their desires. But they can't go back. To some hard-headed observers in the West, they are 'loose molecules,' mindless forces of anarchy or a new primitivism. In fact, the opposite is true: the struggle in Ivory Coast, and perhaps in other parts of Africa, is recognizable as the unlovely effort of individuals to find an identity and a place in a world that has no use for them.

In Abidjan, I spoke with Ruth Marshall-Fratani, a researcher with the French journal *Politique Africaine*. 'The gap between aspirations and possibilities – I think that gap has widened incredibly in the last fifteen years,' she said. 'Access to global images has increased it amazingly.' The phrase she borrowed to describe the situation of the young Africans I had met was *lechè-vitrines* – window-licking. 'It isn't window-shopping,' she explained. 'That means you can go in and buy. This is just licking the window. And, basically, that's this generation's experience.' She went on, 'Everybody wants to get a part of the action. They have these aspirations and they're not prepared to give them up. Politics is one way. Religion is another. And war is another.'

On one of my last days in Ivory Coast, I went back to Koumassi to see Cool B. He wanted to introduce me to two young men he knew; Madness and Yul, twenty-six and twenty-three, had both done time in prison and had the razor scars to prove it. Madness, whose real name is Mohamed Bamba, had been on the street since the age of twelve, working as a petty thief and drug dealer. His eyelids were heavy and his voice slow from years of smoking heroin. Yul, born Issouf Traore, hustled stolen pharmaceuticals. Both of them were trying to go straight as barkers at a woro-woro station, snagging passengers for local runs. Cool B, Madness, Yul, and I sat in a maquis and drank Guinness. Madness was stoic; Yul, whose nickname came from his shaved head, grew frantic as he talked. It was the same story I'd heard from the others – a father who hadn't taken care of him. 'He told me, "If you come back here I'll put you in prison again." I said, "You're my father, you put me in the world."' What agitated Yul to distraction was the fact that his father had gone back to Mali and died and been buried before they could reconcile. 'He died when it still wasn't OK with us. He spoke to me, but I don't know what was at the bottom of his heart.'

> We return again to the fathers who failed their sons. It appears to be partly a metaphor for the way in which the colonising west has failed Africa. He leaves us with an emotional vision of a young man desperate to be a father to his own son.

From his trouser pocket Yul withdrew a piece of folded officialdom. It wasn't proof of citizenship – his father had failed to naturalize him. Nor did Yul have Malian papers. But when his girl-friend gave birth, Yul, who never attended school, needed to establish himself as the legal father. He bribed the police to give him a document stating, falsely, that he had lost his identity card. The document was called a 'Certificate of Declaration of Loss.' It wasn't sufficient to confer his last name on his son, but it was the sum of Yul's identity in Ivory Coast.

'A man has to have a father at his side to help him. If he doesn't –' Yul stared at me a bit wildly, his toothy mouth open. 'Who's going to help me? Who? I don't see.'

Madness said calmly, 'If you talk to a thousand youths, there isn't one who will tell you it's going OK for him.' I asked Madness and Yul what they imagined Americans thought of them. 'They've forgotten us, 'Yul said. 'They don't know what we're living here in Africa,' Madness said. 'Africa is misery. Africa – really – it's hard, hard, hard. People of good will are interested in us. But there are others, with means, who aren't interested at all. Because Africa is a continent of hell.'

© George Packer

6

INVESTIGATIVE FEATURES

Every feature should be investigative. Everything we write, however short, should be answering the questions that people need to ask, or the questions that they are not yet able to formulate. They should ask about what is being done to us, what is being done in our name, who we are and how we live in the world, what is new and whether it is important. Sometimes (though increasingly rarely) a writer gets the time and opportunity to dig down really deep in order to expose matters that others have tried to hide. These special stories don't tend to come your way until you have done your time as a reporter and proved that you can handle the legal, financial and ethical issues that arise. Often these months of work are then regurgitated into print (or more often into pictures on television) in turgid detail that will only be read when it is re-digested and served up in a more palatable form in other media. James Meek is an exception. He digs but he is also a wonderful story-teller capable of bringing the most unpromising material alive.

JAMES MEEK This article is about trains. I am not remotely interested in trains but I read it all and so did my (then) 18-year-old daughter who is even less interested in trains. It is told almost in the form of a thriller, with the writer himself as the protagonist. It is a masterly piece of story-telling. The use of metaphor is restrained and the language is (mostly) understated. There is little possibility here for visual metaphor but where he can find it he uses it and it lifts what might otherwise be a very dry read. Quotes are also used as much to highlight and create emotional effects as to convey information. Look out for the different ways of using them as you read it. I have broken the piece down into ten sections (which are marked) to make it easier to see how it is constructed. Look at the way important pieces of information are signalled by repetition and the use of questions to change the tone. All this and a cracking piece of research that really did need to be done and really does reveal dirty dealings which the public needed to know about.

The £10bn rail crash
Guardian, Thursday 1 April 2004

The consultants charged with finding a way to modernise the crumbling west coast railway thought they'd hit on a magic bullet: a white-hot technology that would allow the huge task to be completed for a song. There was just one problem: it had never worked before. Ten years to the day since Railtrack took over our railways – and after a year-long investigation – James Meek reveals the saga of incompetence, greed and delusion behind Britain's biggest public works project.

The sub editors will have written this stand-first. It establishes the hook. Sets up the goal, establishes villains (the consultants), motive (reducing costs) and means. It then introduces the protagonist – the journalist. It sets up the suspense and hints at jeopardy. It registers the story type: a battle against incompetence greed and delusion (think Westerns, James Bond, etc.). It doesn't establish the 'controlling idea'. That we don't really find out until the end, but if you look back you will find it was there all along, providing the frame from which all the evidence hangs.

Section one: an extended introduction. *This leads us into the story and tells us why it is important.*

On a mild, wet February morning, a work gang of 10 men moves around a stretch of railway line near the village of Goostrey, between Crewe and Manchester airport. Against the extreme green of fields and the whipped grey of rain clouds their synthetic orange work suits shine out violently, like figures in a psychedelic episode. It's hard work. Using thick, weathered, yard-long metal-capped staves, they crank jacks, which raise a stretch of rail, along with its concrete sleepers, up off the bed of stone chips the railway rests on. A bulldozer on rail wheels purrs up on the other line and begins pawing at the stones. The men are to pack fresh ballast in under the rails with hand shovels.

This descriptive introduction is slow for a British newspaper but Guardian *style tends to favour literary introductions and, as the story has already been summarised in the stand-first there is time to linger. The description and the metaphors establish the expectation of an industrial/technological process (even the fields are 'extreme green') and then confounds our expectation by describing hard, manual labour of a very traditional kind.*

These railway workers are engaged in the single most expensive non-military task ever undertaken by Britain alone: the modernisation of the west coast main line. A project that was supposed to cost roughly £1.5bn will, by the time it is finished in about 2008, two years late, have consumed almost £10bn, much of it from the taxpayer. That is £3bn more than the White House considers Nasa will need to send men back to the moon.

> *This was the killer fact. Something important that surprises us and hooks us into the action. Note the change of rhythm from a relaxed, dawdling style to a 'sit up on your seat–this is important' one. The comparison with a moon shot reminds us that it was meant to be a highly sophisticated technological process. Something has clearly gone wrong and we are paying for it. This is the fact on which the whole piece hangs so it is important to get the emphasis right. The reader must not miss it. So the writer goes on to repeat it in slightly different terms in the next paragraph which tells us also why this is so important: it is about good people (reference here to older values and the British liberals love of the genuine worker) as opposed to bad people (greedy capitalist financiers).*

The bizarre story of those multiplying billions, reconstructed here from dozens of interviews and documents, some never before made public, ran parallel to the bloodier history of fatal accidents on the railway since privatisation, and contributed, in equal or greater measure, to the ignominious end of the Railtrack era. It is a tale of incompetence, greed and delusion, driven by the conviction that profit and share value is the only true measure of success; and that the ability to chair a meeting or read a balance sheet is always worth more than the ability to understand how machines and materials will best serve human needs.

It is a story, too, with wider implications about the kind of country that Britain has become: a country that has lost faith in its ability to design, make and build useful things; a country where the few who do still have that ability are underpaid, unrecognised, and un-admired.

> *We now move into story-telling mode. Goostrey is the scene of the 'crime', and as the article opens, our hero detective is found there, looking for clues. We recognise the terse style and immediately settle back expecting an unfolding 'who done it'. The constant reiteration of the 'orange suits' is clearly there to provide a visual reference that will recur later in the piece. Only one adjective stands out – 'quangoid', derived from 'Quango', which is an acronym for 'Quasi Non-Governmental Organisation'. It is a word that has serious business to do. It evokes a kind of shifty incompetence.*

Politics and consultants

Watching over the Goostrey work gang, dressed in cleaner, newer versions of the same orange suits, are three of their bosses, all American, from the

US construction firm Bechtel, brought in two years ago to rescue the project from the incompetence of the collapsed rail company Railtrack. No British company seems now to have the skills required; nor, after Railtrack's systematic efforts to gut itself of in-house specialists, does Railtrack's quangoid successor, Network Rail.

As an extreme measure to try to bring the final bill down, the rail industry agreed to shut the entire stretch of railway we are standing on, from Crewe to Cheadle Hulme, for four months, forcing thousands of travellers on First North Western railways to use coaches while 600 orange-suited men and women work on the line 24 hours a day, seven days a week. Without such radical steps, says Tom McCarthy, the Californian who leads the Bechtel west coast team, the project could have ended up costing £13bn.

It could have cost much, much more. The project now being built is a stripped-down version of a fantasy railway. Railtrack locked itself into a brutal contract to build with Richard Branson's Virgin Trains in 1997. I sat one day with Stuart Baker, the man brought in by the Strategic Rail Authority to survey the wreckage of Railtrack's plans for the west coast in 2002, and read out to him the sequence of growing price tags: £1.5bn in 1996, £5.8bn in 1999, £7.5bn in 2001 …

'None of those numbers delivers the contract,' he said. 'You could talk about numbers six or eight times that. It is into 30 to 40 billion if you were actually to create the infrastructure necessary to fulfil [Railtrack's original] obligations.'

At Goostrey, I try to encourage the Americans to talk about why the project turned out to be so much more expensive than its creators thought. Bob Brady, a Texan from Houston who is managing the reconstruction of this part of the route, begins to answer. 'I think part of the issue was the politics when it was privatised –' McCarthy interrupts him. 'Don't go there,' he says.

Note the use of dialogue. I expect that the Americans had a great deal more to say than this. Meek has chosen just one exchange that serves only to increase the tension by telling us that information is being concealed.

Brady is right, which is why McCarthy doesn't want him to go there. The problem with the west coast project is not that it is going to cost £10bn, but that the original bosses of Railtrack thought it could be modernised at a fraction of the price, and sold this ideology-driven delusion to the public and the City.

'Ideology-driven delusion' – perhaps this is rather overdoing it. I think we have caught the drift of his argument by now and if he keeps on banging on about it we may stop trusting him.

Friday December 23 1994 dawned foggy and almost freezing in central London. The papers reported on Yeltsin bombing Chechnya, on new developments in the Guinness scandal, and on fresh Labour attacks against the millions of pounds made by directors of recently privatised utilities. On the fifth floor of an office building in Hanover Square, London, a group of 15 consultants sat in a room carrying out a strange task. They were writing numbers by hand, in red ink, in the top right-hand corner of a secret 182-page report.

The red numbers were a device to stop the report being leaked, as so many documents were in the course of rail privatisation, the most controversial of all the Conservatives' [the government of the time] state sell-offs. That spring, Railtrack, a new organisation, had taken over British Rail's responsibility for running and maintaining tracks, bridges, signals and tunnels. It was due to be floated on the stock market. It was essential that it now convince the public and the City that it could finance and organise the modernisation of the west coast line – something BR had never been given the money to do – and the report was going to tell Railtrack how it should do it.

Five years later, when the consequences of the report's recommendations became clear but the report itself had been forgotten by the media, a subsequent generation of Railtrack bosses tried to blame it all on BR. In fact, BR had nothing to do with it. Railtrack was determined to prove that it didn't need BR's expertise, so it commissioned a consortium of consultancy firms to do the job.

That Friday, two days before Christmas, the consultants were in festive mood. They had been working on the report since March and as soon as they had finished with the red numbers, off it would go to the government and Railtrack, the job would be done, and the holidays would begin. 'We had to get it finished by noon, and we finished by 11,' one of the consultants recalled. 'I think we all went down to the pub afterwards – the kind of jolly, end-of-project thing that happens.'

On the face of it, the consultants had every reason to celebrate. They had approached a gigantic problem, and come up with an elegant solution.

Here is a hint at conflict ahead and then a neat summary to ensure that we don't forget where we are and that we keep with us the essential facts. Having hooked us into the story, he then goes on to provide some of the detailed background information which will allow us to understand it. If this had come any earlier, many people would have stopped reading.

150 years of decline

For a culture that has been under constant attack from the public and the media for almost two centuries, the rail industry has a surprising love of misleading jargon. The west coast main line, usually known in the business as the WCML, is a case in point. It doesn't run along the west coast, and it isn't a line. It's a 690-mile network of routes between London and Glasgow, connecting them to Liverpool, Manchester, Birmingham and scores of other large towns in the West Midlands and north-west of England.

It is almost the oldest inter-city railway in the world. It was built higgledy-piggledy over three decades, starting in 1833, by entrepreneurs and hard-drinking, red-waistcoated navigators who, if they died on the job, were sometimes buried where they fell. Its narrow tunnels, lines squeezed together, tight curves and eccentric kinks reflect not just the geography of the land but the speed of contemporary trains – 40mph max – and the reluctance of powerful landowners to have clanking, smoky iron horses hauling the proletariat across their estates. Robert Stephenson, son of George, who built the London-to-Birmingham stretch, had to make some of his measurements secretly, by night, to avoid being run off the squireoc-racy's property.

Between 1833 and 1994 the line was modernised, of course, but never rebuilt. Anyone who has lived in a 19th-century house will be familiar with the problem. The arcane wiring when electricity came along, the subsequent clumsy rewiring; the cheap flat conversion in the 1960s; the constant saga of patch and mend from occupants who never have the money or vision to remake the whole thing from scratch – all this, and more, was paralleled on the WCML on an enormous scale.

When the consultants came in, the WCML had been starved of investment by governments for some 20 years. The only significant reconstruction was in the 1960s, when the railway was modified to take electric trains. Repairs and the skills of Georgian and Victorian engineers enabled train speeds to increase until the mid-1980s. Then the network began to deteriorate quickly. The greatest problem was the signalling. It had to be replaced, but to remake that system, with its thousands of miles of cables, coloured lights on poles and elderly signal boxes, would be staggeringly expensive.

A 1992 document, the Hesketh report, classified at the time but later slipped without publicity into the House of Commons library, recounts in bald language the horrific state of WCML signal boxes, on which the safety of passengers depend. They read like despatches from a war zone. Stockport signal box 1 was 'installed 1896. Roof of relay room lets in rain. Cable route heavily damaged ... very few spares. Signal structures have severe corrosion. Power supplies are suspect.' Brewery Sidings: 'Installed 1894 ... severe structural problems ... incapable of modification ... signal structures have severe corrosion and access by staff is by special arrangement.' Miles Platting: 'Installed 1890 ... box and relay room have serious structural damage with propping by the civil engineer to prevent collapse.'

How could Railtrack do it? How could they do what BR had not done and rebuild this tottering railway? The consultants came up with a remarkable scheme which would, besides modernising the WCML without costing the Treasury a penny, enable trains to whizz between London and Glasgow at the unprecedented – for Britain – speed of 140mph, and make the west coast line the envy of the railway world.

The miracle solution

A new idea was being discussed in rail circles in the 1990s. It was called 'moving block', and it was supposed to do away with conventional signals for ever. It was based on the technology used for mobile phones. Normally, trains run on a fixed-block system. A line is divided into stretches called blocks, with signals controlling the entry and exit to each block. If a block has a train in it, the signals prevent another train entering that block and crashing into it.

Moving block abandons conventional signals in favour of computers, track-mounted radio beacons and a cellular radio network. With these, train drivers always know where they are in relation to other trains. They still have a protective block of space around them, but it moves along with the train, and shrinks or grows according to how fast it and the trains in front and behind are going.

Once Railtrack's consultants fed moving block into the equation, the miraculous happened. The numbers made sense. They wouldn't have to remake the signals; they would simply demolish them, and replace them with a few mobile-phone masts and black boxes in existing train cabs, which would be far cheaper to install and maintain. Thanks to moving block, they would be able to squeeze more trains on to the line. The trains would be able to go faster, which would not only justify charging passengers higher fares, but would mean the train operators could run more services with fewer trains. As the final cherry on the cake, the cost of upgrading the route to take 140mph expresses could be defrayed from the extra profits the express operators would make. There was only one problem with moving block, but it was a crucial one: moving block for main-line railways did not exist.

Did you note the change of pace and how it emphasises the important piece of information. Meek describes just how the problem would be solved in clear, simple, factual tones. Then in one sentence he undermines it. In the next paragraph you can almost hear the music rising to a crescendo with the final quote. This is the kernel of the story.

Even now, almost 10 years later, there is not a single main-line railway anywhere in the world, no matter how sophisticated, which uses moving block. It is used only on a few specially built urban transit systems, such as the Docklands Light Railway, a single metro line in Paris, and a new line in Singapore. For full-scale railways it remains where it was, on the drawing board. The consultants did not allow this detail to stop them, and nor did Railtrack.

'When I heard about it from outside: I thought: "Wow, they must have had some amazing breakthrough which means this is now a proven bit of kit." And it wasn't,' said Chris Green, now head of Virgin Trains. 'It was a wish list. To put that wish list on Europe's third busiest railway really was outrageous.'

Section four: the witnesses. Meek now starts to ask why this technology was being investigated. He brings on a number of witnesses. We hear testimony from each. These interviews provide information rather than atmosphere. There is less paraphrasing and more long quotes.

A wing and a prayer

Of the four teams of consultants that prepared the feasibility study, Booz Allen & Hamilton was responsible for coming up with the recommended signalling system. No one from the company would comment for this article, but one of the consultants involved in 1994 did talk. Of the eventual core team of eight consultants, only two had experience of British main-line railways, one at a very junior level. Four of them were American or normally based in the US. Not one had expertise in moving-block signalling on railways like the WCML; most of the experimental work on moving block was being done in mainland Europe.

The consultant asked for his real name not to be used. I've called him Arthur. He said of some of his colleagues: 'My personal view was ... they hadn't got the knowledge to try and do this in any sensible way. Coming from an intensely professional railway background, I was appalled by this. You can imagine. Not knowing what other railways of the world were up to, the consultants did a write-round. 'We did a trawl,' said Arthur. 'We wrote to manufacturers and asked them for information. ... We asked the Japanese what they'd got [in terms of moving block] and they said: "Well, nothing, really." Which amazed us.' Indeed, this would, a lay person would assume, have given the consultants pause for thought. Neither the Japanese, with their 160mph bullet trains, nor the French, with their 160mph TGVs, used moving block in 1994: they still don't.

Yet despite this lack of knowledge, the fact that no railway in the world was using the system, and the fact that the equipment needed was not being made by any manufacturer, the Booz Allen team ended up recommending moving block. Why? Arthur did not say so specifically, but hinted that the remit was not to find the most practical solution and find out how much it would cost, but to find the solution that would make privatisation financially possible. The cost of conventional signalling, had they known it, would have frightened investors off and halted privatisation in its tracks.

'The thing that everybody always theorises is, why did you recommend such a highfalutin-type system or the WCML? And that's a fair question,' said Arthur. 'But it's not a fair question when you actually look at what the remit was. The remit was to come up with the most cost-effective solution.'

The Booz Allen consultants came to another conclusion which, in retrospect, seems extraordinary. Even though they knew what the privatised railways would look like, with Railtrack owning the infrastructure, a horde of private train operators running services, and dozens of other private outfits all taking a cut and all trying not to step on each other's contracts, they based their estimates of how much the WCML modernisation would cost on British Rail history – the bargain-basement modernisation of the east coast main line, and the development of a new type of conventional signalling 20 years earlier. It was as if a western oil company based its cost forecasts in free-market Russia on the way things were done in the Soviet Union.

'What I hadn't understood,' admitted Arthur, 'was that the restructuring of the railway was going to bring a complexity beyond my wildest dreams.' Nor could the consultants have anticipated that the bosses of Railtrack would go on to cherrypick their conclusions.

The bosses

Railtrack was led to privatisation by two men, its chief executive, John Edmonds, and its chairman, Robert Horton. Edmonds was a former senior British Rail executive, Horton the former chairman of BP. Yet it was Edmonds, the former public-sector boss, who was the private-sector fire-brand. Far from being loyal to BR's way of doing things, his experience on the state railways had inspired in him a scepticism towards in-house engineers and safety experts bordering on contempt. They were, he considered, overcautious, conservative, stuck in the mud. It was this which led him, at Railtrack, to shed the nucleus of in-house expertise that left the company unable to understand what its myriad specialist contractors were up to.

Edmonds declined to be quoted for this article. A senior rail manager said of him: 'He was the one who got rid of operations managers and engineers because he didn't believe in them. He thought it could all be contracted out and commercialised.'

'He had a desire to break the mould and change. He was always opposed to the traditional railway. He believed there was a golden panacea in the private world where you just free people up and new technology comes in and the markets come in and it all happens. The railway doesn't work like that. You're not manufacturing baked beans.'

Like Edmonds, Horton was an advocate of privatising Railtrack. But although Horton was happy to play the role of swashbuckling private-enterprise shaker-upper, he was no entrepreneur. He studied engineering in the 1950s but he was no engineering wizard, either. He was, essentially, a highly paid private bureaucrat who made his reputation in the offices of a post-imperial semi-state oil company. He did not make BP; BP made him. It was already a vast, sprawling corporation when he arrived in 1957, and it was still a vast, sprawling corporation when he was sacked in 1992, no matter how much he changed it. He did, at least, know about the oil business. But he didn't know much about trains.

'He wasn't close enough to the railway to know what was going wrong,' said one rail industry source. 'So he was great at privatising, great with the City, good at getting private investment into industry. He didn't understand that he'd lost all his key operators, lost all his key engineers, and was chasing technology that wouldn't work.' Horton also declined to be interviewed for this article. In a brief email, he said: 'I think it is important to understand that the scope of the project changed enormously over time as did the decisions on the technology to be used.'

In 1994, Edmonds, Horton and the latest in a blurry succession of Conservative transport secretaries, Brian Mawhinney, all wanted to hear from the consultants that the WCML could be modernised with privately raised money – by a private railway company. Yet there was still an opportunity for someone to persuade them that the risk they were taking was unacceptably high.

> *This link once again sums up the previous section, by repeating the main conclusion, and takes us on to the next group of witnesses. This section is about all the people who warned against the new technology. These interviews are for information and again longer quotes are used.*

Warnings missed

The key expert standing between Railtrack and the fatal decision to go for moving block at this time was Rod Muttram, the firm's new director of electrical engineering. But he knew little about the railways either: he had just been headhunted from the arms industry, where he had been involved in developing weapons systems, including a new type of artillery rocket. He believed that moving block could work, in theory. As to whether it could work in practice, on such an incredibly complex rail network, he was entirely dependent on what the consultants told him. Muttram, declined to make any public statement for this article.

Yet British Rail still existed in 1994 and 1995, and its board thought the consultants' ideas were far-fetched. John Welsby, then chairman of BR, told me: 'I did have grave concerns about the attempt to integrate a type of technology that had no testing in real, active life in what, in fact, was the most complex railway in the country.'

Welsby was not exaggerating his wisdom after the event. A senior Railtrack figure, one of the key men liaising between Railtrack and the consultants, recalled: 'There were huge rows at the time with the British Rail board, who were completely unsupportive of the project. John Welsby, then chairman of BR, was the most vociferous opponent. He said [moving block] could never be done on a railway like this.'

Welsby and his BR colleagues were unable to get the message through to their private-sector successors. 'You have to remember that we were all, at that stage, unbelievably busy,' he said. 'All my lads had about three jobs. Firstly, they were running a railway. Secondly, they were breaking it up for sale. Thirdly, they were often preparing a management buyout at the same time. People were working seven-day weeks, 12-hour days. Our advice was passed across but then it was up to Railtrack to take that advice or not, as they wished ... of course they would have resented it anyway. The climate has to be remembered: we were big, bad BR, being broken up and done away with, because we were anathema to the government, so the new order was not necessarily going to look very favourably on us.'

Another warning came almost as soon as the consultants handed in their report. It came from Europe. The consultants' report – a copy of which was recently released to the *Guardian* under the 'open government' code – makes little mention of the European dimension. None of the consultants was from mainland Europe. But it was clear from speaking to 'Arthur' that he had assumed other European railways were preparing to introduce the new technology as well, and that Britain, relying heavily on European research, would merely be the first to apply it.

Then, in January 1995, most of Europe's state-owned railways – 19 of them – came to the joint conclusion that moving block was not ready to be used in the real world, and a simpler, transitional form of new technology should be the next step. Again, Railtrack ignored the warning. In fact, Railtrack may never have heard it: at this time the firm had barely any contact with Europe. It was an extraordinary situation, of which the public was ignorant: a group of Anglo-American consultants and executives took for granted European support to develop a technology which those same Europeans openly declared to be premature.

The section ends by summarising the main conclusion. The next section includes some key evidence and so a number of different sources are used. Most are not named but the Guardian *was able to substantiate these anonymous sources by using a copy of the consultant's report which had recently been released under the Freedom of Information Act.*

Section five: the sell (the crime). *This is key part of the investigation. Through close reading of documents, Meek has discovered crucial discrepancies.*

A tale of two reports

On March 22 1995, Railtrack and the government went public with their plans for the west coast main line. Despite the warnings, they endorsed, with few reservations, the consultants' recommendations to make moving block central to the modernisation. John Watts, the Tory rail minister, spoke of an 'innovative signalling and control system' which would be 'at the heart of the proposals' for the WCML. (Interviewed by phone recently, Watts said he could not remember details of this period.)

The consultants' report remained secret. On March 22 Railtrack released what it said was a summary of the report. By and large, it was. But having had a chance, for the first time, to compare the two, the *Guardian* can reveal that there were important changes and omissions in what the public was told compared with what the consultants had said.

The consultants warned, for instance, that if moving block turned out not to work, and conventional signals had to be used, any attempt to try to get trains to run faster than 125mph – always Railtrack's intention – would incur 'exceptionally high costs'. This fateful warning, one of the keys to Railtrack's eventual demise, was omitted from the public summary.

At the beginning of March, signalling-company bosses had told MPs that they might – might – be able to have moving block working and installed within 10 years. In their secret report, the consultants talked, with optimism, of 'a five-year programme' for the development and fitting of moving block. Yet this is what Railtrack told the public: 'The development programme is anticipated to take between three and four years.'

Most surprisingly, Railtrack inserted a line into the public summary that had never appeared in the consultants' report. 'Most of the hardware for this train control system already exists,' it read, 'the technology required being relatively mature.'

I read that line out to Arthur recently. He said: 'Mm. That's interesting.'

Did he find it misleading? Arthur paused for a long time. Eventually he said: 'I don't think there's any doubt, sitting here now, that it was not as far developed as we thought it was ... I'm surprised by those words, I really am ... I am amazed at that statement. Because I don't know where they had any proof of that.'

Neither Horton nor Edmonds would comment on the discrepancies. I asked another senior industry figure, with close knowledge of the subsequent attempt to make moving block work, what he thought. 'To say the technology is mature – yes, I think that was a bit adventurous, certainly in 1995.'

Having shown that the 'sell' to the public did not adequately reflect the consultants' report, Meek seeks to establish what was driving this process. He had already suggested one possible reason: keeping costs down. Now he hints at another: staff cuts. He doesn't develop this line at all. He just leaves it hanging as he returns to a further analysis of the thinking behind the series of decisions. He starts with the justifications of the decisions made.

What happened? The consultants' report never mentioned it, but there was one other factor in the back of the minds of Railtrack and the Tories. 1994 had seen a painful strike by railway signalling workers. Bringing in the new technology would be another step towards ending the unions' leverage, by getting rid of thousands of signalling staff.

Some in the rail industry are inclined to give Horton, Edmonds and their colleagues the benefit of the doubt. 'I think dishonesty does matter, but my suspicion is that it wasn't a question of dishonesty, it was more a question of misjudgment,' a senior rail industry figure told me. 'It was assumed that technology would move very quickly, but it doesn't. That was the problem. That is a bit of an indictment of the calibre of the people running the show at that time in Railtrack.'

Another senior rail industry figure said: 'John Edmonds was keen to get the company privatised and wanted to say things that would encourage people to believe it was bold and dynamic. It was all about creating confidence, which requires bold statements, sometimes.'

Before I knew I would get to see the consultants' report, I spoke to a senior former Railtrack executive. He didn't have a copy of the report, and was trying to remember its conclusions. As I found out later, his memory didn't quite reflect the report; rather, perhaps, it reflected the real back-room conversations going on in Railtrack at the time. 'The basic conclusion was that it was impossible to upgrade the west coast at any sensible cost if you went for conventional signalling,' he said. 'And the only way forward – whether it was feasible or not – was to bring in 21st-century signalling technology.' Whether it was feasible or not: the decision was made, and Railtrack began unconsciously to weave its downfall.

Another summary paragraph ensures that you are following the thread of the argument. It is also a link taking us forward to the next section in which the threads start to be brought together and we see how one set of bad decisions leads inexorably to worse ones as the project slides down hill.

The consultants weren't reckless. They never imagined that Railtrack should manage and finance the WCML modernisation itself. In some detail, they had outlined a scheme whereby Railtrack would get a big, experienced civil-engineering consortium to raise money for and manage the project, thereby assuming most of the risk. But when Norman Broadhurst, then Railtrack's finance director, studied the numbers, he thought the returns looked too juicy to be given away and brought his colleagues round. Yet one member of the board told me that he had argued against the proposal. 'I said at the time Railtrack did not have the management capability to bring that in house,' he said. He was proved right. No sooner had Railtrack committed itself to moving block than it began to waste time in bringing it about. In mid-1995, its rump signalling team had dwindled to the extent that it was possible for it to move office in a single taxi. The following year, a move to Birmingham caused further losses of personnel. One senior Railtrack figure at the time said: 'In resources terms, two years were lost.' It wasn't until March 1996, just a few months before Railtrack was privatised, that the firm picked two consortia of engineering multinationals to develop alternate prototypes of the moving-block system. Things didn't go as planned. Railtrack was beginning to suffer the consequences of Edmonds' determination to gut the firm of its in-house engineering and project-management expertise. 'What Railtrack did in 1996 was quite exceptional, which was to take a really high-calibre engineering team on the BR system and destroy it,' said Chris Green.

Railtrack had assumed that the two signalling consortia would develop similar types of moving-block technology. It assumed their work could then be pooled to provide the foundation for a system that actually worked. But it didn't happen that way. The consortia saw themselves as rivals.

'Not unexpectedly, their work tended to diverge rather than converge,' said a senior figure in the signalling industry at the time. This would not have mattered so much, except that while the moving-block research was meandering, Railtrack made a catastrophic decision. It invited Richard Branson to hold a gun to the company's head.

This is where, in the original, part one of the article ended: on a cliff-hanger. The first two paragraphs of the next section provide a brisk background. The punch comes in the third paragraph.

Section six: the plot twists and the screws tighten.

Catch-22

In February 1997, Richard Branson's Virgin Trains had won the franchise to run fast inter-city services on the WCML. In October, after the newly elected Labour government backed away from its commitment to renationalise the railways, Branson and Railtrack announced how the WCML project was going to be financed. They painted a wonderful picture for inter-city travellers.

Railtrack would spend £1.5bn to restore the worn-out railway to basic reliability, and, in exchange for a slice of Virgin's profits, would lay out another £600m to install moving block and other improvements to make it a high-speed line. By 2002, new Virgin tilting trains would travel the line at 125mph; in 2005, they would accelerate to 140mph. London and Manchester would be only an hour and 45 minutes apart, London and Glasgow less than four hours.

Suddenly, Railtrack found itself locked in a contract with Virgin to deliver a non-existent signalling system on the entire west coast main line by a firm date – 2005 – with crippling financial penalties if it failed to do so.

'They thought, "Oh crumbs, we've just signed [the Virgin deal], we'd better get on with this." There was a realisation the talking had to stop,' said the signalling source.

This quote takes us on to the nub of the problem that Meek then goes on to flesh out. We then get a cascade of different problems encountered by the company – each one leading to another.

Yet Railtrack was locked in a catch-22 situation. It couldn't put a contract out to tender to develop something if it couldn't specify exactly what the thing was. And it couldn't specify exactly what the thing was until it had signed a contract for somebody to develop it.

Furthermore, the two signalling consortia had made the technology look less, rather than more, certain.

'Because we went on divergent routes, because we saw ourselves as rivals, it didn't enable Railtrack to say, "It's obvious, here's the specification,"' said the signalling source. 'What's at the core of this, I think, is that Railtrack did not have its own sufficiently strong in-house knowledge and expertise to be able to use industry for what it was good at, to gather their views in and make a judgment.'

Railtrack did have one ace in the hole. It had, in fact, long since recruited an expert in moving-block signalling. Way back in 1995, the then Conservative government had worried that Rod Muttram's lack of railway experience would put off City investors. At the government's insistence, Railtrack appointed a champion of moving-block technology to be its engineering director. Brian Mellitt was a clever, experienced specialist who had already supervised the early stage of introducing moving block on London Underground's Jubilee line extension, then under construction.

But now, in 1997, just when his expertise was most needed, Mellitt's pet project, moving block on the Jubilee line, was suffering a horrible public failure. Quite simply, it didn't work. Computers that were supposed to talk to each other didn't. Costs soared. Desperately trying to complete the project in time for the opening of the Millennium Dome, engineers had to come up with a crash programme for an old-style conventional signalling system. The number of trains an hour was slashed in half. Westinghouse, the key signalling company responsible, took much of the blame. John Mills, who in 1995 had told parliament that moving block on the west coast main line might be possible in 10 years, was removed as chief executive.

Throughout 1998, as news of the problems on the Jubilee line began to emerge, the newly arrived Gerald Corbett – who took over from Edmonds in late 1997 – became increasingly uneasy about the moving-block plan he had inherited for the west coast. He didn't get on with Mellitt. Corbett was, if anything, even more hostile towards the engineering profession than his predecessor. Railtrack didn't sign a contract to develop the system with the British-French company GEC-Alsthom (later Alstom) until July 1998, more than a year behind schedule. But even this wasn't a proper contract to deliver something; it was a nine-month contract to define the thing that should be delivered.

And the signalling was only part of the WCML modernisation. Much more needed to be done. Tracks needed to be relaid, tunnels modified, bridges altered. This work, too, was behind schedule and over budget. Plans changed constantly. At one point, Railtrack paid £10m to a contractor to develop a new kind of transformer, only to abandon it later and go back to the original type. With every passing day, contractors were finding out how much more seriously the line had deteriorated than Railtrack and the consultants had understood.

At the same time, because Railtrack had shed so much of its engineering and railway operations expertise, it had little ability to judge whether the prices that its myriad contractors were charging were fair. 'It is easy to understand why certain elements within the industry took advantage of that situation,' said one rail industry figure. 'It would have been a great temptation.'

In a recurrent pattern, Railtrack had turned to a US company for project management expertise, but managed to botch that, too. Railtrack hired Brown & Root, a subsidiary of the US engineering group Halliburton, then run by Dick Cheney. Whether Brown & Root, which had grown fat on Pentagon contracts from the Vietnam war and beyond, could have managed the job is unknown, but Railtrack never allowed the company to try.

'Railtrack was half in bed with them and half not,' said an executive who saw the process from the inside. 'Brown & Root had a lot of experience in oil and gas contracts. Railtrack said, "Fine, show us how," but they got cold feet and never signed up.'

Meanwhile, Corbett and his team were becoming horribly aware of the other set of baroque errors that had been made by their predecessors: the Virgin contract, presented to Corbett on his accession as a *fait accompli*.

The Virgin suicide

In a few deft lines the complexity is laid out as a simple problem that a layperson could understand.

Despite Virgin Trains' initial reputation for lateness, there was a general fondness for the Railtrack–Virgin plan, not just in Railtrack, but among politicians, the media and the public. 140mph tilting trains; London to Glasgow in time for lunch; it sounded good. It sounded like progress. But there was a severe problem.

Again, the lay observer would think it was obvious: other trains needed to use the same line. And these other trains did not travel at 140mph. Some of them, freight trains, for example, struggled to reach half that speed. In all, the WCML is used by 120 trains a day. Two thousand different trains travel up and down its various lines, and another 4,000 cross it at some point. They are operated by 14 private train operators, using at least 19 kinds of locomotive, a mix of regional passenger services, local trains and freight – a contractual nightmare. But contracts had been signed. And, in the course of 1998, Railtrack began to come to the terrible realisation that it could not keep to its Virgin contract without breaching some of the others.

The introduction of faster, more frequent Virgin trains on the route meant that Railtrack was obliged to carry out extra work to guarantee that the other, slower trains would still be able to do their job and earn their money. When Railtrack began to look more closely at the Virgin contract, and compared it with the work it had promised to do to the railway, it saw that it was unable to draw up future timetables without breaking at least one of its contractual commitments. Or rather, Railtrack looked, but it refused to see. It was the beginning of the end.

'They had committed to the rail regulator and said that it would work, but everybody knew it was impossible,' said Stuart Baker of the SRA. 'A 140mph train still catches up with a 75mph freight train or a 50mph commuter train rather quickly. So it was a bit of an illusion. The capacity wasn't there for the contracted service without a new railway.'

The speed issue was not all. Railtrack was gambling its future on the highly risky maintenance philosophy that said components should be replaced only when they looked about to break, rather than at fixed intervals. When specialists looked into Railtrack's web of contracts with Virgin and other train operators on the WCML after the company collapsed, they were astonished to see that Railtrack had promised to build a railway that would not need any maintenance at all from 2005 to 2012.

'I don't think anyone denies that the commitment made to [Virgin] was a terrible mistake,' said another senior rail insider. 'It was one of the factors that brought the company down, ultimately.'

Section seven: the crisis/catharsis. *We watch Railtrack implode under the contradictions it has set in motion.*

In 1999, the bubble burst. When Chris Green, who took over as head of Virgin Trains in February, went out and about to see how the epic west coast reconstruction project was going, he received a shock. 'I was surprised at how little physical activity there was. There was nothing happening on the track. I was looking for the big yellow machines ripping up track and signals being replaced and wires being renewed, but everybody seemed to be in endless debate about the scope of the work. There's no doubt that two years were lost. I think as I arrived it was dawning on Railtrack that this was going to be an incredibly expensive and complicated project.'

He quickly found out about the timetabling crisis. 'The basic railway skill ought to be train timetabling, oughtn't it? Railtrack ought to have been able to timetable it themselves and I'm sure they did. When they found it didn't work, they also found they were in a spectacularly tight contract, with massive penalty clauses, up to £250m, with Virgin … every time they went round that situation they found they couldn't afford to break the contract. Which is why they had to implode.'

Heading for the buffers

The tension builds and the pace increases like the plot of a thriller as we head towards the final scene. Now we have a different obstacle in every sentence.

By the spring of 1999, even as Railtrack shares hit a high of more than £17, the project was in turmoil. Brown & Root were dropped and Railtrack drafted in a fresh team of consultants, the Nichols Group, to investigate. The rail regulator was hammering on Railtrack's door, demanding to know how they were going to make the west coast timetables work. Alstom's quest to try to make moving block work was going badly. Nine months of studies had still not produced a clear design for the system, and amid the uncertainty even Railtrack was not about to give them the £750m they were seeking to finish the job. In another blow to the technology, Mellitt quit.

'With him gone, there was nobody championing moving block,' said an insider on the signalling contract, 'and at this time, the Jubilee line was unravelling.'

Why on earth does a meeting have a codename – let alone such a melodramatic one? You can hear the music moving to a crescendo. We have arrived at the dénouement and the detective is confronting the guilty men. He picks them off one by one.

On December 9 1999, at a meeting codenamed Black Diamond Day, Railtrack finally took the decision it had avoided for so long. It accepted that moving block, the technology on which the company had staked so much, was a mirage. The Nichols Group report was painful in its clarity. There was a no better than 5% chance that the system would be ready in time. The Jubilee line fiasco had shown the risks. Alstom had never been able to explain what would happen to a moving-block system in the event of an accident, or if there was a disruption of radio signals. One possibility was that the entire railway network between London and Glasgow would simply grind to a halt.

Nor had Railtrack ever fully grasped the enormous sums it would have to pay train operators for permission to take 2,000 locomotives out of service to fit the new equipment and retrain 4,000 drivers. The implications for Railtrack were catastrophic. They would now have to introduce a different, more conventional signalling system, at vastly greater cost. Installing conventional signalling would mean stretches of railway being closed off, which meant huge compensation payments to the train companies. All Railtrack's contracts with train operators were predicated on moving block. The contracts would either have to be torn up – more huge compensation payments – or a costly extra programme of works would have to be set in motion to reconfigure the entire railway. Instead of the expected £2bn, the new headline figure was a staggering £5.8bn. It quickly turned out that this, too, was a wild underestimate. Without a massive taxpayer bail-out, Railtrack was doomed.

Section eight: the trial. *The guilty men protest their innocence, but the tone has changed, the end is in sight, all that remains is for the ends to be tied up. Almost casually, they are allowed to hang themselves in their own words.*

Five days later, on December 14, Railtrack sent a letter to the rail regulator, Tom Winsor. It was five years almost to the day since those original consultants had explained to Railtrack what a marvellous system moving block was, and more than four and a half years since Railtrack had so misleadingly told the public that it was a 'relatively mature' technology, ignoring the warnings of British Rail, MPs and rail journalists. Now Railtrack wrote: 'No system comparable with [moving block] has been implemented on a main-line mixed-traffic railway anywhere in the world ... the underlying software has never been used previously for a safety critical purpose.' If moving block was installed, Railtrack said, there would be 'a major risk of total disruption' to Britain's most important rail network. At least £65m, and probably more, had been spent on trying to make moving block work, with nothing to show for it that was any use to Railtrack. The final acts of Railtrack's role in the WCML saga, played out until the company went into receivership in 2001, saw an increasingly isolated Corbett go head to head with Winsor, the regulator, confident in his contempt for Railtrack management. In insisting that Railtrack fulfil its contracts to the letter, whatever the financial consequences, Winsor must have known he was contributing to Railtrack's downfall. But he also knew that the Blair government, the public and most of the train companies were fed up with the company, and the City was losing faith.

Railtrack's only ally, Virgin Trains, was full of doubt. In the summer, after Railtrack confessed that the £600m worth of Italian tilting trains he had ordered would not, as promised, be able to reach 140mph on the new WCML, Richard Branson cheerily told an interviewer: 'Do you know why we're changing the name of Virgin Trains? Cos they're fucked.'

Winsor has published word-for-word transcripts of two meetings with the Railtrack leadership at the rail regulator's offices in Holborn in the spring and autumn of 2000. Corbett, wordy, blustering, pleads for more money, and his company's continued existence.

Winsor and his colleagues sit in judgment, terse and sceptical, like magistrates. 'It would have been incompetent if we had just pressed blindly ahead and tried to get moving block to work,' the transcripts record Corbett saying desperately in May, trying to redefine Railtrack's belated recognition of its problems as a triumph of good management. Corbett goes on to plead for a relaxation of contracts with the other train operators to make way for Virgin. Winsor is not impressed. 'Is it reasonable,' he asks Corbett, 'that a party to a contract should expect to have that contract honoured?'

'Yes,' says Corbett. 'That is reasonable. In the real world' – he pauses for a moment, allowing himself a moment of regret – 'in many senses, the railway is not the real world.'

> This is a recap of what we know, in which Meek finally puts the blame fairly and squarely where he thinks it lies. He has provided the evidence, shown where the bodies lie, pointed out who is responsible and now all that is left is for him to tidy up the lurking questions.
>
> **Section nine: the consequences in deaths and rising costs.**

How could it happen?

In June, a fresh horde of consultants, commissioned by the regulator, delivered an indictment of Railtrack's handling of the west coast operation. Some parts of the project, the consultants said, had not been looked at afresh since the original report in 1994. All Corbett could do was choke on the irony that the consultants were from Booz Allen & Hamilton – the same firm that provided the experts which, six years earlier, had recommended to Railtrack that adopting moving block would be a splendid idea.

Away from the WCML, in October 2000, at Hatfield, a GNER express from King's Cross to Leeds derailed, killing four people, when broken rail that Railtrack had failed to repair shattered into hundreds of pieces. It was only a year since the Paddington disaster, which had seen 31 people killed and more than 400 injured when a badly trained driver went through a badly positioned red light. By the spring of 2001, the railways were in chaos and the estimated cost of the WCML project had gone up to £8bn. In October, after one last futile attempt by Railtrack to go behind the backs of the other users of the line and renegotiate the Virgin deal, the government pulled the plug. Railtrack was finished.

As the Strategic Rail Authority, Railtrack's successor Network Rail and, eventually, Bechtel began to investigate the wreckage, the estimated costs of the WCML continued to rise.

Twenty billion pounds was even mentioned as a final price tag. Not until October 2002 did Richard Bowker of the SRA come up with what might be the final figure – £9.8bn – to build a compromise 125mph west coast line by 2008. According to some estimates, a brand-new high-speed railway to the north of England could have been built for half that price.

Section ten: the analysis, lessons learned, equilibrium re-established.

Those who came into Railtrack in the early days, John Edmonds' team, like to blame the fiasco on the Corbett–New Labour era. Dithering over plans, slack financial controls over contractors, political interference, the ever tightening grip of safety regulations – these, they say, added billions to a project that should have cost far less.

Yet all the key decisions that doomed Railtrack were taken before Corbett arrived, before Labour had fully established itself in office, and before the terrible accidents at Paddington and Hatfield: the folly involved in choosing an untried new technology and selling it to the public, the taking over of the WCML by Railtrack instead of letting an experienced engineering consortium handle it, the arrogance displayed in negotiating the Virgin contract.

Throughout Railtrack's existence, the management showed persistent traits – a contempt for engineering wisdom, and a steady refusal to confront the true decrepitude of the railway that they were running into the ground. Even if moving block had come along in time, the rest of the infrastructure would have taken many billions to set right.

'The more we get into it – and facts are still emerging – the more we know the existing infrastructure is completely and utterly worn out,' said the SRA's Stuart Baker. In an imaginary world, if Railtrack had rejected the consultants' advice in 1995 to go for moving block, if it had taken time to investigate the true state of the railway, what would the actual price of WCML modernisation have been? Enough, certainly, to scupper Railtrack's privatisation. And there can be few in Britain today who think that would have been a bad thing. Without privatisation, would the money have been forthcoming to modernise the WCML? Not immediately, perhaps, but sooner or later the Treasury would have had no choice but to put the billions in that it is putting in now; and a commercially run, state-owned Railtrack would not have let £3.8bn in income leak out of the railways in dividends and interest payments over five years.

> *This is the crux of the story. This was not just a saga of 'incompetence, greed and delusion behind Britain's biggest public works project', as promised in the stand-first. It was a failure of democracy. Perhaps that should also have been in the stand-first. Sadly journalists don't get to write their own stand-firsts. Meek now moves away from the role of investigator and ends with an impassioned address to the reader that is rather reminiscent of Martha Gelhorn in 'Visit Italy' (see page 60).*

One of the most disturbing facets of the west coast saga is the failure of democratic government that it represents. Not just of a particular party, but the whole system of government. The administration of John Major was clearly to blame for creating the Railtrack monster. Yet within less than a year of the privatisation of Railtrack, the Conservatives were punished at the polls – and Railtrack, and the WCML project as originally misconceived, went steaming on. No one has answered the question of how governments with five-year terms can be entrusted with responsibility for stewardship of projects whose lifespan is likely to be 15 years or longer. In the dozens of interviews with rail industry figures carried out for this article, it was striking how few ever mentioned transport ministers or political parties. The only government they recognised was the only government that endures: the unelected Treasury.

And yet we cannot accuse our elected representatives of looking the other way. In mid-February and early March of 1995, after the consultants had delivered their report but while Railtrack and the government were still mulling over it, members of the House of Commons transport committee questioned Edmonds, Horton and the heads of some of the big signalling firms about the WCML project.

The MPs did their job well. Gwyneth Dunwoody, the hard-nosed Labour interrogator on the committee, had been briefed by Richard Hope, an expert railway writer, and knew exactly what was at stake. Accordingly, when their report was published that July, the committee gave an uncannily prescient warning of the risk Railtrack was running.

It warned: 'The renewal of the west coast main line is urgent, and reliance on an as yet unproven train control system to underpin the financial case for investment may lead to unacceptable delays in upgrading the nation's principal intercity route.'

Members of parliament had done what they were elected to do, conscientiously and thoroughly scrutinising a big plan by an unelected organisation with power over the lives and purses of the public. It had pointed out its weaknesses. And nobody paid any attention.

What now?

The piece finishes by bringing us to rest again where we started. We have reached equilibrium and we are back out there on the tracks with the men who know about railways and how to look after them.

In 1837 Charles Greville, the racehorse owner, political diarist and intimate of the Duke of Wellington, described his first railway journey – on the west coast line between Birmingham and Liverpool – as a 'peculiarly gay' experience.

'The first sensation is a slight degree of nervousness and a feeling of being run away with, but a sense of security soon supervenes and the velocity is delightful,' he writes. The train travelled at about 20mph, but Greville knew it could go faster. 'One engineer went at the rate of 45 miles an hour,' he records, 'but the Company turned him off for doing so.'

It is not clear when, if ever, the west coast will become a 140mph route. For the time being, all Chris Green can do is take invited guests out on short practice runs in Branson's new red expresses to show them what might have been. 'I went on the 145mph test run last August and it rode beautifully,' he said. 'It was doing 125, and we said, "Please accelerate to 145," and it shot forward like a sports car … we've got this greyhound train which is going to be running around like a labrador for the next 10 years.'

Out in the winter rain on the shut-down Crewe-to-Cheadle line is a British engineer, Roy Hickman, junior now to the Americans from Bechtel but with decades of experience on the railway. He works for Network Rail these days: the slogan of anti-engineering Railtrack's successor is 'Engineering excellence for Britain's railways'. It is spending £3m a day on the WCML project.

'Bechtel are bringing a level of planning we've never seen before,' Hickman said. 'I think Railtrack, in fact the industry, never really fully understood or anticipated the sheer scope or challenge of building the west coast, and only when work started did we begin to understand just what a huge task it was. 'It takes 20 years to wreck the infrastructure, and nearly as long to set it right.'

Guardian Unlimited © Guardian Newspapers Limited 2005

7

PROFILES AND CELEBRITY INTERVIEWS

Celebrity interviews are hard to do well: a few minutes with the subject (often with other journalists in the room) and you are expected to turn out something fresh and insightful. An actor plugging a film or an author peddling a new book will have been interviewed many times – your job is to find a way of getting this person to react to you on an emotional level when she or he may be just longing for a bit of peace and quiet in a hectic day.

Make full use of the interview by doing your research thoroughly before you arrive. You don't want to waste precious minutes checking on information that you could have got from a press release, or the cuttings. If this is an author, make sure you have read not only this book, but several others. If it is an actor, make sure you know what they have done before. If this is a profile (more a feature than an interview), you need to interview friends and colleagues about your subject. Try to do as much of this as you can before the meeting so that you have plenty to talk about and a very clear idea of how you want to guide the interview. Your prior research should have given you a sense of the story line (controlling idea) too, so that you can test it during the interview and make sure your understanding is accurate.

You have to extract every ounce out of the encounter. Note down everything: from what your subject is wearing to the state of his or her nails. If you can do the interview in his or her own surroundings, you will have access to masses of what Tom Wolfe refers to as 'status life' detail (see page 49). If you are stuck with a hotel room, look out for personal details; and if the surroundings are totally sterile, then check out how this person fits in with them: does he or she seem at home or feel uncomfortable? Consider also how people interact with others, from the waiter to the press officer. And of course how they react to you.

LIBBY BROOKS (INTERVIEWING KATHRYN FLETT) When I asked Ian Katz, the editor of

Guardian G2, what he looked for in a writer he said: 'I am a sucker for a brilliant line. I will give writers the benefit of the doubt if they can turn out one or two great sentences – the kind you want to cut out and keep'. Libby

Brooks is always writing lines that he, and I, would like to cut out and keep. But this is not simply a string of one-liners. Her writing has structure, pace and intelligence even when the subject is banal.

Private lives
Guardian (G2), 14 May, 1999

Last week, *Observer* writer Kathryn Flett was leafing through a glossy magazine while she waited to pick up a takeaway. There, in a 100-word review of her forthcoming book, *The Heart-Shaped Bullet*, her life in print was summarised something like this: 'Columnist Kate meets gorgeous Mr Right, they get spliced, he leaves her for someone else, she shouts a lot. Then meets Younger Man, who is Destined to Leave Her, he does, she has a breakdown and checks into a glamorous clinic.' 'And I just had to laugh,' she says, forcing out a weak chuckle, 'because the fact is that nobody is going to care as much about this as I am.'

Since the spring of 1997, Flett has laid the breakdown of her marriage and its devastating aftermath open like a wound, through her newspaper column and now in this more substantial medium. The book is many things – delicate, guileless, occasionally hilarious, worried like a scab and compulsive like a car crash. It is an exhausting read, and her unhappiness sticks in the mind like glue.

The introduction sets up what looks like the story line of a typical 'transformation' (see page 15) in which the heroine has journeyed to the depths of her psyche and learned how to live, but already there is a hint that this story will not stick to the plot.

But primarily this is an ugly book, for the same reason that the most beautiful woman looks dreadful in a meanly-lit public toilet. Midway through her dark night of the soul, Flett turned on the lights. And she chose to see our faces as we watch her fall to pieces. She relies, she says later, on everybody else being as honest as she is.

She takes us through a helter-skelter of emotions and responses. Compulsive car crashes no longer surprise as they used to, but they are more than redeemed by images that stay in the mind like stills from an old movie.

Flett married in September 1995. Seventeen months to the day later, her husband moved out of their flat in west London. He had fallen in love with another woman, to whom he is now married. The book charts her attempts to comprehend the failure of the marriage, in particular assessing the impact of her parents' abusive relationship on her own romantic assumptions. She later embarks on a fresh relationship, which ends abruptly. This second rejection precipitates her nervous breakdown. She is treated as an in-patient for clinical depression. She asks her fellow patients to choose their own pseudonyms for their appearance in her memoir.

> *This is essentially a repetition of the introduction, filling us in with the basic background detail. So far so standard. But then she uses repetition in a different way, to underline what she has taken as the 'controlling idea' (page 41) – that Flett has abused not only herself but also the trust of those who were close to her. It is this that provides the spine of her piece, which is written, unusually for an interview, in 'essay' rather than 'story' form.*

But a life does not unravel in a vacuum. 'Nobody is going to care as much about this as I am.' Unless you are Eric, her ex-husband, at best the wearer of sociology lecturer shoes, at worst 'The Tin Man', emotionally retarded, commitment-phobic, who announces to friends that the marriage is over 'as if he were rescheduling a couple of appointments'. Or The Boy ('just too young, too handsome and too bloody lots of things, really, to be with me'), whose sweetly pompous emails are reprinted without his permission. Or her father, who is exposed in print as a wife-beater.

Why? 'I was astonished by the response that I got to the column. As a journalist you get used to writing into a vacuum. I didn't want the only record to be this one-sided soap opera-ish story.' Flett's butterfly collector approach to memory is a constant throughout the book. Key moments must be captured on video, her wedding service 'gone, all of it', simply because it was not committed to tape.

'The more I learned about myself and the relationship, the more naive and self-deluding it would have been to pretend that I hadn't played a part in the demise of the marriage, and it would have made a very dull and dishonest book. Although this sounds rather unlikely, I was trying to give Eric a bit more respect.' Why? 'On a wider level, I think my generation are very bad at committed relationships and I wanted to explore why that might be, using my marriage as a metaphor.' She sighs. 'I sound like an egomaniac. I had to feel as though I was producing something that was going to go away from me and the people involved, and out into the world to reflect other people's lives and really stop being about us.'…

> *Now a few lines of physical description: economical but as full of information as a Picasso drawing.*

… Sprawling in the tidy, bloodless lounge with her white rescue dog from Battersea, Possum, she is nervously reflective. Her dark crop frames a pale face. The bracken eyes would rather be elsewhere. She looks so young. She fills the room with the bruises on her old heart. She has the most beautiful smile and in other circumstances she must be captivating.

Many argue that Flett is parody on a plate: the shrewish avenger, the pathological solipsist, the pitiably banal product of our equivocal relationship with the piss-and-tell school of lifestyle journalism. But, respect it or damn it, the book is weighty with contemporary resonance. The snapshots of a love in pieces are compulsive.

Note how the pace changes – the piece has built up gradually: introduction, then her subject's account of herself with only the occasional authorial interventions. But now the balance shifts. We are moving from description to interrogation as Brooks takes her subject on.

But pain is not a competition, and honesty is her best policy. Though thick with self-analysis, the book is not self-justifying. The only explanations are those she is searching for herself. And God is in the detail. Flett writes best when she applies a tender eye to the minutiae. But for those she writes about, the Devil is in there too. This is not a vengeful book. Her treatment of others is questing rather than cruel. But she fails to accept that the very act of inclusion is invasion enough.

'I don't think I have invaded other people's privacy because I haven't gone inside their heads. I've presented my life, and it's only where I've touched them or they've touched me.' She pauses. 'But I have to believe that, don't I?' She sent her ex-husband a proof copy, which he returned the following day along with a note which said that he and his wife had decided not to read it. 'I would imagine that he wants it to go away so that he can get on with his life.' Her relationships with her parents are stronger as a result of confronting the truth of her childhood: 'On a personal level, whatever comes out of this process, my small family and I are talking about things and actually healing old wounds.'

And now the pace quickens as Brooks engages with her own analysis of a woman whose actions she considers deeply suspect.

It seems absurd that she has so little conception of her capacity to affect others. The spurious privacy distinction and an insistence that she has not overstepped the mark smack of denial. Is Flett essentially a narcissist who cannot envisage people as anything except players in her own tragedy? Or is she simply supremely naive, lacking any appreciation of her own power? There is a third explanation, which speaks to a deep contradiction in how she views the act of writing itself. Does writing about the thing make it more true? 'Possibly for me … yes. I am pathologically a writer.' She gurgles. She has always written thus. 'As a child, a way of controlling life is by documenting it, feeling that you own it somehow. Certainly now when things get chaotic in my head I find it useful to set them down.' Powerful, but not an act of therapy. It was not cathartic, she insists. 'No. It was just fucking hard.' She remains friends with The Boy, she tells me, although she is aware that he would rather she had not written about him. So why did she, when the book refers to an explicit promise that their relationship would be off-limits. Indeed, she writes of a 'dark little running joke' that The Boy would remain out of print so long as he did not dump her while she was writing the book. 'He broke his promise first,' she whispers.

But why? 'It finished the book. It wasn't the end of the story that I wanted, but I'd had another relationship, I'd been in hospital, I came out and there was a book to finish. He was in it because that was how the plot went.' The plot. Her life. She insists that much was left out, and that 'after the last full stop, everything else is mine. You can't know everything about me.' Both in print and in person, she repeats self-assessments like incantations, one step ahead of those who would judge her. Her conversation is littered with caveats.

> See how she has taken control of the story. It is no longer simply an interview. It has moved on from being a descriptive piece about a woman and her work to an analysis of her personality.

What is evident is that she was unable to control the process of writing; that, as she became increasingly vulnerable and broken, the book gathered a momentum of its own.

'I signed for the book within seven months of my husband leaving, and several months before finishing the column,' she explains, 'although at that stage I was expecting to write a different sort of book.' Constantly writing about emotions, in particular unpacking her childhood demons, exacted a price. 'I was on the slope towards having a breakdown and I think that writing the book precipitated me towards that place.' In the book, her awareness never quite settles into insight. But that was then. Less than a year on from completion, Flett talks of the writer of the book in the third person. 'She's definitely a me that's contained in there, and after the last sentence I'm coming from a different place. She was a more naive, more trusting person. She might have been a nicer person.' Amidst the sound and fury generated by this book, it is easy to forget her impressive career credentials. A pioneer of style journalism, she worked as features editor and fashion editor on the *Face* before becoming the award-winning editor of men's magazine *Arena* between 1992 and 1995. All by the tender age of 31.

She tucks the background biographical detail in so that we somehow absorb it without disturbing the trajectory. Most writers would have introduced this information right at the start, but that would have held up the narrative of her emotional life, on which the story hangs.

'I'm 35, I'm single, I'd be lying if I said I looked forward to a life of doing circuits of Paddington recreation ground with Possum and carrying on being a spare part at dinner parties.' She sounds at once bemused and resigned when she admits that the book is now indelibly marked on her 'emotional and professional CV'. She says that she has written her own death warrant. 'It'll be a very intriguing sort of man who'll have the guts to say, "Never mind the book." I want to get past this', she says. 'I want to get better'. She is still receiving treatment from 'the people with letters after their names'.

'I'd love to have a relationship that was everything that a relationship could be, and I'd love to have kids, but at the moment I know that I'm not able to give and I'm terribly, terribly wary. I've just got to do a bit more growing up I suppose. I can no longer treat happiness as an end in itself. It's the difference between me and the woman who thought she'd be wandering around in a middle-class haze with small and attractive children, that sense of it being bestowed upon you by the God of happiness. It's not something you can go and get, it creeps up on you in small moments.' In time, this interview may become part of Kathryn Flett's plot as well. It will be read by her colleagues, who work two floors above the *Guardian* office. It will be scoured by ex-lovers and nosy acquaintances, in search of further revelations. It will be dismissed at dinner parties. It might by mocked by other newspapers. Circles, in circles, in circles.

Although this started as a traditional story of an emotional journey (a transformation narrative), it plays with traditional structure using our narrative expectations of a happy ending as a way of creating tension and surprise. She ends with another surprise, slipping out of her professional persona and leaving us with a personal reaction that is almost a plea for forgiveness.

I didn't know how to greet her when we met – a professional handshake, a colleague's kiss, a sympathetic hug? I kissed her goodbye. She has very soft cheeks. And afterwards I felt dismal. Because I didn't want to know all those things about all those people.

(*The Heart-Shaped Bullet* is published by Picador, price £9.99)
Guardian Unlimited © Guardian Newspapers Limited 2005

ZOE HELLER (PROFILING TAKI THEODORACOPOLUS)

I love this profile and use it every year in teaching. Zoe Heller is a very different kind of writer from Libby Brooks. Where Brooks engages directly and fiercely with her subject, Heller is an observer. She stands back and toys with her subject, allowing him to un-pick himself as she watches – and reports. Even the interaction between them is turned to good account. Because she isn't initiating, it has a guileless authenticity that is often missing from profiles written by more aggressive writers. Above all, it has a couple of passages that I want to cut out and keep. The first, in paragraph six, is a piece of beautifully observed 'status life' detail elegantly delivered. The second is at the end. Here it is her observation of an interaction in which she seems to pick up her subject and pin him, squirming, on to her specimen board. The beginning and the end are so good that I am ready to forgive the fact that the piece flags a little in the middle. For a while she seems a little too laid back and leaves us to do a little too much of the work of imagining. But then her subject is puffed up enough to fill the space pretty well on his own.

The little emperor
Independent on Sunday (Sunday Review), 31 October 1993

THE NIGHT before he had dined with Baroness Thatcher and the Princess of Wales at a little get-together hosted by his friend, Conrad Black, proprietor of the *Daily Telegraph*. It had been pretty good fun and he had behaved … not badly, although he had refused to stand up when a toast to the American president was proposed. (People no doubt thought he was showing off, but he was damned if he was going to stand up for a non-inhaling, draft-dodging coward.) After dinner he had gone to Annabel's (still the best nightclub in the world, whatever anyone says). He had drunk far too much, stayed far too late, and not got home until the large hours. *Plus ça change.*

There was time for only a quick doze and a shower in the morning before he had had to rush out again for a luncheon engagement with his former editor at the *Spectator*, now editor of the *Sunday Telegraph*, Charles Moore. He was feeling a weency bit grey – at 56, one expects to pay for one's indulgences – but lunch at Christopher's, the Covent Garden restaurant owned by his dear friend Christopher Gilmour, had turned out to be a splendid tonic. He had entertained Charles with all sorts of gossip (including the wonderfully disgusting news that a mutual acquaintance of theirs is a child molester). And he had fancied that Christopher's father, the former cabinet minister, Sir Ian Gilmour, who was sitting at one of the neighbouring tables, overheard some of what he said. This had inspired him to even greater outrageousness. He and Charles had had such a good time, the hours flew by.

Heller's introduction rushes right into the middle of the action by abandoning any sort of chronology. This is clearly Taki's account of the evening before but in paraphrasing, rather than quoting, she has already seized control of the agenda. What we have here is a portrait of an extraordinarily well-connected man running a little faster than his years should allow and clearly in love with himself. She then moves on to a fairly orthodox background paragraph that paints in the biographical details and anchors our understanding of the piece.

Thus it was that Panayotis 'Taki' Theodoracopolus, 'High Life' columnist for the *Spectator*, ex-tennis and karate ace, fabled womaniser, political reactionary and heir to a £200m Greek shipping fortune, observed the first rule of playboy manners and pitched up both late and hung-over for his afternoon appointment with me. While he was still imparting scurrilities on the other side of London, I was being let into his lavish Cadogan Square *pied-à-terre* by a trinity of his nervous retainers. The master would be back shortly, the secretary, butler and maid said.

I waited for Taki in his drawing-room. This is a huge, high-ceilinged chamber decorated in *faux*-18th-century style, with some rather good French paintings, some very fine French furniture and a lot of elaborately swagged silk curtain. On one long shelf Taki has ranged his collection of tennis trophies – most of them dating from the Fifties when he helped win the Davis Cup for Greece and aspired briefly to becoming a Wimbledon champion. The rest of the shelves are devoted to books. Taki's library is rather serious and self-improving. Lots of politics and philosophy, with only the occasional hint of frivolity: *The Complete Book of Insults, The Faber Book of Seductions*. After a bit of waiting I went to explore Taki's bathroom. (There were heaps of crisp, linen towels in the Italian style, hand-embroidered with the letter 'T', but sadly, no nancy toiletries on show – just a lone bottle of Silvikrin hairspray in the cupboard.) After that, I went back to the drawing-room and read a photocopied article by the right-wing American critic, Hilton Kramer. It was entitled 'The Flowers on Sartre's Grave', and Taki, a man who takes his anti-communism seriously, had carefully highlighted passages relating to the vile hypocrisy of the Left, in thick fluorescent pen.

I had just started examining Taki's desk and a pad of joke notepaper headed: 'Everyone's entitled to my opinion', when Taki arrived home. There was a flurry out in the corridor and the pitter-patter of servants' feet. Then he swept in: short, rather beautiful, doused in the complicated smell of wealth. (Roughly: wine, a hint of cologne, the skins of very young animals.) He began immediately to bounce about the high-ceilinged drawing-room like the Infant Phenomenon, issuing instructions to his retinue, barking questions at me and giggling maddeningly at his own naughty jokes.

> Most of these three paragraphs are taken up with 'status life' detail, which places him even more thoroughly than the introduction as a man of wealth and a playboy. The relationship with his servants is particularly telling and her description of 'the smell of wealth' is perfect. Nothing here is borrowed, every word has been carefully considered and every image is newly minted.

'So, Miss Heller, why do you want to talk to me? What is this about? Charles Moore said if I want you to write nicely about me, I must seem like a very unhappy man who's had a hard life. I said – because I'm rather proud, Miss Zoe Heller – 'I don't give a fuck what she writes about me.' I don't give a fuck. I am doing this just because I want to have an affair with you. I am on the make – Ha ha. Is it hot in here? I don't know why I have a soft spot for Charles – but he has everything I like. He's a gent, he's extremely handsome … I say that, even though, unlike most Englishmen, I don't like being buggered …

'… Fiona. Fiona. Were there any messages? I am not feeling very well today. I have a little asthma. … You know, I put on 10 pounds while I was in Greece just now – stuffing myself at all those boring, working lunches … Andrew. Did you get Miss Heller a drink? Yes, Charles is so moral and good. He thinks gossip is bad, which it is of course. I mean, gossip in the newspapers …'.

To call Taki's conversation digressive, would be to suggest that it has an intended course from which to digress. But his choppy locutions betray no sign of forward planning whatsoever. They skip from idealet to idealet, from morsel to morsel, with a sort of restless hedonism, rather as Taki conducts his life.

> Note how Heller uses quotations, not necessarily to further the story, but to illustrate it. Sometimes they are just throw-away asides, sometimes they are anecdotes, but mostly they are used to give us a sense of character.

With the exception of four months in 1984, which he spent in Pentonville Prison for being caught at Heathrow airport bringing 20 grams of cocaine into the country, Taki has spent his entire adulthood in a ceaseless, global commute: a few weeks in Athens taking care of business, a weekend round-and-about the Greek islands in his yacht, a fortnight in Manhattan with his family, a month of parties in London and always – failing natural disaster – winter in Gstaad.

'Why stay in the same place,' Taki asks with a shrug, 'when you can move around? It's like what Swifty Lazar (the celebrated Hollywood agent) said. Someone asked him once, tell me, Shitty Lazar, why do you go out every night? Now Shitty is obsessed with money – he knows nothing else – but like all these people who're obsessed with money, he comes up with great wisdoms. He said: 'Why stay in when you can go out?' Just like that. That's the smartest thing I've ever heard. Including Plato and Socrates.'

The story line here is the hardest one to bring to life. Taki is a man who rose without effort on the tide of his father's wealth. How do you bring narrative tension into something like this? Heller goes for a 'coming of age' narrative and a story structure, with a hero whose life is a series of (mostly) fortunate coincidences oiled by his own wit and peopled by larger than life characters. He is the quintessential Jack (from Jack and the Beanstalk): self-serving and cheeky, he enrages his father (the giant) but still ends up with his wealth and the love of not just one woman but a harem full.

Of course, one needs fairly large amounts of money in order to test this wisdom. The funds for Taki's ne'er-do-wellery are derived from the immense wealth of his late father, John Theodoracopolus, a tough, rather distant character who was thrown out of home as a teenager but went on to marry the daughter of a Greek Prime Minister, Pangiottis Poulitsas, and to build himself a fortune in textiles, hotels and, principally, shipping. Taki, who has one brother, Hari, three years his senior, was always the family bad boy. Starting with his expulsion from his American prep school, Lawrenceville, at the age of 12 (his father had sent him and his brother abroad, fearing Stalinist incursions into Greece) Taki's youth was one long list of black-sheep misdemeanours. Hari was the stolid, fair-haired sibling who seemed to take after his father's German side of the family. He kept his head down, his nose clean, and in due course entered the family business. Taki, on the other hand, pursued a career of resolute foppishness. He was forever getting himself into scrapes with girls and money – forever being hauled back home to Athens and threatened with having his trust fund cut off.

When Mr Theodoracopolus died in 1986, however, he surprised everyone – except perhaps readers of romantic fiction – by leaving all his worldly goods to Taki. In the end, the youngest son's mischievous spirit won out against the more frigid virtues of poor Hari. Taking pity on his brother, Taki offered to share his inheritance and split the business down the middle. But arguments about the way in which the two sides of the business should be run began almost immediately, and Taki has regretted his fit of magnanimity ever since. His public denunciations of his brother have led to Hari threatening litigation. At the heart of the feud is Taki's contention that Hari has never properly acknowledged his indebtedness to the father. During my visit, Taki had a long and explosive phone-call about the latest fraternal spat with his business manager in Athens.

'Ah, my brother has a lot of resentment towards me,' he said when he had got off the phone. Having been snubbed as Hari was would tend to breed a certain resentment, I suggested. 'Yes,' Taki agreed impatiently, 'but the idea that this man who has never, ever worked for anybody except my father won't even allow a ship of ours to be called John Theodoracopolus. Everything he has comes from my father. It doesn't come from him. He is a ludicrous individual. I'm as ludicrous as he is, but at least I admit it.'

> It would be easy for this story to become dull. Here is a man who started rich and has remained that way ever since. Heller manages to create momentum from the minor ups and downs of his life and the wry comments of his friends and acquaintances. To start with we hear about Taki's life from his own standpoint.

Taki's keen sense of his own privilege and the ignoble fact of never having earned his own living has prompted various efforts over the years to try to 'make something of himself'. At the age of 30, he made his first stab at a proper job with a brief and disastrous experiment in photo-journalism. Soon after that, he fell into the first of a series of freelance reporting jobs for William Buckley, an old friend from Gstaad and editor of the grotesquely conservative *National Review*. Buckley made him his Mediterranean correspondent and commissioned him to write a letter from Jordan on the 1970 War. There followed various foreign reporting jobs, the high point of which was an assignment in Vietnam. Taki is immensely proud of his experiences 'in combat', but in truth they were pretty short-lived. He found his proper journalistic niche as a columnist when, in the late Seventies, Alexander Chancellor, then editor of the *Spectator*, commissioned him to write the weekly 'High Life' column. Loath to publish a rather turgid piece about Greek politics that Taki was pressing upon him, Chancellor suggested that Taki would be much more amusing on the subject of his own decadent social life.

Taki has gone on to write columns for the *National Review, Interview, Esquire, Vanity Fair* and the *New York Observer*, but it as the *Spectator*'s bragging, bibulous and libellous chronicler of what he still quaintly calls, 'the international jet-set', that he has really made his name. He takes the column – and the fact of being employed – tremendously seriously. 'When Taki first started "High Life",' Chancellor recalls, 'I thought he was rather idle. His English was not so good then and I would have to spend hours translating his copy. I thought he was a playboy, not bothering. But then I discovered that he would stay up all night labouring over his prose, surrounded by screwed-up balls of paper. I was rather touched.'

Taki's take on the smarty-pants circles in which he moves is unashamedly treacherous: he has been called 'a terrorist among the rich'. This attitude is partly born of snobbery, partly a more genuine moral unease. Taki is unhappy about the seedy, uncultured atmosphere that the nouveau riche have brought to smart living. If he is to be a rake, Taki wants to be one in the Flaubertian not the Jackie Collins tradition. But he is also prey, as his prison memoirs, *Nothing to Declare*, published in 1985, make clear, to feelings of mortification and worthlessness. His father worked for the Resistance when Germany occupied Greece during the war; and he built an empire. What, Taki asks himself, has his wayward son achieved? 'At least I've been employed,' he is fond of saying. 'I've been fired five times so that means I've been employed six times.' But the sense of his own 'ludicrousness' haunts him.

His own view of himself as louche but essentially moral is then endorsed by the other characters in his life who are brought on to support him.

'It sounds silly,' his second ex-wife, the Austrian princess, Alexandra Schonberg says, 'but Taki is actually a profoundly moral man, a very serious person.' This is some testimony, coming from a woman who has put up with 30 years of Taki's philandering. Alexandra, the mother of Taki's two children, Mandolina, aged 17, and John-Taki, aged 12, officially divorced Taki in 1986. She had grown weary at last of his public infidelity. Like his father before him, Taki has always kept mistresses and always been entirely honest about doing so. 'It is,' he says, 'the Greek way. The Greek male way.' In pressing his suit with young women, he has relied for many years on the seductive charms of one form letter which – having written out a copy the night before – he was happy to share with me.

This is the first turning point in the piece, where it becomes clear that Heller finds her subject not so much engaging as ludicrous. From this point she starts to play, not only with the pomposity of her subject, but also with the assumed outrage of her liberal readership. She picks out his most outrageous remarks and drops them in front of her readers for them to do with as they please.

'Dear X, There's a marvellous line in *Romeo and Juliet* where Romeo – having avenged Mercutio's death – is advised to flee Verona. 'But heaven's here, where Juliet lives' he cries. However corny and sudden this may sound, this is how I've felt since the moment I met you. Love Taki.'

Taki beamed as he finished reading. 'It's a wonderful letter, isn't it?' he said. 'It's so sweet, isn't it?'

If the epistolary method doesn't work, Taki has other ways of wooing. 'He is incredibly straightforward,' says one ex-mistress who prefers not to be identified. 'He comes up to you and says: "I'm crazy about you and I want to have an affair." It's very seductive.' Those who have received such attentions, have, for the most part, been upper-class English women. This, according to his friend, the journalist Charles Glass, is because Taki considers the upper-class English female the 'easiest' – that is of the loosest morals – in the world.

> *Note how the comments from friends and ex-wives are dropped in to provide evidence for his view of himself.*

'Yes, that's right,' Taki says complacently. 'And besides, it is difficult to sleep with maids. I mean … the smell is not good.' But he is not so narrow as to restrict himself to England, he assures me. Any nationality will do – except American. 'They are the only women I refuse to sleep with. It's a crime against humanity to sleep with an American woman. I've never seen a ghastlier form of woman. I tell you, I see an American woman in front of me and I start shaking. They deny everything I was brought up to adore – beauty, the feminine aesthetic, sweetness … Come on Miss Heller, name me one attractive American woman.'

I cast around for a name. 'Nora Ephron,' I say. Taki explodes. 'Nora Ephron? Listen. I was in boarding school for 11 years and I spent four months in prison and never have I looked at a man – but I promise you I would rather sleep with Nora Ephron's husband than with her.' He goes on cast a series of extremely unpleasant and libellous aspersions on Nora Ephron's person. At such moments it is difficult to fathom exactly what Taki's wife might mean by describing Taki as 'profoundly moral' and 'deeply serious' unless it is in the sense suggested by Charles Moore, who regards Taki as subscribing to an exact inversion of conventional morality: 'His vows are the exact opposite of poverty, chastity and obedience, but he is as serious about carrying them out as any monk.'

> *Once again the piece changes direction, providing a moment of surprise as Heller appears to discover something contradictory in her subject.*

There is, however, if one watches out for it, the occasional pocket of scruple in Taki's cheery wickedness. Although he and Alexandra are divorced, they do in fact still live together for large chunks of the year, and up until quite recently they were trying to have another child together. Their house in Manhattan may have been converted to provide Taki with a bachelor pad, but Taki still refers to Alexandra as his wife, and although ostensibly not answerable to anyone, he does in fact observe a marital etiquette of sorts. He will not, for instance, answer my questions about how long his affairs with women tend to last, or what sort of gifts he purchases for his girlfriends. 'It would,' he says, 'be an insult to my wife if I answered the question. If I said yes, it would hurt her and my children. If I said no … well, I refuse to answer.'

How to explain this outbreak of sensitivity, given the declarations of lust with which Taki indiscriminately sprinkles his column? 'I never name the women. It's all without naming.' Taki insists. This is not true. I say so. 'Well I name women I lust after,' he concedes. 'But I don't say I have been with particular women. You know, the smartest thing that's ever been said is that you can be a faithful husband but a very bad husband and you can be an unfaithful husband but a very good one. I like to think that I am the latter.'

However sceptical one chooses to be about Taki's husbandly virtues, his arrangement with his wife clearly isn't as straightforward – as straight-forwardly unfair – as it looks. And Taki isn't quite as thorough-going a cad as at first he seems. 'The two of them play a sort of game together,' one friend explains. 'Alexandra pretends to be the squaw – the oppressed wifey, but it's all very jokey.' While Alexandra whoopingly agrees that Taki is 'absolutely impossible' about women – 'He is,' she says, 'a Neanderthal man. He thinks he can walk around with fur on his shoulder and bat women about' – it is evident that she doesn't stand for any such nonsense. Taki, who once claimed never to have met a woman who was his intellec-tual equal, will, when pressed to earnestness, concede that he regards Alexandra as his intellectual superior. 'She's become my intellectual supe-rior, I'd say. She did something. She pulled some number on me and sud-denly I found that, whereas before she was just a very pretty girl who was moody – I think she used those fucking shrinks or whatever – she became suddenly understanding and above it all.'

In fact, Taki's 'batting about' of women appears to be a lot of mouth and very little trousers. 'There are lots of men who pretend to respect women, but don't really,' one of the former girlfriends says. 'Taki is exactly the oppo-site. He pretends not to respect women but he does.' It would be going too far to imagine that all of Taki's reactionary pronouncements were simply ironic camouflage for a liberal teddy-bear beneath. But it is rather amazing to hear Taki, the scourge of 'poofters', admit that if his son turned out to be homosexual, he could learn to live with it, as long as his son was happy. He grows uncomfortable when trapped into saying reasonable things, however. As quickly as possible he will revert to the jollier business of epatering the bien-pensants.

It's a man's role to defend women from 'nigger muggers' he'll tell you – he's proved it by watching elephant behaviour at his friend John Aspinall's zoo. Or: Mussolini was very good for Italy – he just had a bad army. Or: sexual harassment is a load of bullshit – he longs to be had up on harassment charges, so that he can stand in the dock and declare: 'Yes! Yes! I did it!' Or: he is embarrassed that his daughter is fat.

Everyone has their breaking point.

'Taki, that is a revolting thing to say. Don't you know that girls are destroyed by their fathers saying things like that to them?'

'Well, I wouldn't say it to her. No, actually I do. I say: 'You're wasting away, darling.' And she laughs. She's always screaming at me about how fat and hairy I am. We're very close … Oh, shut up Zoe Heller, I don't want to talk about my children because I love them, and I don't want to sound warm and nice and compassionate and all that bullshit.' Aha. At last. A way to wind Taki up. 'What do you mean, 'bullshit', Taki? Hey, you're just being honest. That's okay.'

'I don't want to be honest' he practically screams. 'I won't even open up to my wife – why should I open up to you? Spilling the beans is a cowardly thing to do. I think most people who spill the beans are lying anyway. This is my public face – a drunken, arrogant buffoon, who shits on women and blacks – that's what I show and all I care to show. It's like Barbara Walters (the presenter of an interview programme on American television) who asks questions like: 'If you were a tree, what kind of tree would you be?' You want to say: 'A tree that was shoved up your arse, you dumb bitch …'

Taki giggles into his collar for a bit and then shouts for his butler to bring us drinks. They come – a glass of water for me and a cup of tea for Taki – served on a silver salver. The butler, a young amiable Australian, seems vaguely embarrassed to be participating in this archaic *Upstairs Downstairs* ritual. He wears the same expression of sheepish amusement that people have when they are pulled out of the audience at pantomimes and made to dance with Widow Twankey. But then, Taki is smirking slightly too – camping up the little emperor act for my benefit. 'At first,' he says, nodding at the butler's retreating back, 'he kept calling me Taki. Which is outrageous, really. I mean, I am many years older than he is. In Greece, when someone is older than you, even if he is the gardener, you show them respect. I spoke to him about this. Now he always calls me Mister Taki.'

The 'coming of age' story usually ends when the son overthrows the father, grabs the riches and then the girl. In this version we discover what happens afterwards.

Taki is all too aware that he is getting on in years. A couple of years ago he suffered a heart attack. Sometimes now, when he is out carousing, he gets frightening pains in his chest. He still chases women compulsively, he says, but 'more and more unsuccessfully … I am old. Fifty-six. Old.' And even as he feels his value on the sexual marketplace declining – 'I am not sure how many women would go with me now if I wasn't rich' – he finds himself more and more interested in the idea of … er, meaningful sex. 'I don't like prostitutes any more – well, sometimes when I'm drunk. But I find now that I'm randier with a girl if I'm emotionally involved.'

The vulnerabilities of age seem to make the buffoon mask more necessary than ever, the showy incorrectness more vital. His friends admire the fact that the old trouper is still trouping. 'Mortality is approaching now which makes him a more touching figure,' Charles Moore says. 'It makes his bad behaviour seem more gallant.'

'Can we go now?'

For the last half hour of our conversation, Taki has been itching to go outside and have a walk. At last I agree. Like a schoolboy released from detention, he leaps up, puts on his jacket and whisks me out into the bleak, autumn afternoon. We head for Knightsbridge.

This last passage, still equally restrained, is a beautifully observed moment that skewers her subject and shows him for just what he is – a pathetic, ageing man who is in the process of being overthrown by a new generation.

Taki races along the pavement, chattering away very loudly. Now and then he peers at me sideways. He is trying, he says, to determine which one of his ex-girlfriends I resemble. Every time we get to a road, he takes my arm with an elaborate flourish and shepherds me across. It is in the same spirit of chivalry that, when we say goodbye on the corner of Knightsbridge, he makes a rather obscene joke about the possibility of our sleeping together. This isn't a pass – it is Taki's idea of politeness, a formality that doesn't require or expect a response. But the boys who are stationed at the traffic lights cleaning car windscreens have overheard and are outraged. 'Dirty old man,' one of them comments. Taki doesn't hear. He is already trotting away, back up the street. Very soon, his trim little figure has been swallowed up by the crowd.

Later, speaking to Taki's wife on the phone, I ask her whether she thinks Taki's son, J.–T., will grow up to be like his father. She laughs uproariously. 'No, J.–T. won't follow in his footsteps,' she says. 'He couldn't. Women don't put up with behaviour like Taki's any more. Men like him are a dying breed.' She sighs. 'Taki,' she adds, a little sadly, 'is one of the last.'

© Zoe Heller

LANGDON WINNER (PROFILING DON VAN VLIET, AKA CAPTAIN BEEFHEART)

Langdon Winner wrote this piece, he told me, 'As a labour of love'. He was, he said, 'interviewing by day, sleeping nights under the grand piano at Van Vliet's house in Woodland Hills, California, during a period of history when anything seemed possible.'

I found this piece when searching for good music writing. As music writing, it is excellent. As a profile, it is flawed, but I included it because it is a portrait of a very particular moment in cultural history, a quality which seems to be missing from much of today's popular music press. It is entirely unlike the last two pieces. It was written before the publication of Tom Wolfe's *New Journalism* in 1975 and it has none of the literary quality of that writing. There is practically no description – apart from description of the music which is wonderful – but it is lively, well constructed and full of anecdote and testimony from friends and associates.

The odyssey of Captain Beefheart
Rolling Stone, 14 May 1970

'Uh oh, the phone,' Captain Beefheart mumbled as he placed his tarnished soprano saxophone in its case. 'I have to answer the telephone.' It was a very peculiar thing to say. The phone had not rung.

Beefheart walked quickly from his place by the upright piano across the dimly lit living room to where the telephone lay. He waited. After ten seconds of stony silence it finally rang. None of the half dozen or so persons in the room seemed at all surprised by what had just happened. In the world of Captain Beefheart, the extraordinary is the rule.

At age 29, Captain Beefheart, also known as Don Van Vliet, lives in seclusion and near poverty in a small house in the San Fernando Valley of Los Angeles. Although it appeared on several occasions in the past that he would rise to brilliant stardom as a singer and bandleader, circumstances have always intervened to force him into oblivion. In his six years in the music business he has appeared in public no more than 25 times.

Since virtually no one has ever seen him play, stories about his life and art have taken on the character of legend, that is, of endless tall tales. People who saw him at the Avalon Ballroom in San Francisco three years ago will now tell you, "I heard that he's living in Death Valley somewhere' or 'Didn't he just finally give up?' But there is considerably more to the man than the legend indicates.

The fact is that Don Van Vliet is alive, healthy, and happy, and putting together a new Magic Band to go on tour soon. As his recent album 'Trout Mask Replica' testifies, he is one of the most original and gifted creators of music in America today. If all goes well, the next six months should see the re-emergence of Captain Beefheart's erratic genius into the world and the acceptance of his work by the larger audience it has always deserved.

The crucial problem in Beefheart's career has been that few people have ever been able to accept him for what he is. His manager, musicians, fans, and critics listen to his incredible voice, his amazing lyrics, his chaotic harp and soprano sax, and uniformly decide that Beefheart could be great if he would only (1) sing more clearly and softly (2) go commercial, (3) play blues songs that people could understand and dance to. 'Don, you're potentially the greatest white blues singer of all time' his managers tell him, thinking that they are paying him a compliment. Record companies eagerly seek the Beefheart voice with its unprecedented four and one half octave range. They realize that the man can produce just about any sound he sets his mind to and that he interprets lyrics as well as any singer in the business. Urging him to abandon the Magic Band and to sing the blues with slick studio musicians, record producers have always been certain that Don Van Vliet was just a hype away from the big money.

> *The Beefheart philosophy is crucial to the trajectory of this story: here is a man who won't sell out to commerce. It is this that makes him a hero, this is the 'controlling idea' and here Winner expresses it via a quote which, by its very weirdness, helps to build up the character of the man.*

But Beefheart stubbornly continues what he's doing and waits patiently for everyone else to come around. He has steadfastly refused to leave the Magic Band or to abandon the integrity of his art. 'I realize,' he says, 'that somebody playing free music isn't as commercial as a hamburger stand. But is it because you can eat a hamburger and hold it in your hand and you can't do that with music? Is it too free to control?'

> *Now we have the classic story structure which, having established the character of the hero, moves back in time to paint in the background to his life.*

Beefheart's life as a musician began in the town of Lancaster nestled in the desert of Southern California. He had gone to high school there and become the friend of another notorious Lancasterian, Frank Zappa. In his late teens Don Van Vliet listened intensively to two kinds of music – Mississippi Delta blues and the avant-garde jazz of John Coltrane, Ornette Coleman and Cecil Taylor. Although he was attracted to music and played briefly with a rhythm and blues group called the Omens, he did not yet consider music his vocation. He enrolled at Antelop Valley Junior College in 1959 as an art major, and soon grew suspicious of books and dropped out. For a brief while he was employed as a commercial artist and as a manager of a chain of shoe stores. 'I built that chain into a thriving, growing concern,' he recalls, 'Then as a kind of art statement I quit right in the middle of Christmas rush leaving the whole thing in chaos.'

In the early Sixties Don Van Vliet moved to Cucamonga to be with Frank Zappa who was composing music and producing motion pictures. It was at about this time that Van Vliet and Zappa hatched up the name Captain Beefheart, 'But don't ask me why or how,' Beefheart comments today. The two made plans to form a rock and roll band called the Soots and to make a movie to be named 'Captain Beefheart Meets The Grunt People', but nothing ever came of either project. In time Zappa left for Los Angeles and formed the Mothers. Beefheart returned to Lancaster and gathered together a group of 'desert musicians.' In 1964 the Magic Band was ready to begin playing teenage dances in its home town.

The one stage appearance of the first Beefheart ensemble was bizarre to the point of frightening. All members of the Magic Band were dressed in black leather coats and pants with black high heel boots. The lead guitar player had a patch over one eye and long dangling arms that reached from his shoulders to half way below his knees. At a time that long hair was still a rarity, the Captain sported long dark locks down to his waist. It was simply outrageous.

The band was an immediate sensation in Lancaster and very soon its fame began to spread through southern California. Beefheart's brand of abrasive blues-rock was truly a novelty to young listeners in 1964. Record companies interested in the new sound began to take notice. In mid-1964 Beefheart entered into the first of a long series of disastrous agreements with record producers.

His first release on A&M was a new version of 'Diddy Wah Diddy' made popular by Bo Diddley. It featured his own style of frantic harp playing and an incredibly 'low down' voice hitting notes at least half an octave lower than the lowest notes ever sung by any other rock performer. The record was a hit in Los Angeles and for a while it appeared that Beefheart was going to be a brilliant success in the music business.

But it was not to be. Beefheart recorded an album of new music and took it to Jerry Moss of A&M (Alpert and Moss). Moss listened to the songs – 'Electricity,' 'Zig Zag Wanderer,' 'Autumn's Child,' etc. – and declared that they were all 'too negative.' He refused to release the album. Beefheart was crushed by this insensitivity and abruptly quit playing. A&M released the remaining single it had in the can. The words to 'Frying pan' now seemed strangely prophetic: 'Go down town / You walk around / A man comes up, says he's gonna put you down / You try to succeed to fulfil your need / Then a car hits you and people watch you bleed / Out of the frying pan into the fire / Anything you say they're gonna call you a liar.'

The record went nowhere and neither did Beefheart. For almost one year he lived in retirement back in Lancaster.

But our hero rallies and come back to fight again. In an almost throwaway paragraph Winner paints in the musical background, making clear his own intimate knowledge of the genre but without labouring the point.

The second break in Beefheart's career arrived in 1965 when producer Bob Krasnow of Kama Sutra agreed to release the same material that A&M had rejected. Beefheart reassembled the Magic Band and returned to record the twelve cuts of 'Safe As Milk' (Buddah BDS 5001), an album which is still one of the forgotten classics of rock and roll history. Even though the album had been delayed for a year, it was still far ahead of its time. It featured the unmistakable Beefheart style of blues and bottleneck guitar, the first use in popular music of an electronic device called the Theremin, and the first effective synthesis in America of rock and roll and Delta blues.

For the first time also, Beefheart was able to demonstrate the power and range of his voice. On one song, for example, Beefheart's vocal literally destroyed a $1200 Telefunken microphone. Hank Cicalo, engineer for the sessions, reports that on the song 'Electricity' Beefheart's voice simply wouldn't track at certain points. Although a number of microphones were employed, none of them could stand the Captain's wailing 'EEEE-Lec-Triccc-ittt-EEEEEEEE' on the last chorus. This, incidentally, can be heard on the record.

With an excellent album under his belt Beefheart felt confident enough to go on the road. In early 1966 he went on a tour of England and Europe where Safe As Milk had attracted considerable attention. When he returned to the States he played gigs at the Whiskey A-Go-Go in Los Angeles and the Family Dog in San Francisco. Well received in the burgeoning psychedelic rock scene, it seemed once again that Beefheart was on the verge of success. The Magic Band was scheduled to play a gig at the Fillmore and to appear at the Monterey Pop Festival, both of which could have been springboards to the top.

Note the way the piece is structured through optimistic ups and then sudden downs. With each downturn the rhythm of the writing changes: a short choppy sentence introduces the bad news.

Then disaster struck. Beefheart's lead guitar player suddenly quit the band leaving a gap which could not be filled. The unusual nature of Beefheart's songs make it necessary for him to spend months teaching each new musician his music. The departure of the lead guitar destroyed Beefheart's chances in the San Francisco scene. The Monterey Pop Festival went on without him. Those who attended it never knew what they had missed.

From this point in the story, events become even more chaotic and difficult to unravel. Beefheart returned to Los Angeles and tried to put together a new band and a new set of songs. His producer, Bob Krasnow, was to arrange the second Beefheart album on Buddah. According to sources in the Los Angeles record industry, Krasnow deliberately allowed the option on Beefheart's contract to expire. When this happened he signed Beefheart to a personal contract and then sold the rights to Beefheart's next album to both Buddah Records and MGM. Tapes of the album were then made at two different studios, apparently at the expense of both companies. When the sessions were finished in the summer of 1968 Beefheart left for a second tour of Europe.

In Beefheart's absence Bob Krasnow released the album 'Strictly Personal' under his own label, Blue Thumb, without Beefheart's approval. As lawsuits filled the air, Beefheart himself was left in bewilderment. The record had been electronically altered through a process called phasing which totally obliterated the sound which he had been striving to put down. 'That's the reason that album is as bad as it is,' he sighs when asked about the incident. 'I don't think it was the group's fault. They really played their ass off – as much as they had to play off.'

Again Winner accepts at face value the complaints that the music was tampered with (even though he cannot himself hear any problems with it) and that was why, in spite of all the early promise, Beefheart failed again.

But despite the electronic and legalistic hanky panky surrounding its production, 'Strictly Personal' is an excellent album. The guitars of the Magic Band mercilessly bend and stretch notes in a way that suggests that the world of music has wobbled clear off its axis. Beefheart's singing is again at full power. In songs like 'Trust Us' and 'Son of Mirror Man – Mere Man' it sounds as if all the joy and pain in the universe have found a single voice. Throughout the album the lyrics demonstrate Beefheart's ability to juxtapose delightful humor with frightening insights – 'Well they rolled around the corner / Turned up seven come eleven / That's my lucky number, Lord/ I feel like I'm in heaven.'

The unfortunate fact about the second album was that few people were able to get into it. Apparently, the combination of Beefheart's musical progress and Krasnow's electronic idiocy made the album too much for most listeners to take. 'Strictly Personal' sold poorly and did nothing to advance the band's popularity.

Having established his subject's credentials, the writer now feels able to stand back a little. Here we get a rather more nuanced exploration of Beefheart's behaviour.

To this day there exists a strange love/hate relationship between Beefheart and Krasnow over the record. Krasnow claims that Beefheart still owes him $113,000 and that as a result of Beefheart's disorganized way of handling money, he has been thrown in jail twice. Beefheart, on the other hand, usually cites Krasnow as a charlatan and pirate – the man most responsible for destroying his career. At other times, both men speak of each other with genuine respect, sympathy and affection. 'I'd really like to have him back with me,' Krasnow said recently. 'He's actually a good man,' Beefheart will tell you.

Most of the Captain's relationships with those close to him are of this sort. Everybody's a despicable villain one day, a marvellous hero the next.

The current focus of Beefheart's love/hate dialectic accounts for much of his current activity and inactivity. This time the prime protagonist is Frank Zappa.

Zappa has always had a great admiration for his old friend from Lancaster – an admiration often bordering on worship. Like so many of those around Beefheart, Zappa considers the man to be one of the few great geniuses of our time. When the smoke had cleared from the Blue Thumb snafu, Zappa came to Beefheart and told him that he would put out an album on his label, Straight Records. Whatever Beefheart wanted to do was O.K. and there would be no messing around with layers of electronic bullshit. The result was 'Trout Mask Replica', an album which this writer considers to be the most astounding and most important work of art ever to appear on a phonograph record.

When Beefheart learned of the opportunity to make an album totally without restrictions, he sat down at the piano and in eight and a half hours wrote all twenty-eight songs included on 'Trout Mask'. When I asked him jokingly why it took that long, he replied, 'Well, I'd never played the piano before and I had to figure out the fingering.'

This extraordinary quote was thrown away without explanation which does seem a shame. I want to know how come he has never played the piano before and why, if he hasn't, he chose to do so now? But Winner doesn't question his subject and, in a sense, that is part of the charm of this piece. Everything is taken at face value, we are not subjected to long explanations and analysis. What you see is what you get. This is how Captain Beefheart sees himself.

With a stack of cassettes going full time, Don banged out 'Frownland,' 'Dachau Blues,' 'Veterans' Day Poppy,' and all of the others complete with words. When he is creating, this is exactly how Don works – fast and furious. 'I don't spend a lot of time thinking. It just comes through me. I don't know how else to explain it.' In his box of cassettes there are probably dozens of albums of 'Trout Mask Replica' quality or better. The trouble is that once the compositions are down it takes him a long time to teach them to his musicians. In this case it took almost a year of rehearsal.

'Trout Mask Replica' is truly beyond comparison in the realm of contemporary music. While it has roots in avant-garde jazz and Delta blues, Beefheart has taken his music far beyond these influences. The distinctive glass finger guitar of Zoot Horn Rollo and steel appendage guitar of Antennae Jimmy Semens continues the style of guitar playing which he has been developing from the start. It is a strange cacophonous sound – fragmented, often irritating, but always natural, penetrating and true. Beefheart himself does not play the guitar, but he does teach each and every note to his players. The same holds true for the drums. Don does not play the drums but has always loved unusual rhythms and writes some of the most delightful drum breaks in all of music.

These next paragraphs are wonderfully evocative writing, a blend of knowledge and observation which, although it cannot help us to hear the music, takes us as close as possible. We feel we are there in the room with him and that it really matters that we should be there.

On 'Trout Mask Replica' Beefheart sings 20 or so of his different voices and blows a wild array of post-Ornette licks through his 'breather apparatus' – soprano saxophone, tenor saxophone and musette. When Beefheart inhales before taking a horn solo, all of the oxygen in the room seems to vanish into his lungs. Then he closes his eyes, blows out and lets his fingers dance and leap over the keys. The sound that bursts forth is a perfect compliment to his singing – free, unrefined and full of humor.

'Trout Mask' is the perfect blend of the lyrics, spirit and conception that had been growing in Don Van Vliet's mind for a decade. Although it is a masterpiece, it will probably be many years before American audiences catch up to the things that happen on this totally amazing record.

Here the structure changes again. The dispute between Beefheart and Zappa is not a simple case of man against the Establishment, here we get a flavour of his complexity. He may be a genius but he is pathologically unable to operate within social conventions, and Winner now presents us with a series of anecdotes about his hero which build on our knowledge of him as a character while at the same time taking us through the next plot twist as he finds success – and then lets it slip from his grasp.

For the first time in his career, Beefheart was entirely satisfied with his album. Zappa had made good his promise to give him the freedom he required and in fact issue the record in a pure and unaltered form. Nevertheless, the Beefheart/Zappa relationship is presently anything but an amicable one. Beefheart claims that Zappa is promoting 'Trout Mask Replica' in a tasteless manner. He does not appreciate being placed on the Bizarre–Straight roster of freaks next to Alice Cooper and the GTO's. He constantly complains that Straight Records' promotion campaign is doing him more harm than good.

Straight Records on the other hand claims that Beefheart's problems are all of his own making. He refuses to go on tour and procrastinates about making a follow-up album. 'What can we do?' a Straight P.R. man asked me. 'Beefheart is a genius, but a very difficult man to work with. All we can do is try to be as reasonable as possible.' Straight's brass recall that during the recording of the parts of 'Trout Mask' which were done in Beefheart's home, Don Van Vliet asked for a tree surgeon to be in residence. The trees around the house, he believed, might become frightened of the noise and fall over. Straight refused to hire the tree surgeon, but later received a bill for $250 for such services. After the sessions were over Beefheart hired his own tree doctor to give the oaks and cedars in his yard a thorough medical check up – his way of thanking them for not falling down.

In another classic story of this sort, Herb Cohen of Straight recalls that one day he noticed that Beefheart had ordered 20 sets of sleigh bells for a recording session. Cohen pointed out that even if Frank Zappa and the engineer were added to the bell ringing this would account for only 14 sleigh bells – one in each hand of the performers. 'What are you going to do with the other six?' he asked. 'We'll overdub them,' Beefheart replied.

> *The next few paragraphs could only have been written in the early 1970s, when total weirdness was seen as a badge of authenticity rather than signs of a nervous breakdown. The description of his peculiar relationship with his parents and the world is written without judgement and as such it stands as a metaphor for a particular way of living and thinking. Beefheart encapsulates the hippy dream of a life lived through creativity without recourse to such banal necessities as business plans and bank accounts. From this distance the writing seems naive and uncritical and yet it delivers an evocative sense of that time.*

The fact of the matter seems to be that precisely the same qualities of mind which make Beefheart such an astounding poet and composer are those which make it difficult for him to relate to Frank Zappa or anyone else in the orthodox music business. Like many notable creative spirits, Beefheart's personality is not geared to the efficient use of time or resources. For this reason and for the reason that he has often been burned by the industry,

Beefheart is very suspicious of those who try to influence the direction his career takes. To see why he has such continual trouble adjusting to the practicalities of his vocation, it will do well for us to look briefly at the incredible story of Beefheart's life before he became a musician.

Don Van Vliet was born in 1941 in Glendale, California, to normal middle-class parents. He grew up without problems as any child would in Glendale – until the age of five. It was then that he decided that civilized American life was a gigantic fraud. Don noticed that this society had established a destructive tyranny over nature; over all the animals and plants of Earth. He also became aware of the fact that America extended this tyranny over each man and that it was apparently out to include him in 'the great take over.' They wanted to teach him proper language, social rules, arithmetic and all of the other noxious techniques required to live in this country. Young Don suddenly rebelled and refused to go along.

Looking back on it now Beefheart recalls one day of enlightenment. 'My mother, who I called "Sue" rather than "mother" because that was her real name, was walking me along a path to school – the first day of kindergarten. We came to an intersection and she walked right out into the way of a speeding car. I reached up with both hands and pulled her out of the way. She could have killed us both. It was then that I thought to myself, "And she's taking me to school."' So Don did not attend school, at least not regularly. Instead he took up sculpting all the birds of the air, fish in the sea and animals on the land. Because he refused to come out for dinner, his parents were obliged to slide his meals under the bedroom door to him. It was Don's belief that he could re-establish ties to everything natural through the art of sculpture.

Soon he was good enough at what he was doing to attract the attention of professional Los Angeles artists. One day during a visit to the Griffith Park Zoo he met and befriended Augustino Rodriquez, the famous Portugese sculptor. Together they did a weekly television show in which Don would sculpt the images of nature's art while Mr. Rodriquez looked on.

Understandably, Don's parents were concerned about the unusual inclinations of their son. When at age thirteen he won a scholarship to study art in Europe, they took strong steps to discourage him. 'My parents told me all artists were queers,' Beefheart recalls. 'They moved me to the desert, first to Mojave and later to Lancaster.'

But even though Don's life as a sculptor had ended, he never gave up the vision of art and nature that he had discovered in life. Neither did he forsake the wonderfully unstructured consciousness with which he had been born. 'I think that everybody's perfect when they're a baby and I just never grew up. I'm not saying that I'm perfect, because I did grow up. But I'm still a baby.'

Beefheart still believes that in nature all creatures are equals. Man in his perversity forgets this and builds ridiculous hierarchies and artificial systems to set himself apart from his roots. 'People are just too far out. Do you know what I mean? Too far out – far away from nature.' He still sets out sugar for the ants, creatures that he considers most similar to man in their mode of life. 'If you give them sugar,' Beefheart contends 'they won't have to eat the poison.'

In songs like 'Wild Life,' 'My Human Gets Me Blues,' and 'Ant Man Bee' Beefheart presents with great subtlety the truths which students of ecology are just now beginning to recognize. 'Now the bee takes his honey / Then he sets the flower free / But in God's garden only man 'n the ants / They won't let each other be.' It is entirely possible that it is in this area that Beefheart will eventually attract a wide audience. If those who are delving into ecology would listen carefully to 'Trout Mask Replica', they could advance their understanding by leaps and bounds. Beefheart lived these crucial lessons from his very first days.

Another definite carryover from Beefheart's unusual childhood can be seen in the marvelous quality of his lyrics and poems. Since young Don Van Vliet decided that civilization was a trap, he refused to use civilized English in a linear, logical way and learned the entire language as a vast and amusing game. As a result, virtually everything that he says or writes turns out to be poetry. In a conversation with Beefheart the entire structure of verbal communication explodes. A barrage of puns, rhymes, illogicalities, absurd definitions, and unending word play fills the dialogue with a wonderful confusion.

All of this wonderment, of course, comes through very clearly in Beefheart's lyrics. In 'My Human Gets Me Blues,' for example, the Captain sings, 'I saw yuh dancin' in your x-ray gingham dress I knew you were under duress/I knew you under your dress.' One way of getting into songs like this is to understand that Beefheart is primarily fascinated with the sounds of words and their many ambiguities rather than the explicit meaning of terms. He believes that all truth comes from playing rather than from planning. Playing is what children do, what lovers do and what musicians and poets ought to do if they could escape the chains of structure and see the light. In both his music and his lyrics Beefheart is constantly engaged in an ongoing process of play. Behind the onslaught of words stand certain insights that Beefheart wishes to communicate.

The secret is, however, that they can be communicated only after the listener surrenders his neurotic reliance on words and established forms. 'I'm trying to create my own language,' Beefheart observes, 'a language without any periods.'

In his discouragement with the music business Beefheart has now turned much of his energy to writing as an outlet for his creative demon. The closets of his house are strewn with thousands upon thousands of poems and at least five unpublished novels. The song 'Old Fart at Play' from 'Trout Mask Replica' is a tiny excerpt from a long novel of the same name which Beefheart hopes to publish soon.

The formlessness and intensity of Beefheart's music have often led people to conclude that he is merely another product of the drug culture. Sadly, much of the promotion material on him in past years has implied that he is the king of the drug heads and hip freaks. Nothing could be further from the truth. Don Van Vliet does not use drugs and does not allow members of the Magic Band to do so either. Like his friend Frank Zappa, Beefheart admonishes everyone to stay away from LSD, speed and marijuana. The reason for this is not only that he believes that drugs have harmful and irreversible effects, but also that each person has the power to get 'there' all by himself.

In my conversation with the man, Beefheart would often smile broadly and tilt his head far back on his neck and say, 'You know, I'm not even here. I just stick around for my friends.' Moving his hand up and out from his temple and wiggling his fingers (the Beefheart 'Far Out' sign) he would then say, 'You not even here either. You know that. Don't kid yourself. You just stick around for your friends too.'

Like Socrates, Beefheart believes that everyone knows everything he needs to know already. What he tries to do is to make them realize this. Most people, he reports, fight it every inch of the way. They refuse to be free even when they see what it's like. 'They just have too much at stake.'

At this point I start to long for a short suspension of the breathless enthusiasm. These days Winner is an academic specialising in 'the politics of technology'. I can only hope that this next paragraph was written ironically!

The absolutely boundless character of Beefheart's mind has taken him into investigations of extra-sensory perception, clairvoyance and even reincarnation. In addition to his ability to answer the phone before it rings, Beefheart is apparently able to foretell parts of the future. On all of my visits to his house in the San Fernando Valley, Beefheart told me he knew in advance that I was coming. On one occasion he was able to prove it to me by showing that he'd put on 'The Florsheim Shoe' and bright red socks that we had joked about on my earlier visit. 'I wore them just for you, he said, holding out his foot. Beefheart also maintains that he has led previous lives. At present he believes that he is a reincarnation of a man named Van Vliet who was a friend of Rembrandt's. 'Van Vliet was a tremendous painter who could never finish anything. Rembrandt used to write him letters saying: 'I am pretty good, but if you ever got it together ... wow!'

In order to pursue the possibilities of this previous existence, the Captain has recently begun painting again. Like everything else he does, his paintings are simply astounding. During one of our conversations he went to a two foot tall stack of poster paper and pulled out one of his recent works. Holding it under his chin and peering over it at me, Beefheart asked, 'Well, what do you see?" I stared into the spots and blobs of yellow, green and red and had to confess that the painting said nothing to me. With that Beefheart reached around and pointed to a small object in the middle of his masterpiece. 'See the little finger with the decal ring?' He asked. I looked carefully. Sure enough, there in the midst of the chaos: a little finger with a decal ring! 'Is that what it's about?' 'It sure is,' he replied.

What, then, of the future of Captain Beefheart? What are the chances that he will leave his self-imposed house arrest and begin to spread his music and magic more widely into the world?

At present the Captain stands at a crucial turning point. On the face of it everything seems to be in his favor. His new Magic Band is probably the best he's ever had and may be one of the best in the country. He has recently added drummer Art Tripp, formerly of the Mothers of Invention, who provides exactly the right blend of rhythmic novelty and imagination to the groups' sound. Zoot Horn Rollo and Rockette Morton, musicians that Beefheart taught from scratch, have reached musical maturity and are eager to get out before the public. Both of them are remarkably talented and love the music they play with an unwavering passion. The captain himself is clearly at the peak of his creativity in terms of both composition and performance. His new songs in rehearsal – 'Woe Is A Me Bop', 'Alice in Blunderland' and others – are even better than the tunes on 'Trout Mask Replica'. I have heard the new Magic Band play this music in the shelter of Beefheart's living room and, believe me, it's simply incredible.

Beyond this, Beefheart now has around him a group of associates that he should be able to trust. His new manager, Grant Gibbs, is both honest and thoroughly sensitive to the special needs and foibles of his artist. Previously an unbiased observer of Beefheart's career, Mr. Gibbs is now trying to untangle the web of contractual knots which the Magic Band had stumbled into over the years. Although Beefheart thinks otherwise, Straight Records is probably giving him as good and forthright a deal as he'd find anywhere in the business and there's no dearth of opportunities either. Beefheart is very much in demand both in the United States and in Europe. Offers for a tour of England and the continent have come from five different agencies in recent weeks. He could also do well touring college campuses and jazz and pop festivals in America. All Don has to do is say yes.

As we near the end of the piece it looks as if the transformation will fail to materialise and that we will be left with a tragedy: a man brought down by his own delusions.

At the point of decision, Captain Beefheart wavers erratically. He hires and fires musicians with great abandon and then says that the group is not yet ready. He also creates imaginary enemies in his mind and then spends his days trying to figure out ways to fight them off. During the writing of this article, for example, Van Vliet became convinced that I was public enemy number one. For days he brooded about the crimes that I was supposedly committing against him. ... What Beefheart cannot seem to understand is that he has nothing like the number of foes he thinks he has. There are literally dozens of people who would do anything to enable him to perform on stage again. All those who may have had evil designs on him have long since retired in frustration.

But this is America in the 1970s and we are provided with a happily ever after, Hollywood ending, in which the man is saved from the abyss by the love of a good woman who suddenly pops up from behind the curtain. Where has she been all this time?

Fortunately, it appears that Beefheart is regaining the necessary confidence in himself and his surroundings. He has recently married a lovely girl named Jan who is a constant companion in the wild and delightful realm of Beefheartism imagination. He has also made tentative preparations for a tour and a new album. All of it hangs on choices that he will make in the next several weeks.

But who knows? Perhaps 1970 will be the year that we finally catch a glimpse of the man behind the Trout Mask. Maybe this will be the year that all of us can experience the amazing wisdom and humor that Captain Beefheart has in his grasp. Clearly though, it's strictly up to him.

© Langdon Winner

Certainly this piece is flawed but, its weaving together of cultural history, personal anecdote and descriptive writing lifts it above the dreary hagiographies that comprise most music writing today. Above all it is written with unabashed enthusiasm and without intervention from PR minders.

8

ARTS, SPORTS AND MUSIC

TV CRITICISM: NANCY BANKS SMITH

I love Nancy Banks Smith: a mixture of the anarchic and the erudite, she writes about popular culture with rapt attention and a sly giggle. Checking her revues on the *Guardian* website, since 1999 I came across only one reference to Harold Pinter and 118 to *Coronation Street* (a popular soap opera). When she does focus on high culture she is constantly referencing the popular. Take this extract from a review of 18 January 1999.

> I would rather have relished Stephen Poliakoff's *Shooting The Past* (BBC2) than reviewed it. Talking brushes the bloom off, and this is such a plum of a play.
>
> A library of 10 million photographs is to be junked to make way for a business school. The collection has grown like a coral reef. Sometimes a few faces are fanned out before us like a winning hand of cards. Elizabeth Taylor, forever young; Marlene Dietrich, forever beautiful; Jean Harlow, whom her studio called 'the baby'. (They say that when the baby died nobody in the commissary spoke a word).
>
> If junking photographs seems a crass thing to do, you should see the tapes the BBC has wiped. Or, rather, you can't see them.
>
> *Shooting The Past* has a superb performance by Timothy Spall, as the sort of disconcerting eccentric you might find breaking a code. He looks as if he sleeps in his socks. He has – what else? – a photographic memory. (Nancy Banks Smith, *Guardian*, 18 January 1999)

Her reviews are like rows of pearls. Each item is separate and complete: snippets of show business gossip sitting side by side with quotes from the Classics, and all strung together to create a tightly crafted whole. They don't dazzle and glitter, they have warmth and weight: definitely the real thing. I couldn't choose one. I love them all. The one below was suggested by *Guardian* literary editor, Claire Armistead. Its unusual in that it only covers one event but it demonstrates the way in which Banks Smith weaves together visual metaphors and cultural references and always celebrates 'the popular' rather than the precious.

The funeral of Diana: trail of tears
Guardian (TV Review), 8 September 1997, page 12

'Cover her face.
Mine eyes dazzle.
She died young.'

The Duchess of Malfi

This quotation is a stunningly apt introduction. There was no need to mention the death of Diana, Princess of Wales. Only someone who had been in a coma would have been unaware of it.

For the first time I remember, television seemed a second best. I would have liked to be part of it, to take part in it. Be where a million people were moving together, being moved together.

Her key idea is, as always, the triumph of the ordinary, and it is 'the people' who are the protagonists of this 'transformation' story – written as a chronological account of the day. Note how people are represented first of all with flower metaphors.

You can't, for instance, throw flowers at a TV screen. I have thrown ping-pong balls at it but that is another story.

Flowers were a powerful symbol of the public sorrow. Diana, like Proserpina, kidnapped by death, left a trail of fallen flowers which could be followed.

She doesn't flaunt her knowledge, she shares it. You may not know that Proserpina is the Roman goddess of Springtime, but the analogy still works.

At Kensington Palace where, in a classically Freudian slip, David Dimbleby [a TV announcer] said 'The Queen's body has been lying all night', the bees were having a bonanza in the sudden herbaceous border.

Now Bank's Smith crashes in with one of her characteristic asides. It's as though she is having a chat around the kitchen table with her mates, but these digressions are tightly controlled and lead us back into the story.

Somewhere en route to St James' one brash, pink, proletarian carnation, thrown at the gun carriage, stuck among the magnificent wreath of lilies. You could hear them putting their heads together. 'Who is it? Don't talk to it, Muriel. You don't know where it's been.' Nothing abashed it or shook it off. Pink and perky, it was there as the six-foot guardsmen shouldered the lead coffin. It entered the Abbey without a by-your-leave. It left for Althorp in the hearse. For all I know, it is lying on the grave on the island in the lake. Somebody's thoroughly common or garden carnation.

As the hearse headed home surrounded – your skin prickled – by seven motor cyclists, showers of flowers were thrown like confetti. It soon began to wear a rackety hat like a battered Easter bonnet with all the flowers upon it. The driver, who seemed on the small side, was bouncing up and down trying to look over or peer through the flowers his windscreen wipers could not shift.

At Lord's [a cricket ground], young lads, who will give Australia a fright one day, flung gladdies with wicket-shattering accuracy. At the start of the M1, startled road workers had an impromptu bouquet laid at their feet as the hearse's windscreen was cleared. The whole day was impromptu. 'We've been caught by surprise by everything,' said ITN.

Where Have All The Flowers Gone? could be rewritten as Where Did They All Come From? They all came from the people. Even on the inhuman motorway flowers rained on, fell off, fell under the hearse. Arthur C Clarke, who ponders the mysteries of this and other worlds, might like to look into it.

This next paragraph contains four different stories, each one spinning off the last, and each evoking a different kind of emotion.

The horses that pulled the gun carriage had had flowers thrown at them all week – and that is something else I would have liked to see – to accustom them to a rose up the nose. They advanced with muffled hooves like the surrey with the fringe on top bringing home a tired girl in Oklahoma. ('Hush, you team, my baby's a sleeping. Hush, you team, and just keep a-creeping with a slow clip clop.') Prince Harry's round wreath, stuffed with plump buds and with Mummy written on it, looked like a child's cake. Sixteen years ago, when Lady Diana and Prince Charles did their first television interview, she talked about being sent small iced cakes from children. 'Covered with Smarties,' she said and laughed, being too young then, too young always, to know that one doesn't mention brand names.

Thinking themselves unobserved in the darkness of an arch, Earl Spencer patted Harry's shoulder encouragingly. Prince Philip touched William and snatched his hand away as if stung. (It may be said, on behalf of old-style stoicism, that this walk was not easy for him either. He is 75 and arthritic.) There were four sudden bursts of applause from the congregation outside the Abbey. For Richard Branson, striding along on foot, waving cheerfully, wearing the tie no-one knew he possessed. For Pavarotti, leaning heavily on two stick-thin young women and wearing an expression no-one knew he possessed. For the Union Jack being lowered to half mast at Buckingham Palace. And for Earl Spencer, who has leaped onto the public stage with an exhilarating flash and bang.

After his speech (in which press and royals, to their mutual embarrassment, both got a piece of his mind), the crowd outside stood up and applauded with their hands above their heads. In the Abbey, Chris de Burgh, who had been giving a comradely thumbs-up to Elton John, heard the sound coming in the west door like a wave and rushing up the nave to the coffin. 'It made,' he said 'your hair stand on end.' Unless, of course, you were Elton John.

Even at this moment she cannot quite resist a quip – at the expense of hairless Elton John.

People had been extremely quiet, all the reporters remarked on it. When they raised their voice, it raised your hair. There's a story in the Bible about Paul trying to preach in Ephesus but the Ephesians already had their own goddess. 'And all with one voice about the space of two hours cried out "Great is Diana of the Ephesians".' And Paul gave up and got out.

© The Guardian

And so she returns to her thesis: this was the moment when the people won the day. Having started with poignancy of the Duchess of Malfi, she ends with a triumphant quote from the Bible and they both seem to fit perfectly alongside the supermarket carnation which may, who knows, have been lying on Diana's grave.

SPORTS: SIMON BARNES

I cannot pretend to be an avid reader of sports reports. Simon Barnes, Chief Sports Writer of *The Times*, was on a shortlist drawn up by some of my students of the people who they regard as the greatest. In sports, the writing is at its best when the writer is allowed to be completely partisan. Covering an international game is the point at which any thought of neutrality goes out the window (usually along with any restraint in the use of superlatives). Using wordplay, puns and war metaphors, sports reporters seem to be trying to make up with words what their subject lacks in depth or subtlety.

The narrative here is a 'transformation' and the form is a simple story. There wasn't much to say: the heroes, Liverpool, nearly lost the game in the first minute and then went on to win in the second half. Making up for a paucity of information, Barnes simply repeats the story, four times. I read a number of reports of this event and this one topped them all for its sheer exuberance.

Gone in 50 seconds, back in six minutes
The Times, 26 May 2005

FOOTBALL. Bloody hell, the printable expletives are utterly inadequate for the task of summing up a night of football mayhem. Bring out the asterisks: it was a night when football brought us the utterly impossible on a night of perfect insanity as Liverpool won the European Cup final on penalties after doing their best to lose it.

> *A simple summary introduction that tells us what happened and raises our curiosity as to how it happened. We have to assume that nobody reading the paper that day would need to have been told that the OTHER team was the Italian club Milan. After that we have an explanation of the events: not once but three times with increasing detail in each.*

Liverpool produced one of the greatest comebacks in the history of football. They created for themselves an utter disaster and somehow rose to find hope, and with it, power and effectiveness and purpose and direction. They turned a lost match around in six impossible minutes: one of those periods of total enchantment that happen in football, but very rarely.

> *Now we have a slightly fuller version.*

Yet it seemed that they had managed to lose everything in less than a minute. After a season of ever-growing hope and burgeoning expectation,

Liverpool looked as if they had lost the lot in a matter of 50 seconds. They conceded a goal more or less before a Liverpool player had touched the ball and were 3–0 down at half-time. It was humiliation.

But before you could say 'Football. Bloody hell' they were back in it again. After being made to look like small-timers and second-raters, they came roaring back as if they were the old champions of the Eighties, the Liverpool side that expected to win European Cup finals as a matter of course. They drew level in that period of magic and took the game into extra time, a spooky period played in a mood close to emotional exhaustion.

Okay, this is clichéd, but it works like a football chant. Thousands of (mainly) men in stripy scarves, all yelling wildly and waving things is also clichéd as an image – but it happens every week.

The match proper finished at 3–3, but not before Jerzy Dudek had made a remarkable double save from Andriy Shevchenko that suggested the force was with the Pole. Then came the penalties and Dudek, a goalkeeper often and fairly criticised this season, saved two of them, enough for Liverpool to win the shoot-out 3–2.

Now the story unfolds again in more detail. Like Banks Smith, Barnes uses references to other events. Perhaps he hopes that he can count on his Times *readers to remember the most famous use of the slogan 'no passaran' by anti-fascists at the time of the Spanish Civil War in the 1930s. Certainly it is an apt metaphor for a team considered to be the plucky underdogs. Sadly it stops there. The anti-fascists lost that time.*

There was a Liverpool banner in the stadium that bore the legend *no passaran* – they shall not pass – a tribute to the startling and complete impregnability of the Liverpool defence over the previous three matches in this competition. Plan A was obvious, then: don't concede a goal and so the favourites will get worried and grow vulnerable.

As plans go, it had a lot going for it, but it was less than a minute before Liverpool were on to plan B. It is the nature of football that things can go very wrong very quickly. Liverpool were a goal behind while still wondering what the opening ceremony was all about.

The goal was simplicity itself. A foul: Djimi Traoré on Kaká. A free kick, and Andrea Pirlo swung it in. Paolo Maldini was supposed to be a weak link at 36, but his legs had not got tired in three quarters of a minute. He hit a spirited right-foot volley and topped the ball rather than met it sweetly.

As so often happens in such circumstances, it crashed into the ground and rose steeply in a fashion that was hard to read. And on this occasion it found the net and Liverpool's day was ruined before it had rightly started. The Liverpool supporters had out-sung the Milanese before the start: their silence was shocking. It reflected a feeling of deep dismay and it reflected perfectly the dismay of the Liverpool players.

So much for Rafael Benítez, the Liverpool manager, and his sudden recognition as a tactical genius. You can't fault him for effort, but he was presiding over a disaster at half-time and his ploy of putting Harry Kewell in his starting line-up looked like an act of folly.

They shall not pass, indeed. Liverpool hardly passed at all in the first half. Liverpool had come with a reputation for outstanding defence, Milan showed that the traditional continental virtues of tight, intelligent passing are worth a mention. Shevchenko, in a moment of gliding wit and invention, set up Hernán Crespo for a tap-in, then Kaká pushed through a sweetly timed pass. This one required a bit more of a finish. Crespo provided it and in the process made Liverpool look like a team playing a little way out of their class.

Then the tide turned in a manner that defied logical and even tactical sense. It was simply as if God had changed sides. The force, long absent, was suddenly with Liverpool. Steven Gerrard was the man who started it with a looping header from a cross by John Arne Riise. Then it was Vladimir Smicer, who had come on as a 23rd-minute substitute for the hapless Kewell. He reduced the deficit to one with the goal that threw Milan into a state of confusion.

So much so that they promptly conceded a penalty and Xabi Alonso put that one away on the rebound. Three goals within six minutes: rout had become fightback and fightback had become epic.

© The Times

MUSIC: SASHA FRERE-JONES

What is happening to the music press? It seems increasingly to be written for those who are totally uncritical fans and yet it is at the same time strangely disengaged. Popular music is about youth and passion and I looked everywhere for the kind of writing that leaps off the page and engages its readers. Leafing through the pages of old copies of *Rolling Stone* I found much to engage me. It didn't confine itself to music but took music as a place from which to reach out and engage its readers with discussions of contemporary life and politics.

Langdon Winner, writer of the piece about Captain Beefheart in the profiles section of this book, told me: 'The music business redefined rock writing and put out the flame. I quit and went back to the university as pressures from the biz took over in the early 1970s'. I asked what he thinks of rock journalism these days: 'I can't suggest anything that I find especially interesting in rock criticism these days. Greil Marcus is a master. Alas, Lester Bangs, really the best of them all, tragically left the planet long ago.'

I don't share his passion for Bangs. Although his writing is certainly exuberant, it feels too noisy to me (Bangs by name ...). Marcus is indeed a master and well worth looking at if music journalism is where your heart lies. What I was looking for here was a writer who could bring music to a new audience. Someone who enthuses but also engages. I found it in the shape of Sasha Frere-Jones, ironically writing in the *New Yorker*.

1979: the year punk died, and was reborn
New Yorker, 1 November 2004

In 1979, The Clash were experiencing some pressure. Whether they wanted it or not, punk rock had become their responsibility. In New York, the Ramones had come up with the musical idea of reducing rock to three chords, doubling the volume, and accelerating songs until they sounded like Morse code. In London, the Sex Pistols had turned disgust into an ideology and made punk a historical moment, inspiring teenagers across England to start bands. But by March of 1979 the Ramones had become more interested in being themselves than in changing the world, the Sex Pistols disbanded and The Clash, feeling burned out, had fired the manager who helped put the band together, in 1976. Yet they still owed CBS a record.

This is a summary introduction. The New Yorker *readership are of an age to be comfortable with a piece starting 'In 1979', which ought to be, but somehow isn't, a complete turn-off. The paragraph uses the rhetorical device of a list of three things (twice) and then drops in the inciting incident in at the end, as the rhythmic reply.*

The Clash were able to fit more music and faith through the keyhole of punk than anyone else. Their debut album, 'The Clash,' was a brick in flight, fourteen songs, half of them under two minutes long. The lyrics talk about the riots the band members want to start, American imperialism they want to stop, and England's general lack of 'career opportunities.' It is an act of political resistance and pure pleasure. Their second album, 'Give 'Em Enough

Rope,' was criticized for having an allegedly American sheen, but you'd have trouble hearing that now. The music is hard and echoey, barking but sweetly melodic. Actually, no – the hierarchy is more specific than that. Someone is singing sweetly way in the back, behind the loud guitars, and there's a very loud singer in the front who sounds like he's going to die if he doesn't get to sing right now. The one in the back is Mick Jones, the guitarist, who wrote most of The Clash's music, and the one in the front is Joe Strummer, who wrote and sang most of the lyrics, if singing is the right word. Strummer delivered words as if there were no such things as amplification and he would have been willing to run around town singing through a tube if he had to.

> *This is the backgrounder but it is so much more than that. When Ian Katz of the* Guardian *said that he looks in a writer for 'lines I want to cut out and keep', I think he would have included the first three lines of the last paragraph. They are perfectly crafted, the metaphors are fresh, original and absolutely on target. And he really knows the music.*

Strummer's moral authority, coupled with Jones's ability to synthesize decades of rock music without seeming too clever, made people care about The Clash, personally, intensely, and totally. When the band, not yet a year old, signed with CBS in 1977, the London fanzine writer Mark Perry said, 'Punk died the day The Clash signed to CBS.' Perry was only taking the band as seriously as they took themselves. Strummer, especially, believed that punk should be available to all, and felt inherently hostile to authority. Paradoxically, it was the corporate paymaster CBS that eventually ran ads for The Clash with the tagline 'The only band that matters.' In March of 1979, everyone, including The Clash, knew that the hype might be more than hype. But how could a rock band possibly live up those expectations?

> *This is when we realise that he is himself a musician, with this call and response link between two paragraphs.*

By releasing 'London Calling,' sixty-five minutes of rock music that never goes wrong. Without self-importance, the music covers huge amounts of ground. The stories hang together with the weight of commandments and the serendipitous grace of a pile of empty bottles. Montgomery Clift becomes a folk hero ('The Right Profile'), the myth of Stagger Lee is resurrected for a new audience ('Wrong 'Em Boyo'), and London burns. Nothing sounds forced or insincere, not the breezy cover of an obscure English rockabilly song ('Brand New Cadillac') or fantasies of being a Jamaican bad boy ('Revolution Rock'). Hyperbole itself cannot diminish this record. Each of us is invincible when it's playing.

Note the rhythm of this last paragraph – how it rises and falls and sweeps the reader
along. It never falters, or snags.

Now reissued as a boxed set, 'London Calling' comes with a bonus CD of rehearsals and a DVD documentary about the making of the album and original promo clips. This generosity would have pleased Strummer, who died in 2002, but he would have been less thrilled that the set lists for $29.98. When the album was originally released, as a two-LP set, the band felt that records had to be priced for punks and insisted that CBS sell it for $9.98.

Here at last is the hook, so banal that it is hidden in the middle, just an excuse to write
about a band he loves. He then goes on to describe first the DVD and then the music.
But he doesn't avoid the politics. He knows what drove The Clash.

The documentary and the rough rehearsal demos make the same point: The Clash worked fiendishly hard to be magical. In an on-camera interview, Strummer say, 'For some reason, we weren't night-clubbing people. All I can remember is writing and rehearsing and recording. A real intensity of effort.'

The rehearsals are evidence that the songs on 'London Calling' were almost entirely worked out before the records producer, Guy Stevens, was even hired. The only remaining task was to record the music. How Stevens, who died of an overdose of an anti-alcohol medication two years later, helped to do this is unclear; thanks to this DVD, history will remember him as the guy who threw chairs and swung ladders about while The Clash recorded.

On 'London Calling,' Strummer remakes his major points: the police are on the wrong side, wage labor will crush your soul, and sometimes people need to destroy property to be heard. His sense of righteousness is enhanced by the album's sequencing, which feels Biblically logical and begins with one of the best songs of any record ever, the title track. The songs starts cold. Two guitar chords ring on the downbeats, locked in step with the drums, marching forward with no dynamic variation. A second guitar introduces difference, coming toward us like an ambulance Dopplering into range. The bass guitar, sounding like someone's voice, heralds everybody over the hill and into the song. If you can listen to it without getting a chilly burst of immortality, there is a layer between you and the world. Joe Strummer simultaneously watches the riots and sloughs off his role as de-facto punk president: 'London calling, now don't look at us / All that phoney Beatlemania has bitten the dust / London calling, see we ain't got no swing / 'Cept for the ring of that truncheon thing.' The chorus forms a keystone for the whole album: 'A nuclear error, but I have no fear? London is drowning and I, I live by the river.' The clash are laughing at Margaret Thatcher and will be dancing long after the police have come and gone.

In the next paragraph we are treated to an analysis of the music itself. It is knowledge-able, beautifully written and completely accessible.

And what can you call this generous mountain of music, this sound that levitates around its own grievances like a plane on fire? Is it chopped-up rock? Very loud reggae? Some kind of devotional punk? The sensation of hearing several kinds of music at once runs through the album. Reggae is a force that permeates much of it, both as a source of topical song writing and as a sound, but nothing on the album is strictly reggae. A song like the massive 'Clampdown' shifts naturally through three sections: the four huge, descending chords big enough to open a season at Bayreuth; the dancing, pendulous rock of the verses; and the taunting funk of the bridge. The song fades away in a vamp that sounds like disco, so light you might get the impression the band had forgotten everything they'd just sung about: insti-tutional racism, political brainwashing, and the creeping compromise of working life. 'You start wearing the blue and brown / You're working for the clampdown / So you got someone to boss around / It makes you feel big now.' The hectoring is never so simple that you don't wonder if they're directing it partly at themselves.

The album's soul might be found in 'Guns of Brixton,' by the group's bassist, Paul Simonon. It's reggae thickened up and filtered by musicians who don't exactly know how to play reggae but love it completely. Their heavy hands make it something new. Simonon is a croaky and untrained singer, and this only enhances his convictions: 'When they kick at your front door / How you gonna come? / With your hands on your head / Or on the trigger of your gun?' Threatening your rivals and writing scatological lyrics is one way to be 'controversial.' Staring down the riot police is another.

And now we find out what the controlling idea is. Punk is dead: long live punk.

If Strummer's instincts were not his alone, then somewhere right now a kid is throwing a fancy, overpriced package of twenty-five-year-old material across the room and pledging to reinvent punk rock once and for all, doubting her heroes while carrying their astonishing music in her whole body.

© Sasha Frere Jones

9

PERSONAL AND COMMENT COLUMNS

Newspapers and magazines are increasingly filled with personal columns. For many journalism lecturers, personal pieces are not really journalism. For most editors, they are the beating heart of a features section. Readers love them. They draw people to the page like no other form. They attract huge post-bags of letters. They provide a sense of intimacy that most people only get from talking to their closest friends. The subject of such pieces may be moving, gripping or just funny. Sometimes they do nothing but help us pass the time, allow us to chuckle as we sit on the bus, or grab a coffee in a break from work. Sometimes they help us to deal with our own worries, or deeply submerged fears, by providing a point of identification.

More serious personal columns, usually placed in the middle pages of the newspapers, are called comment columns and they are there to provide, and stimulate, political debate. These spaces probably come closer than anything else to replicating what Habermas described when he discussed the coffee shops of eighteenth-century England in his essay 'The Public Sphere' (Habermas, 1989). They are not open to public participation in the way that the letters pages are: they are more like a membership club than a public house, and they are clearly partisan, but their role, in advising, and holding politicians to account, is an important one. Other comment pieces have a more light-hearted purpose. They are also advisory in a sense, but they are addressing, not politicians but citizens. Their debates are about who we are and the way we live our lives.

GARY YOUNGE Gary Younge is one of the most thoughtful columnists around. He writes with a serious clarity. No cheap laughs here. Every sentence is weighed and considered. You feel that he is mulling things over in front of you. These arguments are real, live and happening now. They haven't been passed down in a textbook. Regular readers of the *Guardian* will know that Younge is black, which gives this piece an additional resonance.

Terms of abuse
Guardian, Monday 25 February 2002

About every three months I am accused of being an anti-semite. It is not difficult to predict when it will happen. A single, critical mention of Israel's treatment of Palestinians will do it, as will an article that does not portray Louis Farrakhan as Satan's representative on earth. Of the many and varied responses I get to my work – that it is anti-white (insane), anti-American (inane) and anti-Welsh (intriguing) – anti-semitism is one charge that I take more seriously than most.

> A 'one-liner' introduction, a tough clear statement that carries with it a wealth of deeply held prejudice – and then he turns it on its head. It is written in essay style, each argument is opened up, discussed and disposed of before the debate moves on. The controlling idea is raised in that last line, but only made clear at the end of the piece.

This is not because I believe I consciously espouse anti-semitic views, but because I do not consider myself immune to them. There is no reason why I should not be prone to a centuries-old virus that is deeply rooted in western society. That does not mean that I accept the charges uncritically. I judge them on their merits and so far have found them wanting. But I do not summarily dismiss them either; to become desensitised to the accusation would be to become insensitive to the issue. It is a common view on the left that political will alone can insulate you from prejudice. It stems, among some, from a mixture of optimism and arrogance which aspires to elevate oneself above the society one is trying to transform.

> Younge is always sparing in his use of the first person. On this occasion his own experience is the jumping-off point for the piece but he moves quickly into a debate on the issues. He may have a particular position but the debate belongs to everyone.

Last month's *New Statesman* front page of a shimmering golden Star of David impaling a union flag, with the words 'A kosher conspiracy?' was a case in point. Some put it down to an editorial lapse of judgment. But many Jews saw it not as an aberration but part of a trend – one more broadside in an attack on Jews, not from the hard right but the liberal left. The *New Statesman's* editor apologised, but the response of some progressives has been defensive and confused, because they fail to see that the more they accommodate, excuse or ignore anti-semitism, the less they are qualified to preach about Israel.

Anti-semitism existed long before Israel did and played the decisive role in winning over the vast majority of Jews to the Zionist cause. But Judaism is not Israel. And while it is difficult, in the current climate, to understand the Jewish community's concerns without reference to Israel, it is vital not to confuse the two. To do so opens the door for both anti-semites and apologists for Israeli aggression in the Middle East.

'Signs of leftist and Islamist anti-semitism are rife in Britain these days and Jews are worried,' claimed an article in Israel's most leftwing mainstream newspaper, *Ha'aretz*, a few weeks ago. Sadly, the facts which might verify these claims were, for the most part, lacking. Research conducted by the Community Security Trust, an organisation which aims to provide advice and security for British Jews, showed a 'sharp increase' in anti-semitic attacks over the past four years. But the groups which are by far the most vulnerable to racist attack remain Pakistanis and Bangladeshis, who are overwhelmingly Muslim.

Since there is no suggestion that the left is responsible for these anti-semitic attacks, the evidence of an anti-semitic revival among its numbers remains anecdotal. The British left has a strong record of fighting anti-semitism, but there can be little doubt that today anti-semitism does find a specific expression among the left. Believing that wealth disqualifies Jews from being among the oppressed, leftwingers fail to take anti-semitism as seriously as other forms of discrimination. Based on the stereotype of 'the wealthy Jew', such a view is not just insulting but ignores the nature and history of anti-semitism and the considerable pockets of poverty within the Jewish community. Moreover, Jews on the left complain of feeling themselves under suspicion for their private attachment to Israel, and their presumed support for all that it does.

Such presumptions and prejudices are morally wrong. And because they are wrong in principle they remain a liability in politics. In the same way that the racism and historical amnesia of the right weaken its arguments against Robert Mugabe and Zimbabwe, every example of anti-semitism devalues whatever opinions are given about Israel's role in the Middle East. It does not invalidate the arguments – Mugabe is a despot and Israel's occupation an outrage – but the question mark hanging over the motivation of the proponent inevitably taints the pronouncement.

The conflation of Judaism and Israel – as though they are interchangeable – prompts a spiral of mutual recrimination. Israeli hawks and Zionist hard-liners brand any criticism of Israel anti-semitic, regardless of its merits. Their accusations become so frequent that the term becomes devalued. Then Israel's detractors dismiss every allegation of anti-semitism, regardless of its merits, as a cynical attempt to stifle legitimate dissent. And so it goes on, until what should be a complex debate descends into polarised positions – 'Zionism is racism' on the one hand, 'anti-Zionism is anti-semitism' on the other.

Zionism is a political position, not a genetic given. It did not always command majority support among Jews. The minority of Jews who are anti-Zionist today might be accused of being psychologically unstable 'self-haters', but the Board of Deputies of British Jews did not have a Zionist majority until 1939. Nor has Zionism ever held a monopoly on Jewish thought here. According to a poll by the Institute for Jewish Policy Research, about 20% of British Jews surveyed in 1995 said they had negative feelings towards Israel (3%) or none at all (16%). But Israel nonetheless commands the affection of the vast majority of Jews in Britain.

That doesn't mean that gentiles have to support Zionism or Israel just because most Jews do. But it does mean that they cannot simply dismiss Zionism if they are at all interested in entering into any meaningful dialogue with the Jewish community. And it means that they have to be sensitive to why Jews support Israel in order to influence their views. To deny this is to maintain that it is irrelevant what Jews think. It is to move to a political place where Jews do not matter – a direction which they will understandably not follow, because they were herded there before and almost extinguished as a people. To declare 'Zionism is racism' offers little in terms of understanding racism, anti-semitism or the Middle East. It is not a route map to debate, liberation or resistance but a cul-de-sac.

The same can be said for its opposite: 'Anti-Zionism is anti-semitism'. Anti-Zionism, up to and including opposition to the existence of the state of Israel, is a legitimate political position, with roots in the Jewish and non-Jewish communities. That does not mean that Jews have to support it. But to equate it with bigotry is unsustainable. 'It is easy to forget that Zionism and the possibility of a sovereign Jewish state were once deeply divisive issues in Jewish life in this country,' according to a 1997 Institute of Jewish Policy Research document on the attachment of British Jews to Israel.

Such engagement will not be easy, for the semantic differences reflect fundamental disagreements. But if it cannot be achieved in Britain, what hope is there for the Middle East?

Guardian Unlimited © Guardian Newspapers Limited 2005

CATHERINE BENNETT

Catherine Bennett squats snappishly in the G2 section of the *Guardian* newspaper, firing at whatever foible of middle-class London life happens to irritate her most that week. I have to confess to having loathed her for years for her sneering appetite for demolition. Is it me who has changed or is it her? These days she seems to be part of what she is laughing at rather than a morally superior bystander. She is rueful rather than plain vicious and I think it works better. I laughed out loud the first time I read the piece below. It is written with a knowing sense of complicity with the largely London-living, left-leaning, readers of the *Guardian*.

Pay more, worry less? Not after Sudan 1
Guardian, 24, February 2005

Experts have already reassured us that, taken in microscopic doses, the prohibited food colouring Sudan 1 is quite harmless. Personally, having ingested quite a few microscopic particles of the boot polish dye, concealed inside Waitrose Thin and Crispy Cheese and Tomato Pizza, I must confess that I have never felt better. A bit on the lustrous yellow side, perhaps, but apart from that, tip-top. Others, who share my enthusiasm for Waitrose Perfectly Balanced Tuscan Bean Soup, report a similarly overwhelming sense of emergent health and general wellbeing. For us, these unwitting encounters with Sudan 1, that sovereign pick-you-uppo, have succeeded, as nothing has before, in firming our resolve to eat wholesomely, and, when that proves too challenging, to eat only the very cheapest of additive-laden convenience food, sourced, where possible, from the cheapest of supermarkets. Why pay more for your carcinogens?

Sudan 1 has also been a tremendous tonic for food writers, who have crowed – with complete justification – that it just proves what they have been saying for years. We only had to listen. Haven't they told us, over and over, to renounce the food industry and turn our backs on supermarkets, replacing unethical swill of dubious origin with bread from farmers' markets, dirty vegetables out of central casting, and meat from butchers whose cows all have a minimum of three As at A-level (excluding general studies)? But lazily, many of us have compromised, buying organic milk and meat, but reasoning, in an abject, Islingtonian way, that if we throw enough money at a shop that has a reputable ring to it and nice manners, there is no need to get too precious or puritanical. Isn't this local produce, farmers' market thing getting a bit Marie Antoinettish? What about the poor? And what harm can there be in, say, a small tin of Perfectly Balanced Tuscan Bean Soup from my local Waitrose? It has practically been on holiday with us.

> *The old Catherine Bennett would have settled for poking fun at people who only buy meat from 'clever cows'. The new one recognises, from the inside, the soup of guilt and compromise in which middle-class, left-leaning, parents swim. She then goes into a perfectly argued demolition of the kind of snobbery that mistakes good design and high prices for moral superiority. She locates this kind of thinking in Islington, a smart but slightly bohemian, area of London.*

Similarly, no matter what Jamie Oliver feeds his own superhuman, guaranteed sugar-and additive-free toddlers, can there be any reasonable objection to the occasional slice of Waitrose Thin and Crispy Cheese and Tomato Pizza? It is not as if it comes from Morrisons. It is thus that, alongside its chunks of pain Poilane, organic salmon and Neal's Yard baby products, the Islington Waitrose also manages to shift thousands of cod fish-fingers, out-of-season strawberries and towers of Thomas the Tank Engine Pasta Shapes (with added vitamins).

This form of perfectly balanced shopping is apt to instil such a false sense of security, or complacency, that it was some days before I thought of searching for Waitrose on the list of afflicted supermarkets. Its appearance, with a dismayingly large number of very familiar products, seemed condign punishment for a person who buys ready-made pizza and who is reassured by the appearance of any one of the following words on a tin: Tuscan, Waitrose, Perfectly, Balanced, Bean and Soup. Rather more chastening, however, was the appearance of four products from the Waitrose cute, healthy range of Food Explorers: 'good food for children'.

> *Having skewered the Islingtonian, Waitrose-shopping intelligentsia, herself among them, she then goes on to put the blame where it should really lie – with the food manufacturers who are so ready to exploit our guilt, laziness and snobbery.*

Food Explorers meals are aimed at parents trying to buy their way out of the guilt of not cooking all their children's food themselves. The meals have a dedicated website, featuring an enchanting floating balloon, teaching materials for schools ('discuss the attributes of the vegetables'), and this promise: 'The Food Explorers range: Contains no artificial sweeteners, flavourings or colours.'

As we know, this is not true. Batches of the Food Explorers Cottage Pie, Shepherd's Pie, Cheese and Tomato Pizza and Spaghetti Bolognese have all contained Sudan 1, courtesy of Crosse & Blackwell's adulterated Worcester sauce. At Waitrose customer services, a courteous person agrees that Food Explorers do promise not to contain things like Sudan 1 and, after consulting a food technologist, he explains that Waitrose could not have known about the Sudan 1 in the Worcester sauce, which was only discovered by chance testing by the FSA. This still leaves you wondering a) what else is in the meals that they could not possibly know about? and b) why is a strong seasoning, such as Worcester sauce, even in its additive-free incarnation, zinging up a range aimed at toddlers? What is this chilli-laced condiment doing in the babies' wee pizzas and junior portions of bolognese sauce? Softening them up for Bloody Marys? It means that the healthy, Food Explorers Shepherd's Pie, for example, is seasoned with salt four times over, once in the potato, once in its lamb sauce, once in the vegetable stock and once in the Worcester sauce. A course in nutrition might be more in order than a website telling teachers how to discuss the attributes of the vegetables.

But the people who put that great smugness-corrector, Sudan 1, in the chilli powder, join the ranks of the great food educators. There is, they have reminded us, no superior processed food, just processed food. And without them, I might never have discovered that the secret for a really authentic-tasting, perfectly balanced Tuscan bean soup, is a nice big dash of Worcester sauce. Someone ought to tell the River Cafe.

No drum-banging conclusion. It would have been quite unnecessary. More a rueful recognition of the controlling idea: those who advocate 'dirty vegetables out of central casting' may be right after all.

Guardian Unlimited © Guardian Newspapers Limited 2005

BORIS JOHNSON

Boris Johnson is probably best know in the UK as the blond, mop-headed Conservative member of parliament for Henley on Thames. He started his career as a journalist on *The Times* and *Daily Telegraph* and became editor of the right-wing political magazine *The Spectator* in 1999, resigning in 2005. Only *GQ* readers will know of his motoring column – there is no evidence that he has any particular expertise. As with everything else he does, Johnson uses this as a opportunity to talk politics. What he doesn't do is preach. He makes us laugh but underneath there is a message. The hook for this story is the launch of a new car.

Go forth and multiply
GQ, March 2004, page 174

Shall I tell you how you feel, when you bomb down the motorway in the Chrysler Grand Voyager Limited XS? You feel terrific. You feel a bit like a whale, but a sleek, porpoising whale, nosing aside the BMWs and the Ford Focuses as if they were minnows. You feel a bit like a Zeppelin, whooshing aloft, your eyeline higher than everyone else's. But the main reason you feel terrific is that you feel fertile.

> Straight to the point, Johnson will never lose an opportunity to poke fun at 'liberals'. This article is clearly aimed partly at annoying anyone with a concern for the planet, partly at lampooning the pretensions of MPV owners but the controlling idea – is a concern about population decline and the pensions' crisis.

Whatever else the Chrysler Voyager says about you, this car tells the world that you are not firing blanks. You don't need one of those irritating yellow Lib Dem-type signs saying, 'Baby on board'.

The Chrysler Voyager is a mobile advertisement for the fact that you have been repeatedly engaged in the noble business of reproducing the human race.

> Jokes about sex, and an ease with sexual slang are de rigueur for GQ. It sets out to create a blokey intimacy from which women are excluded. Boris manages also to poke fun at the genre he is working in.

Many a car is designed to make the driver look sexy. Every year there are dozens of sleek models constructed as if to proclaim that there is a 'Bonker on board'. If you drive the Chrysler Voyager, with its seven seats and 14 (count 'em! 14!) cupholders, the world rather gathers that you have been bonking for Britain. Let us imagine that you bought a Voyager without first acquiring some kids to fill it.

I am not saying that would necessarily be a foolish thing to do. This vehicle has all kinds of attractions for the bachelor of the parish. It goes like the clappers for an object of this size, what with the 3.3-litre engine. It has a cool eight-way adjustable driver's seat, with the arm rests like the ones on the chair Hemingway used to fish marlin. It has a state-of-the-art stereo and air con and everything else.

And yet I suggest that there might come a time, as you toddled along on your own, when you felt that you were not exhausting the potential of the machine. There are ten hi-fi speakers dotted around the vast cabin. There are three separate zones for the air con. There is an in-car DVD entertainment system for anyone sitting in the back rows. You remember in Richmal Crompton's *Just William* books, when William gets a penknife that has one of those special blades for getting the stones out of horses' hooves. He feels a bit depressed about this accessory, and then it hits him that he must get a horse to go with it! That's how you will feel: a couple of days sitting at the wheel of the Voyager, and you'll be yearning to punch out some babies to go with the cup holders.

The reference to Just William (pretty meaningless for anyone who wasn't brought up in a British middle-class home) is a 'remember when we were all lads together?' moment; the moment of intimacy with the reader which characterises writing for consumer magazines. It is also the twist in the tale. We discover that Boris is not merely upholding the Voyager as the symbol of fecundity for the middle-class male, but as a policy instrument. Here, mixed in well with the irony, is the evidence.

It is my view, in fact, that Voyagers and MPVs like it are not just a response to the needs of families. They promote that need. They encourage fecundity. Get a family with one or two children into a Voyager, and I guarantee there will come a moment when mummy looks at daddy in a smouldering way, and they decide that they might as well make use of the three seats at the back. In so far as this analysis is correct, these MPVs are playing a vital part in the future of our nation, and I've the statistics to prove it.

You'll be familiar with the catastrophic decline in the fertility of the average British woman from 1964 to 1978. As we all know, our parents were going at it hammer and tongs in the early Sixties, and the tongs were vibrating most vigorously against the hammer in 1964. This was in many ways a vintage year; not only the year in which your motoring correspondent drew his first breath, but it was also the year of maximum productivity by the average British woman, who was then popping out a Stakhanovite three babies. Then something terrible happened.

Maybe it was the pill. Maybe it was feminism. Maybe some foreign power put something in the water supply. Whatever the reason, the fertility rate slumped to about 1.7 babies per woman of childbearing age. And that's not enough to replenish the population, even assuming that people live longer.

From that moment, we have been living with a worsening dependency ratio. We have more and more old people, who depend on the taxes generated by the earnings of fewer and fewer young people. Panic!

Some politicians, such as David Willetts, the Shadow [opposition] Work and Pensions Secretary, have suggested that Britain needs Mussolini-style have-a-baby bounties. But there may be other options that don't involve more public spending. Look at the fertility chart over the last 50 years, and you will find astonishing evidence that the MPV is an incentive to reproduction. After they slumped to 1.7 babies per mother in 1978, the Brits got bonking again. By 1981, they were up to 1.9 babies per mother; and why? It's obvious, innit? It was about that time, of course, that the first people carrier, the Renault Espace, appeared on the market.

> Now we are into pure farce but the piece ends by returning us to the point. There really is [in Boris's opinion] a problem about population decline. We may not agree with him but he has managed to plant this little seed of fact inside his confection – it slips down far more easily than a treatise would.

By the early Nineties, as the novelty of the Espace was wearing off, the graph begins to slip again. Then, round about 1994, it kicks up. Why? Because of the impact on the British market of this US machine, the Chrysler Voyager. According to Trevor Creed, Senior Vice President of Design, Chrysler has sold ten million Voyagers since 1983. Now imagine that, in every case, there was a family that decided to expand by two kids to make use of some of the cupholders. That means, at a conservative estimate, that the Voyager has been responsible for the creation of 20 million human beings. Let us assume that Britain has one twentieth of the market for Voyagers: that means the machine has added a million kids to our stock of human capital. There, my friends, in the gloom of the pensions crisis, is the glimmering of hope. It's the car that thinks it's a maternity ward.

© Boris Johnson and GQ Magazine.

MARCELLE D'ARGY SMITH

Marcelle D'Argy Smith worked for *Cosmopolitan* through the 1980s and 1990s, becoming features editor and then editor. She now freelances and is often called upon as a commentator. She worked on *Cosmo* during its heyday, when the magazine felt that it had a duty to inform women about the world – as well as providing them with information about sex, clothes and make-up – and did it with humour. This piece is an ironic 'transformation story' with a twist. By early 1984 the relatively innocent sexual freedom of the 1970s had been undermined by the threats of sexually transmitted disease (AIDS had recently been identified) and a growing fear of sexual violence, articulated by feminists such as Andrea Dworkin and Catherine MacKinnon. D'Argy Smith is writing about parallel concerns about health, but it is the New Puritanism of the 1980s which is the driving idea behind the piece.

When a lovely flame dies
Cosmopolitan, May 1984

I don't suppose it interests you very much. It's of little interest to me. Giving up things isn't fascinating. But I have to tell you that, as I stubbed out my last cigarette about six months ago, I told myself it was a sign of the times. I stared at the stub in the brown and white ashtray, the one that has Buca di Santanonio, Lucca written on it, and felt nostalgic, wistful, older.

A downbeat first line followed by an inciting incident and then she establishes the mood of the piece: nostalgic. As with most women's magazines, there is no obvious hook – just a sense of the moment. This piece captures a moment of doubt in the onward rush of sexual liberation.

Because I remembered when – and they were different days – cigarettes (dare I say it?) were romantic. They were to do with the mysteries of sex and the fumbling beginnings of sophistication. My first love affair began on a beach in southern France. I was stretched out in the hazy heat of the Antibes midday sun re-reading *Tender is the Night*. My accessories were a small bikini, blue sunglasses and a packet of Gitanes, lying provocatively half in and half out of my beach bag. There was something urgently attractive and worldly about a person who smoked Gitanes. The rough tobacco was an acquired taste. But then, Gitanes smokers had usually acquired a taste for Sartre and intense conversation. I met 'the man' when I reached for the cigarettes. He appeared and offered me a light. He looked into my eyes and smiled. I inhaled … and we *knew*.

We dined that evening and the smoke from our cigarettes drifted hazily in the still air of the restaurant garden. A wispy sensual intermingling. I remember our tanned bodies lying on crumpled sheets with the brilliant blue and white packet of Gitanes next to us. Cigarettes were what you did afterwards. You talked, you stroked, you lingered, you smoked. It's what anyone with even a notion of *savoir-faire* did. And it was terrific, I tell you. Simply terrific.

My first affair stretched over the long French summer and into rusty autumn. Him, me and the Mediterranean blue and white packet of Gitanes.

We did everything together, we discussed practically everything you could think of. Yet the subject of heart disease did not crop up and in our most intimate moments he never mentioned lung cancer.

> *A simple structural device: using cigarette brands to evoke place, mood and men. The tone is ironic but also wistful. Her opening scenario is clichéd, but knowingly so. She references all the metaphors used by cigarette companies in those bygone days when it wasn't yet illegal to sell them by reference to romance and sexuality. The men, and the moods she evokes are those that the cigarette companies were indeed selling with their branding.*

Of course I had to change my brand when I came home to England. The Gitanes were too fraught with memories. And, anyway, I needed something warmer-looking to counteract London's leaden skies. Dunhill seemed to suit my mood. The shiny crimson and gold packet. Expensive, traditional, cosseted-looking. I met elegant Dunhill lighters and the men who owned them. Men with Turnbull shirts, dark suits and creative hands.

It was good to sit in Wilton's or the Connaught and gaze first at the menu and then at the packet of Dunhill on the starched tablecloth. Even if you were an absolute gourmet, the crimson and gold packet was a delicious reminder that the best was yet to come. Dunhill men sent flowers, gift-wrapped presents from Bond or Jermyn Street and asked you to marry them. Being English, they may not have understood women, but they did appreciate the subtle and wonderful difference between the sexes. These sophisticated smokers did not expect to get their women on the cheap, either financially or emotionally. The smoking bonded you somehow and they recognized this. It was easy to talk and be romantic while smoke softened the atmosphere. They inhaled and thought what they were going to say, exhaled and said it. Or you did. Dunhill meant a dialogue and it was delicious. During the crimson and gold period no one accused anyone of tasting like an ashtray or having hair that reeked of smoke.

Then there were the raunchy, racy Rothmans men. A different breed altogether. Younger, more relaxed, less willing to impress. But very willing to fall in love. They were as sharp and crisp as the navy and white packet. Decisive and enthusiastic. They said, 'Let's'. And you did. You raced to crowded, noisy Italian restaurants and to each other's flats and on to planes together – because naturally you had airline tickets to romantic places. And Rothmans were smoked incessantly through all the intense interaction. You spent lazy weekends in bed making love, smoking and daring to talk about the rest of your lives. Very sensual and emotional men sometimes blew smoke rings across your body. That was heady stuff. Love, sex, optimism and cigarettes were all mysteriously intertwined.

It was harder to understand people who didn't smoke. They were accepted, of course. We were liberal. But you felt they weren't embracing the good things in life with the same uninhibited fervour as the rest of us. Non-smokers went home a little earlier, drank a lot less and married people who were 'safe'. A non-smoker *never* complained about a smoker. Non-smokers were the very opposite of the macho Marlboro man. He treated his women with a certain rough charm and he was only ever available on his own terms. He handled the sexually aggressive, scarlet and white packet with New World nonchalance and he usually used matches. When he wasn't riding cowboy country in Arizona, it was rumoured he was great in bed and amazingly gentle and tender to his Chosen Woman. I never knew one well because I was romantically involved with the Rothmans men. And you get used to a certain brand of men.

Now we get the change of direction with the argument against smoking. No finger wagging here, just a regretful sense of an era being over. Readers who smoke could read this without fear of being told off. Cosmo, and Marcelle in particular, was like them, on their side, suffering with them. This ability to be 'on side' is probably the single most important aspect of writing for women's magazines. Writers should talk to you like a friend – never like a mother.

Then it happened. The ugly rumours were officially confirmed. Cigarette smoking was Bad for your Health. Overnight it became a dirty, anti-social, lethal habit.

Well, naturally we all tended to ignore it for a while. Denial is a way of handling grief. Cigarettes *bad* for you? Those pure white, orally gratifying little sticks that were popped into our mouths at every meaningful moment in our lives? Those vital accessories for communication and togetherness? We carried on sucking and blowing and flicking gentle ash and saying it didn't matter. But it did. Next thing you knew was that man after gorgeous man was laying down his cigarettes and saying, 'But not for me.'

Some of the more defiant among us persisted for years, but it became an increasingly lonely crusade.

Romantic meals began to die a death. People thought more about their health, their weight, what they were eating and very little about their dining companion. It was hard to get personal over a Perrier and as for a cigarette – heaven forbid! Of course you sometimes had the drinks before and during the meal, but the sweet promissory note of a lingering sexual aftermath had vanished. If the topic of sex cropped up and you went home and tried it, there was no sensual chatter afterwards. It seemed that without the curly lazy smoke, the essential *après* atmosphere between lovers was not possible. Tender words were left unsaid. Sex, in many cases, became perfunctory.

'What of soul was left, I wonder, when the kissing had to stop?'
Not much, Mr Browning. Not much.

> I am not sure a reference to Robert Browning would stay on the page these days. And now a twist in the tail. It is signalled by a change of pace. The sentences are shorter and choppier as we are steered to the finale. This is certainly a transformation story but one with a rather different moral at the end.

Well, you know the rest. It was only a matter of time before people began to lose interest in sex because sex without romance is de-personalising and depressing. A few people had sex because it was rumoured to be good for you – a form of relaxation and exercise. Heaven help us. Spinach is good for you.

Look, I'm contemporary, flexible. A 1984 person. My finger, albeit a little wobbly, is on the pulse of modern life. I understand that lung cancer, heart disease and blocked arteries are bad for your health. I read the health columns. It's terrific news that there is a breakthrough for herpes. My spirits soar. It's just that I can't help noticing that sex and cigarettes seemed to go out of fashion at about the same time and I thought I should point out that there seemed to be a very definite connection.

Think what you will, I'm wistful about the bygone era of a drink before and a cigarette after. Those golden days of Rothmans and romance, Gitanes and *je t'aime*. The days when smoke got in your eyes and men lingered over you. That era is finished, gone. Manly men are pumping iron at the local health club, getting up early to jog or do press-ups.

To hell with killer diseases. The fact is I do not want packets of painful nostalgia lying around my flat. I do not want a low tar tug at my memory. Cigarettes remind me of times that no longer seem to be available to a romantic sensualist.

And I do not wish to be reminded. So I've given up smoking.

©Marcelle D'Argy Smith

JAMES SUROWIEKI

All newspapers and magazines have specialist writers who write regularly on a particular topic. Their value is that they know their subject and are authoritative but they must also be able to explain the intricacies of their specialism to a lay audience. Doctors, nutritionists, gardening experts, business gurus – if you have an area of expertise, it is marketable. Some journalists become experts through many years of covering the same 'beat' and some are simply crowned as experts because they know a bit about their field and they can turn around a witty 500 words every week. Whatever the field of expertise, the skill is to be accessible. I always read the financial page of the *New York Times*. Economics is to most people impenetrably difficult. It involves huge numbers and concepts that have evolved somewhere far above street level. Surowieki can always find a convenient analogy that reduces the most abstruse concept to an understandable story. He has a chatty easy style that never talks down.

Hello, Cleveland
New Yorker (Financial page), 16 May 2005

In the summer of 1924, a Kansas City band called the Coon-Sanders Original Nighthawk Orchestra did something unusual: it went on tour. Popular as live music was, bands in those days tended to serve as house orchestras or to play long stands in local clubs; there was hardly even a road to go on. But Jules Stein, a booking agent from Chicago, convinced the Nighthawk Orchestra that it could make more money by playing a different town every night. The tour, which lasted five weeks, was a smash. Soon, bands all over the country were hitting the road to play ballrooms and dance halls.

Stein's original vision hasn't changed much, despite some modifications over the years–parking lots, hair spray, the disposable lighter. Consider Metallica, the Coon-Sanders Original Nighthawk Orchestra of our day. Though Metallica still sells a fair number of CDs from its back catalogue (it has made just one album in the past six years), it makes most of its money from concerts. Two years ago, the band brought in almost fifty million dollars with its Sanitarium tour. Last year, it brought in sixty million with its Madly in Anger with the World tour. God knows what it would take to make Metallica happy.

Scratch a forty something in a suit and you will have no difficulty cutting through to the rocker beneath. New Yorker style favours long, lingering intros, even on relatively short pieces, and this one, written with the ease of a man who is very familiar with the territory, will appeal directly to its largely middle-aged male readership. He then moves into simple essay mode.

The music industry may be in crisis, what with illegal file-sharing, stagnant CD sales, and the decline of commercial rock radio, but the touring business is as sturdy as ever. In some ways, it is healthier than some of the mediums (radio, recorded music) that at one point or another were supposed to render it obsolete. Since 1998, annual concert-tour revenue has more than doubled, while CD sales have remained essentially flat. Last year, thirteen different artists grossed more than forty million dollars each at the box office. (Prince made eighty-seven million.) Consumers who seem reluctant to spend nineteen dollars for a CD apparently have few qualms about spending a hundred bucks or more to see a show.

> *This paragraph provides the hook and the 'killer fact'. The piece will then go on to explain why musicians will survive the file-sharing era. The next paragraph provides a clear example.*

There are still artists who make huge sums of money selling records, but they are the lucky few. A longtime recording industry rule of thumb holds that just one in ten artists makes money from royalties. Today, it's probably less than that. So the best model, if you're in it for the money, may be the Grateful Dead. Although the Dead didn't sell many records or get much airplay, they worked the big stadiums and arenas long enough and often enough to become one of the most profitable bands out there. As in politics and sales, nothing beats meeting the people face to face.

> *The next three paragraphs provide the background, which in a specialist column, is the bread and butter of the piece. They explain why a record contract may not be the stairway to heaven that every garage band hopes for. The explanation is clear and robustly evidenced. This is not just an opinion piece but it is written in an easy, conversational style.*

Most musicians, from a business perspective, at least, would wish it otherwise. Selling CDs is, as economists say, scalable: you make one recording, and you can sell it to an uninvited number of people for an unlimited amount of time, at very little cost. A tour, on the other hand, is work. You have to perform nearly every night, before a limited number of people, for hours at a time. You can knock a few seconds off each song, fire a percussionist, or sell more T-shirts, but in the end efficiencies are hard to come by.

The trick is that musicians get a much higher percentage of the money from concerts and merchandise than they do from the sale of their CDs. An artist, if he's lucky, gets twelve per cent of the retail price of a CD. But he doesn't get any royalties until everything is paid for – studio time, packaging costs, videos – which means that he can sell a million records and make almost-nothing. On tour though, he often gets more than half of the box office, so even if he grosses less he can profit more.

Traditionally, tours were a means of promoting a record. Today, the record promotes the tour. The decline in record sales has shrunk the size of the pie for labels and artists to fight over, so they've had to find new ways to make money, and artists have come to see how lucrative touring can be, given what people will pay to see them live. (Ticket prices for the top hundred tours doubled between 1995 and 2003.) And, while high prices may be starting to put a dent in attendance, the dollars keep pouring in. Last summer's concert season was considered a dismal one, yet, according to Pollstar, the industry's trade magazine, concert revenues rose for the year.

Now having established how the industry has changed, we are told who is reaping the benefits.

Inevitably, touring rewards some artists better than others – graying super-stars, for example, with their deep-pocketed baby-boomer fans and set lists full of sing-along hits. The economist Alan Krueger has estimated that the top one per cent of performers claim more than half of all concert revenues. But even indie rockers are reaping the benefits, with bands like Wilco and Modest Mouse selling out venues like Radio City Music Hall, at decidedly non-indie prices.

The conclusion reiterates the point he set out to prove. His controlling idea is that musicians are taking music back from big business and he rounds his piece off by returning to Metallica.

The upshot is that the fortunes of musicians and the fortunes of music labels have less and less to do with each other. This may be the first stage of what John Perry Barlow, a former lyricist for the Dead, once called the shift from 'the music business' to 'the musician business.' In the musician business, the assets that once made the major labels so important – promotion, distribution, shelf space – matter less than the assets that belong to the artists, such as their ability to perform live. As technology has grown more sophisticated, the ways in which artists make money have grown more old-fashioned. The value of songs falls, and the value of seeing an artist sing them rises, because that experience can't really be reproduced. It's funny that, in an era of file-sharing and iPodstealing, the old troubadour may have the most lucrative gig of all. But then Metallica knew it all along. 'Send me money, send me green,' the group sang in 'Leper Messiah' twenty years. ago. 'Make a contribution, and you'll get a better seat.'

© New Yorker

REFERENCES

Aristotle (1998) *Poetics*. Trans Kenneth McLeish. London: Nick Hern Books.

Barber, L. (2004) 'Growing Pains', *The Observer*, 22 August.

Barthes, R. (1972) 'Myth Today', in *Mythologies*. London: Jonathan Cape.

Bird, E. and Dardenne, R. (1988) 'Myth, chronicle and story: exploring the narrative qualities of News', in Carey, James W. (ed.), *Media Myths and Narratives: Television and the Press*. Sage Reviews of Communications Research Vol. 15. Newbury Park, CA: Sage, pp. 67–86.

Booker, C. (2004) *The Seven Basic Plots: Why We Tell Stories*. New York: Continuum.

Booth, W.C. (1961) *The Rhetoric of Fiction*. Chicago: University of Chicago Press.

Brooks, L. (2005) 'The girl who fell to the earth' *Guardian*, 18 May.

Cartner-Morley, J. (2005) 'Bird of paradise', *Guardian*, 8 October.

Cohen, N. (2005) 'Capital punishment', *The Observer*, 6 November.

Didion J. (1987) *Miami*. New York: Simon & Schuster. Republished in Granta (2005) *Classics of Reportage*. London: Granta.

Engels, M. (1996) *Tickle the Public*. London: Orion.

Fenton, J. (1989) 'The Fall of Saigon', in *All the Wrong Places*. London: Granta, p. 88.

Frank, A.W. (1995) *The Wounded Story Teller*. Chicago: University of Chicago Press.

Franklyn, B. (1997) *Newzak and News Media*. London: Arnold.

Geertz, C. (2000) *Available Light: Anthropological Reflections on Philosophical Topics*. Princeton, NJ: Princeton University Press.

Gelhorn, M. (1944) 'Visit Italy', *Colliers* (magazine), February. Republished in M. Gelhorn (1986) *The Face of War*. London: Virago.

Gelhorn, M. (1945) 'Dachau', *Colliers* (magazine), May. Republished in M. Gelhorn (1986) *The Face of War*. London: Virago.

Hall, S. (1996) 'Encoding decoding', in Marris, P. and Thornton, S. (eds), *Media Studies: A Reader*. Edinburgh: Edinburgh University Press, pp. 51–62.

Hall, S. et al. (1978) *Policing the Crisis: The State, and Law and Order*. London: Macmillan.

Herr, M. (1969) 'Khesanh', *Esquire*, September. Republished in Wolfe, T. (1975) *The New Journalism*. London: Picador, p. 123.

Hull, A. (2001) 'Divided feast', *Washington Post*, 1 April. Republished in Woods, K. (2002) *Best Newspaper Writing 2002*. St Petersberg, FL: The Poynter Institute for Media Studies/Chicago: Bonus Books.

Hull, A. (2001) 'An American dream, slightly apart', *Washington Post*, 27 October. Republished in Woods, K. (2002) *Best Newspaper Writing 2002*. St Petersberg, FL: The Poynter Institute for Media Studies/Chicago: Bonus Books.

Kerrane, K. and Yagoda B. (1998) *The Art of Fact*. London: Pocket Books.

Lloyd, A. (2005) 'Earthquake survivor lay buried for 27 days', *The Times*, 18 November, p. 3.

Lule, J. (2001) *Daily News Eternal Stories: The Mythological Role of Journalism*. New York: Guilford Press.

McKee, R. (1999) *Story*. London: Methuen.

O'Kane, M. (2001) 'No man's land', *Guardian*, 3 October.

O'Kane, M. (2001) 'Vulnerable given a cold welcome in Britain', *Guardian*, 3 December.

Orwell, G. (1950) 'Politics and the English Language', in *Inside the Whale and Other Essays*. London: Secker & Warburg. Article originally published in 1946.

Parker, P. (1999) *The Art and Science of Screenwriting*. Exeter: Intellect.

Phillips, A. (2003) *Children Before Money*. London: Guardian Unlimited/Analysis, 30 July.

Rofel, L. (1999) *Other Modernities: Gendered Yearnings in China after Socialism*. Berkeley, CA: University of California Press.

Rowan, D. (2006) 'Downloading Mr Right', *Sunday Times* (magazine), 8 January, p. 18.

Said, E. (1994) *Culture and Imperialism*. London: Vintage.

Silverstone, R. (1988) 'Television myth and culture', in James W. Carey (ed.), *Media Myths and Narratives: Television and the Press*. Sage Reviews of Communications Research Vol. 15. Newbury Park, CA: Sage, pp. 20–37.

Sparks, C. and Dahlgren, P. (1992) *Journalism and Popular Culture*. London: Sage.

Sparks, C. and Tulloch, J. (2000) *Tabloid Tales*. Oxford: Rowman & Littlefield.

Steele, J. (2005) 'Puzzle over shot Brazilian's visa as his body is flown back to grieving family', *The Daily Telegraph*, 26 July.

Thompson, D. (2005) 'England has a terrible crisis of identity', interview with David Starkey, *Daily Telegraph*, 9 September.

Thompson, J.B. (1995) *Media and Modernity*. Cambridge: Polity Press.

Todorov, T. (1977) *The Poetics of Prose*. Oxford: Blackwell.

Willis, P. (1971) *What is news*? Working papers in cultural studies. Birmingham: Birmingham University.

Wolfe, T. (1975) *The New Journalism*. London: Picador.

Woods, K. (2002) *Best Newspaper Writing 2002*. St Petersberg, FL: The Poynter Institute for Media Studies/Chicago: Bonus Books.

Examples of Good Writing

Banks Smith, N. (1997) The funeral of Diana: trail of tears', *Guardian* (TV Review), 8 September, p. 12.

Barnes, S. (2005) 'Gone in 50 seconds, back in six minutes', *The Times*, 26 May.

Bennett, C. (2005) 'Pay more, worry less? Not after Sudan 1', *Guardian*, 24 February.

Brockes, E. (2001) 'Call me sergeant', *Guardian* (G2), 13 December.

Brooks, L. (1999) 'Private lives', *Guardian* (G2), 14 May.

Burkeman, O. (2004) 'The fatal step', *Guardian*, 5 August.

Cusk, R. (2005) 'Sweetness and lights', *Vogue*, January.

D'Argy Smith, M. (1984) 'When a lovely flame dies', *Cosmopolitan*, May.

Frere-Jones, S. (2004) '1979: the year punk died, and was reborn', *New Yorker*, 1 November.

Gelhorn, M. (1944) 'Visit Italy', *Colliers* magazine, February 1944. Republished in Gelhorn, M. (1986) *The Face of War*. London: Virago.

Heller, Z. (1993) 'The little emperor', *Independent on Sunday* (Sunday Review) 31 October.

Johnson, B. (2004) 'Go forth and multiply', GQ, March, p. 174.

Lloyd, A. (2004) 'Kalashnikov matriarch emerges to tell of her life as an Afghan warlord', *The Times* (London), 21 October.

Meek, J. (2004) 'The £10bn rail crash', *Guardian*, 1 April.

Packer, G. (2003) 'Gansta war', *New Yorker*, 3 November.

Roberts, Y. (2006) 'Focus: Cannabis psychosis – off your head?', *The Observer*, 19 February.

Steavenson, W. (2004) 'Osama's war: on getting to know an Iraqi terrorist', *Granta*, No. 87, September.

Surowieki, J. (2005) 'Hello, Cleveland', *New Yorker* (Financial page), 16 May.

Wainwright, M. (2005) 'Villagers clean up after flash floods', *Guardian*, 21 June.

Winner, L. (1970) The odyssey of Captain Beefheart', *Rolling Stone*, 14 May.

Younge, G. (2000) 'This is not racism, it's polities', *Guardian*, 20 April.

Younge, G. (2002) 'Terms of abuse', *Guardian*, 25 February.

INDEX

extended anecdote 46–7
eye-witnesses 21–3, 40

Fenton, James 49
financial writing 210–12
Flett, Kathryn 155–61
Frank, Arthur 15
Franklyn, B. 2, 33
Frere-Jones, Sasha 191–5

Gelhorn, Martha 49, 60–7
Gladwell, Malcom 37
GQ 202–5
Granta 101–9
The Guardian 70–3, 74–80, 95–101,
    131–61, 185–8, 196–202

Hadar, Mary 1, 29–30
Hall, S. 8, 10
Heller, Zoe 161–71
heroes
    character as story 34
    news focus 81
    profiles 172–84
    sports writing 189–91
    story archetypes 13–23
    war reporting 60–1
Herr, Michael 36
hook 27–9
    comment columns 198
    financial writing 211
    investigative features 132
    news focus 81
    personal columns 200
    profiles and interviews 172
    topical features 91, 102
Hull, Annie 36, 50, 51
Hussein, Khalid 35–6
hybrid structure 45, 81

inciting incident 43
    comment columns 198
    introduction 46, 47
    news features 75
    personal columns 206
    reportage 58, 68, 71
    topical features 96, 104, 112, 119
Independent on Sunday 161–71
informational form 44–5
interviews 38–41
    celebrities 155–84
    character as story 34–5
    gathering facts 30
    investigative features 134, 138–42
    news features 74

interviews *cont.*
    news focus 80, 82
    rewriting 54
    topical features 101–30
introductions 43, 45–8
    comment columns 197
    financial pages 210
    investigative features 132–3
    news features 75
    personal columns 200
    profiles 156–7, 161–2
    rewriting 54
    sports writing 189
    topical features 101, 110
    war reporting 61
investigative features 37, 44, 131–54

Jenkins, Simon 2–3
Johnson, Boris 202–5
Jones, Dylan 31–2
Jones, Francis 16

Katz, Ian 155
Kerrane, Kevin 4
killer fact 43, 68, 85–6, 133, 211

Loyd, Anthony 35–6, 68–70
Lule, J. 13, 17

McKee, Robert 12, 41–2, 43
malevolent stranger 13–14, 21–3
Meek, James 131–54
Menezes, Jean Charles de 21–3
metaphor
    characters 34, 35–6, 102, 103
    clichés 51–2
    investigative features 131
    mixing 51
    sports writing 189
    topical features 112, 122, 124, 129
    war reporting 68
minorities 13–14
Moore, Charlotte 32
morality 13–14, 15–16
motoring 202–5
music writing 171–84, 191–5
myth 8–9, 11, 12–4

narrative
    collective 8–9
    definition 7
    framing 11
    narrative quality 11
    news conventions 9–10
    story archetypes 12–24